THE

AMERICAN FRIENDS'

Peace Conference

HELD AT

PHILADELPHIA

TWELFTH MONTH 12TH, 13TH AND 14TH

1901

Philadelphia:
PUBLISHED BY THE CONFERENCE
1902

Copies of this Report may be secured at the office of either the *Friends' Intelligencer* or the *American Friend*, Philadelphia.

Press of Ferris & Leach, 29-31 North Seventh Street, Philadelphia.

Introduction.

ORIGIN AND ORGANIZATION OF THE CONFERENCE.

The first step toward the organization of the Peace Conference, the proceedings of which are given in this Report, was taken at the time of the Seventh Annual Conference on International Arbitration, held by Albert K. Smiley at Lake Mohonk, N. Y., on the last three days of Fifth month, 1901. At this Conference a meeting of Friends present was called to discuss the question of holding a peace conference in which members of all the religious bodies in America calling themselves Friends should be invited to participate. The following were present at this meeting:

Alexander C. Wood and wife, Camden, N. J.; Arthur Perry and wife, Brookline, Mass.; Hannah J. Bailey, Winthrop Centre, Maine; D. Wheeler Swift and wife, Worcester, Mass.; Benjamin F. Trueblood, Boston, Mass.; John B. Garrett, Rosemont, Pa.; Frances B. G. Branson, Rosemont, Pa.; Philip C. Garrett, Philadelphia; Wm. P. Bancroft and wife, Wilmington, Del.; Clement M. Biddle and wife, Lansdowne, Pa.; Charles Richardson and wife, Philadelphia; Howard M. Jenkins and wife, Gwynedd, Pa.; Margaretta F. Atkinson, Philadelphia; President William W. Birdsall and wife, Swarthmore, Pa.; Rufus M. Jones, Haverford, Pa.; Joshua L. Baily, Philadelphia; Alfred H. Smiley, Minnewaska, N. Y.; Sarah Collins, Purchase, N. Y.

Benjamin F. Trueblood was appointed chairman and Howard M. Jenkins secretary. After a free interchange of views, a committee consisting of Benjamin F. Trueblood (chairman), Arthur Perry, Howard M. Jenkins, Philip C. Garrett, Hannah J. Bailey, William W. Birdsall and Rufus M. Jones was appointed to take into further consideration "the holding of a conference of Friends of all bodies in America on the subject of peace and arbitration, with authority to add to their number, and also with authority to make arrangements for such conference, if in the judgment of the committee it should seem proper to hold one."

This committee, in order to obtain the opinions of Friends throughout the United States and Canada, published the following circular in the Friends' papers in Seventh month.

PROPOSED FRIENDS' NATIONAL PEACE CONFERENCE.

To Friends in America:

It has been felt by a number of Friends that the opening year of the Twentieth Century ought not to be allowed to pass without some general public manifestation, on the part of all in America who call themselves and are known as Friends, of their peace principles and faith. The hour is a most important and even critical one in the history of Christian civilization, and demands the active and speedy movement of all the forces of righteousness, love and peace.

Throughout their history Friends have stood for goodwill and fellowship among the nations as well as between individuals, and for the settlement of international disputes by the friendly, rational method of arbitration. In addition to their direct peace work as a religious body, they have furnished a number of the leaders and organizers of the general peace movement, and their large and constant influence in opposition to war as radically inconsistent with both Christianity and humanity has been widely recognized and felt.

The body of Friends in America is in a position to-day to speak with greater intelligence and wisdom, and therefore with greater power, than ever before in its history. It has spread across and over the continent, grown in numbers, and in recent years developed much in its intellectual resources. Its history and the history of the world during its existence have been full of instructive lessons as to the power of peace principles and the evils of war, the force of which ought to stimulate to new and better service. Do we not owe it to ourselves, to our history, to our profession before the church and the world, to the American public and to mankind everywhere, to declare ourselves anew to-day—and in a united way, as we have never done before—on the great and pressing question of the peace of the world, of the rescue of mankind from the awful iniquities and crushing burdens of modern militarism?

So far all to whom the idea of such a conference as that proposed has been suggested, have expressed the heartiest approval of it, and also their readiness to co-operate as far as possible in promoting it. At the time of the recent Arbitration Conference held at Lake Mohonk, N. Y., some thirty Friends, of different bodies, who were present, met, and, after earnest consideration of the subject, came to the unanimous conclusion that it was not only very desirable, but a clear and positive duty, that such a national conference be held, provided Friends throughout the country in sufficient numbers approve of the project, and are ready to co-operate in it as they may be able. The persons named below were appointed to constitute the nucleus of a national committee, with power to add to their number, to lay the subject before Friends in general, and if, after the consultation, it should be deemed wise to go forward, to have charge of the arrangements for the conference; the committee to be enlarged into a representative national one.

It is proposed to hold the conference in Philadelphia, the city of William Penn, some time near the end of this year, for about three days.

The plan is to make it a mass conference, that all interested Friends may attend as members, without the necessity of any official appointment.

The program, it is thought best, should consist of carefully-prepared papers, by the ablest and most experienced thinkers and workers in the peace cause to be found among Friends (to be selected by the National Committee), upon various phases of the peace question,—religious, historical, sociological, educational, political, etc.; a limited amount of time to be given to general discussion; the proceedings to be afterwards published for distribution.

If the conference is held, it will be necessary to have a local committee of Friends in and about Philadelphia, to provide a suitable hall, make arrangements for the entertainment of visitors, etc.; and also a finance committee to secure through voluntary contributions funds for defraying the expenses of the meeting—rent of hall, advertising, printing of proceedings, bringing speakers from a distance, etc.

The Provisional Committee, whose names are given below, desire to hear at once, in response to this circular, from Friends in all parts of the country, and invite the freest expression of opinion, in brief form, as to the proposed conference.

Address all communications to Benjamin F. Trueblood, Chairman, 3 Somerset Street, Boston, Mass.

> HANNAH J. BAILEY, Winthrop Centre, Me.
> WILLIAM W. BIRDSALL, Swarthmore, Pa.
> PHILIP C. GARRETT, Philadelphia.
> HOWARD M. JENKINS, Philadelphia.
> RUFUS M. JONES, Haverford, Pa.
> ARTHUR PERRY, Brookline, Mass.
> BENJAMIN F. TRUEBLOOD, Boston.

The responses to this circular were so numerous and cordial that the committee felt the duty to be clear to proceed with the arrangements for the Conference. A second circular, stating that it had been decided to hold the Conference, was published in *The American Friend* and *The Friends' Intelligencer* at the end of Eighth month. The provisional committee then enlarged its number and constituted the following General Committee, which proceeded to prepare the program and make other necessary arrangements for holding the Conference:

> ELIZA C. ARMSTRONG, Centre Valley, Ind.
> HANNAH J. BAILEY, Winthrop Center, Me.
> PRESIDENT W. W. BIRDSALL, Swarthmore, Pa.
> HANNAH W. BLACKBURN, Zanesfield, Ohio.
> WILLIAM G. BROWN, Toronto, Canada.
> EMILIE U. BURGESS, Highland, N. Y.
> CLARKSON BUTTERWORTH, Waynesville, Ohio.
> ELIZA H. CAREY, Wichita, Kan.
> WILLIAM R. CLARK, Emerson, Ohio.
> ELIZABETH H. COALE, Holder, Ill.
> J. ELWOOD COX, High Point, N. C.
> SARAH ANN DALE, Pickering, Ont., Can.
> L. MARIA DEANE, Pleasant Plain, Iowa.
> JANE EDGERTON, St. Clairsville, O.
> PROF. A. M. ELLIOTT, Baltimore, Md.
> ALLEN J. FLITCRAFT, Oak Park, Ill.
> PHILIP C. GARRETT, Logan (Philadelphia), Pa.
> JOB S. GIDLEY, North Dartmouth, Mass.
> ABIGAIL J. HADLEY, Clarksville, O.
> MARGARET W. HAINES, Cheltenham, Pa.
> JOSEPH HILL, Emerson, O.
> PROF. C. W. HODGIN, Richmond, Ind.

WILLIAM M. JACKSON, New York, N. Y.
DR. O. E. JANNEY, Baltimore, Md.
SUSAN W. JANNEY, Philadelphia, Pa.
ALLEN JAY, Richmond, Ind.
HOWARD M. JENKINS, Philadelphia, Pa.
RUFUS M. JONES, Haverford, Pa.
HARRIET COX MCDOWELL, New York, N. Y.
PRESIDENT EDWIN MCGREW, Newberg, Ore.
ELIZABETH B. MILES, Newberg, Ore.
DR. WILLIAM L. PEARSON, Oskaloosa, Iowa.
ARTHUR PERRY, Brookline, Mass.
ESTHER PUGH, Selma, O.
PETER W. RAIDABAUGH, Plainfield, Ind.
ELEANORA H. ROBINSON, Richmond, Ind.
ELIAS H. ROGERS, Toronto, Can.
DANIEL SMILEY, Lake Mohonk, N. Y.
PRESIDENT EDMUND STANLEY, Wichita, Kan.
PRESIDENT CHARLES E. TEBBETTS, Whittier, Cal.
RICHARD H. THOMAS, Baltimore, Md.
BENJAMIN F. TRUEBLOOD, Boston, Mass.
PRESIDENT J. B. UNTHANK, Wilmington, O.
ELLA C. VEEDER, Whittier, Cal.
ELISHA H. WALKER, Baltimore, Md.
JANE WHITE, Baltimore, Md.
JAMES WOOD, Mount Kisco, N. Y.
MARY C. WOODY, Winston-Salem, N. C.
SAMUEL P. ZAVITZ, Coldstream, Ont., Can.

A Finance Committee, consisting of Alexander C. Wood, chairman, Camden, N. J.; Robert M. Janney, treasurer, Philadelphia; Joshua L. Baily, Philadelphia; William P. Bancroft, Wilmington, Del.; Isaac H. Clothier, Philadelphia, and Asa S. Wing, Philadelphia, was appointed, and through their solicitation ample funds were secured to meet all the expenses of the Conference.

The Local Committee of Arrangements chosen, to whose earnest, self-sacrificing and wisely-directed efforts in arranging for the meetings and providing for the entertainment of members from a distance the success of the Conference was so largely due, consisted of the following persons:

John B. Garrett, chairman; Samuel S. Ash, Mordecai T. Bartram, Clement M. Biddle, Benjamin Cadbury, Hannah W. Cadbury, Arabella Carter, Isabel Chambers, Julia Cope Collins, W. W. Comfort, Howard M. Cooper, Joseph Elkinton, Sarah W. Elkinton, Sarah B. Flitcraft, Joseph E. Haines, Edward H. Magill, John B. Rhoads, J. Henry Scattergood, Isaac Sharpless, Walter P. Stokes, Agnes L. Tierney, Mary Travilla, William S. Vaux, Jr., Emma Waln, Joseph S. Walton, Emma S. Webster, Mary R. G. Williams,

John C. Winston, Stanley R. Yarnall and William Y. Warner. With this committee the local members of the General Committee, William W. Birdsall, Philip C. Garrett, Susan W. Janney, Howard M. Jenkins and Rufus M. Jones, regularly met.

The program as finally revised and completed when the Conference opened was as follows:

WITHERSPOON HALL, PHILADELPHIA,

Twelfth month 12th, 13th, 14th, 1901.

Program.

FIFTH-DAY MORNING.

JOHN B. GARRETT (Philadelphia), Presiding.

10.00. Devotion.

10.10. Address by the Chairman.

Announcements.

10.30. " The New Testament Grounds of Peace."
PROFESSOR ELBERT RUSSELL, recently of Earlham College.

10.55. " Elements of Peace Doctrine in the Old Testament."
DR. GEORGE A. BARTON, Bryn Mawr College.

11.15. " The Failure of the Christian Church in Regard to Peace Principles."
MARY CHAWNER WOODY, Winston-Salem, N. C.

11.35. Discussion of Papers.

12.30. Adjournment.

FIFTH-DAY AFTERNOON.

HOWARD M. JENKINS (Editor of " Friends' Intelligencer "), Presiding.

3.30. Remarks by the Chairman.

3.45. " The Early Friends' Conception of War and Peace."
WILLIAM G. HUBBARD, Lansing, Mich.

4.05. "The Growing Iniquity of War."
    PRESIDENT A. ROSENBERGER, Penn College, Iowa.

4.25. "The Inherent Immorality of War."
    MARIANA W. CHAPMAN, Brooklyn, N. Y.

4.45. Discussion of Papers.

5.20. Adjournment.

FIFTH-DAY EVENING.

President JAMES B. UNTHANK (Wilmington College, Ohio), Presiding.

8.00. Remarks by the Chairman.

8.15. "Early Christianity and War."
    JAMES WOOD, Mount Kisco, N. Y.

8.40. "Attitude of Christians as to War and Peace."
    DR. JESSE H. HOLMES, Swarthmore College.

9.05. "The Christian Idea of Force."
    DR. RICHARD H. THOMAS, Baltimore, Md.

9.30. Discussion of Papers.

10.00. Adjournment.

SIXTH-DAY MORNING.

President M. CAREY THOMAS (Bryn Mawr College), Presiding.

10.00. Devotion.

10.10. Remarks by the Chairman.

10.25. "Importance of teaching Peace Principles in Bible Schools."
    PETER W. RAIDABAUGH, Plainfield, Ind.

10.45. "The Principal Influences Making for Peace, and How They May be Strengthened."
    PRESIDENT EDMUND STANLEY, Friends' University, Wichita, Kan.

11.10. "Woman's Responsibility and Opportunities for Promoting Peace Principles."
    MARY JANE WEAVER, Batavia, N. Y.

11.30. Discussion of Papers.

12.30. Adjournment.

SIXTH-DAY AFTERNOON:

President WILLIAM W. BIRDSALL (Swarthmore College), Presiding.

3.30. Remarks by the Chairman.

3.45. " Present Encouragements for the Friends of Peace."
    PROF. ELLEN C. WRIGHT, Wilmington College, O.

4.10. ." Internationalism."
    HANNAH J. BAILEY, Winthrop Center, Maine.

4.30. " Peace Principles in Political Life and Institutions."
    AUGUSTINE JONES, LL.B., Principal Friends School, Providence, R. I.

4.50. Discussion of Papers.

5.20. Adjournment.

SIXTH-DAY EVENING.

JOSHUA L. BAILY (Philadelphia), Presiding.

8.00. Remarks by the Chairman.

8.15. " To What Extent are Peace Principles Practicable? "
    PRESIDENT ISAAC SHARPLESS, Haverford College.

8.40. " William Penn's Peace Work."
    PHILIP C. GARRETT, Philadelphia, Pa.

9.05. " The Present Position of the International Peace Movement."
    DR. BENJAMIN F. TRUEBLOOD, Boston, Mass.

9.30. Discussion of Papers.

10.00. Adjournment.

SEVENTH-DAY MORNING.

ARTHUR PERRY (Boston, Mass.), Presiding.

[Meetings on Seventh-day in Twelfth Street Meeting House.]

10.00. Devotion.

10.10. Remarks by the Chairman.

10.20. " The Duty of the Christian Church at the Present Time in the Movement to Abolish War."
    HENRY W. WILBUR, New York City.

10.40. "Mistakes and Failures of Friends in Their Peace Work."
   PRESIDENT JAMES B. UNTHANK, Wilmington College, O.

11.00. "The Makers of Peace."
   DEAN ELIZABETH POWELL BOND, Swarthmore College.

11.20. "The True Spirit of Peace."
   DR. WILLIAM L. PEARSON, Penn College, Iowa.

11.45. Discussion of Papers.

12.30. Adjournment.

SEVENTH-DAY AFTERNOON.

SUSAN W. JANNEY (Philadelphia), Presiding.

3.30. Remarks by the Chairman.

3.45. "The Relation of Quaker Women to Peace."
   EMILIE U. BURGESS, Highland, N. Y.

4.10. "War Inconsistent with the Genius of Quakerism."
   PRESIDENT CHARLES E. TEBBETTS, Whittier College, Cal.

4.20. "Constancy in our Peace Sentiment and Effort."
   PRESIDENT EDWIN McGREW, Pacific College, Oregon.

4.30. Discussion of Papers.

5.00. Miscellaneous Business.

5.20. Adjournment.

SEVENTH-DAY EVENING.

President ISAAC SHARPLESS (Haverford College, Pa.), Presiding.

8.00. "Remedies for the Prevailing Militarism."
   JOSIAH W. LEEDS, West Chester, Pa.

8.20. "The Influence of Quaker Peace Ideals in Our National Life."
   DR. O. EDWARD JANNEY, Baltimore, Md.

8.40. "Peace as Involved in the Christian Method."
   DR. RUFUS M. JONES, Haverford College, Editor of "The American Friend."

9.00. Discussion of Papers.

9.30. Closing Remarks by the Chairman.

THE AMERICAN FRIENDS' PEACE CONFERENCE.

First Session.

The American Friends' Peace Conference, the calling of which is explained in the Introduction to this Report, met for its first session in Witherspoon Hall, Philadelphia, Twelfth month 12th, 1901, at 10.00 a.m. John B. Garrett, of Philadelphia, presided. In opening the Conference the Chairman said:

We all recognize that the only proper beginning for such a Conference as this upon which we are entering is the seeking of the favor of Almighty God; and as true spiritual worship is a matter between the individual soul and the Creator, I suggest that a few moments be first given to silent communion with Him. While we are so engaged, should there be a feeling on the mind of any of the duty of vocal prayer, we shall all appreciate its appropriateness and endeavor to be baptized into the spirit of it.

During the period of devotion prayer was offered by Rufus M. Jones and James Wood. Stephen R. Smith, of Pleasantville, N. Y., in a few brief sentences said that it was fitting that they should all come with feelings of self-abnegation and of true humility of soul before Him who had called them to serve Him; that they should seek the outpouring of His infinite life and love and power in their midst, that they might be able to enunciate the doctrines of the fatherhood of God and the brotherhood of man in such a way as to make some impression not only in the United States, but also in other parts of the world; that the day might be hastened when " the kingdoms of this world should become the kingdoms of our Lord and of His Christ."

THE CHAIRMAN: The Local Committee of Arrangements has designated, as Secretaries for the Conference, Elizabeth Lloyd and Elizabeth B. Cadbury. Their duties, they may feel assured, are not likely to be onerous, seeing that the papers which have been prepared have been handed in, in manuscript or typewriting; and because we have also a stenographer to take reports of extemporaneous remarks.

Most of us are aware that under divine blessing the origin of this Conference is due to one who has spent many years in studying the great problems of internationalism, war and peace, historically and otherwise. He is now the General Secretary of the American Peace Society. I am sure it is due to you, as also to him, that you should hear from his own lips the account of the beginnings of this movement. I will therefore call upon Dr. Benjamin F. Trueblood, of Boston, to speak to us before we undertake other business.

BENJAMIN F. TRUEBLOOD: I cannot tell you, dear friends, how great pleasure it gives me this morning to meet so many of you here, from so many different parts of the country. To see you here is sufficient compensation for anything that I may have been permitted to do in the origination of the Conference.

Only a few words are needed as to the origin of the Conference. For some months of last year I felt that the time had come when the various religious bodies in this country calling themselves Friends should unite, both for the sake of their own membership and that of the public at large, in a fresh declaration of their views on the subject of peace. The Society in its different branches has spread, as you know, over almost the entire continent. No attempt, so far as I know, had ever been made to get members of all the branches together and have them speak in a united voice on the great subject of peace. I had felt for many months that the time had come for something of the kind to be done. I approached a few Friends of the different bodies, and found them all in sympathy with the idea.

At the time of the Lake Mohonk Arbitration Conference, held by our friend Albert K. Smiley, at the last of May this year, I ventured to call together the Friends who were there, representing the three principal bodies of Friends. I found them, without exception, in sympathy with the thought as it had formulated itself in my mind. It was decided by those present to appoint a Provisional Committee, with power to add to its number, and to issue an address to the Friends of the continent, in order to learn whether they felt as we did about it. The address was duly issued, and published in the Friends' papers. The result was that from East and West, North and South, there came such a voice of approval that the Provisional Committee felt that it was right to go forward with the subject. A second circular was issued, saying that it had been definitely decided to hold the Conference, and the Provisional Committee proceeded to constitute a General Committee on Organization (see Introduction), a Local Committee of Arrangements, a Finance Committee, and to make preparations for the Conference.

The Committee, in making arrangements, preparing the program, etc., have endeavored to have not only the Friends of all bodies, but, as far as possible, the Friends of all sections of the country, represented. Of course we could not use all the Friends of the country either upon the committees, or upon the program, but we have tried to get representative men and women from the different bodies, and from different sections of the continent. This has been a somewhat difficult and delicate task, as you will all recognize.

We have found it to be necessary, in making up our program, in order to get as wide a representation and as great a variety of thought as possible, to limit the papers to twenty minutes in length.

As we gather together this morning, I feel sure that it is in the divine ordering. God has led us in the organization of the Conference, and I believe He will lead us in the accomplishment of the work for which we have met, and that He will enable us to do something that shall be of influence in the spread of His kingdom of righteousness, love and peace. I hope that throughout the entire Conference we shall all abide under a sense of His presence, His power and His guidance.

I want to say one word more: We wish you all to feel that this is your Conference. If at any time during the discussions which will follow the papers you feel that you have something to say, we want you to feel perfect freedom to speak. We do not wish you to throw the responsibility of the meetings too much on those of us who have organized the Conference. Now that the Conference has met, it is yours as well as ours; it belongs to all of us; and let us all put an amount of devotion, thought and prayerful interest into it which shall make it a very great success under the blessing of God.

I want to thank you all this morning for your presence here, and as Chairman of the Committee on Organization to give you a most hearty welcome.

THE CHAIRMAN: There are several announcements that ought to be made at this time, and in view of the fact that it is now within three minutes of the time designated on the program for the reading of the first paper, I will ask you to excuse me from making any remarks at this time, as the opening has been so well done by our friend Dr. Trueblood. I will watch my opportunity to say anything that is on my mind as the discussions of the papers go on.

In the first place, I want to ask that those coming from a distance will make themselves known to the Entertainment Committee, of which our friend William Y. Warner, sitting at my left, is Chairman. If they have not homes already they will be provided for.

Let me remind all that punctuality is one of the graces in which we Friends are supposed to have been educated. As the doors will be closed during the period of devotional exercises each morning, it is desired that all in attendance shall have entered the room and taken their seats before the designated hour of 10 o'clock.

It is the wish of those who have organized the Conference that the name and address of every one in attendance shall be left here. If you will kindly write your names and addresses distinctly on the cards which have been, or will be, handed to you, and give them to one of the secretaries or ushers, we shall feel grateful.

When we enter upon the consideration of the papers, some one who has been designated to open the discussion will occupy not to exceed ten minutes, after which the subject will be open to the whole house. If we are to get through in three days the large amount of work before us it will be necessary to limit the speeches during the discussions to five minutes. Those who rise to speak, unless known to the Chairman, are kindly requested to give their names and addresses, as this will make you known to the audience, and thus greatly add to the interest of the occasion.

One of the first matters of business is that of the appointment of a Committee on Credentials.

ISAAC WILSON: I offer the following: " Resolved, that a Committee on Credentials, consisting of five members, be appointed by the Chair, to which credentials of delegates are hereby referred for examination, with instruction to present to a future session a list of all duly-appointed delegates, their post-office addresses and the communities which they respectively represent."

THE CHAIRMAN: You hear the resolution which has been offered by Isaac Wilson, of Canada.

BENJAMIN F. TRUEBLOOD: I second the resolution, and desire to say that I hope it will give rise to no misunderstanding. While there are certain meetings and groups of persons which, in order to be represented, have joined in sending delegates, it is, I hope, understood that this is a mass Conference and open to all Friends. Any member of any branch of the Society who is present is just as much a member of the Conference as anybody appointed by a quarterly, yearly or monthly meeting, or by any group of Friends.

The resolution offered by Isaac Wilson was adopted.

THE CHAIRMAN: I ought to add that we are not exclusive by any means. The Conference has been widely advertised in and about Philadelphia, and not a little at a distance. We hope that our Christian brothers and sisters who are about us will come in with the utmost freedom and share with us the benefits of this occasion. Our purposes are largely educational, and they are to be realized in a great degree by the attendance of those who are about us.

The Chairman then named the following as the Committee on Credentials: Isaac Wilson, Chairman; Timothy B. Hussey, Emma Waln, Joseph Potts and Hannah Collins.

BENJAMIN F. TRUEBLOOD: I offer the following: " Resolved, that a Business Committee, consisting of not less than seven members, be appointed by the Chair, to which shall be referred without discussion all resolutions offered in the Conference. Said Committee shall prepare a Declaration, to be submitted to the Conference towards its close for its consideration and possible adoption, and the Committee shall have power to add to its number."

The resolution was adopted, and the Chairman named, as the Business Committee, Dr. Benjamin F. Trueblood, Chairman; President William W. Birdsall, Howard M. Jenkins, Susan W. Janney, Philip C. Garrett, Dr. Rufus M. Jones, Dr. O. Edward Janney and Professor Ellen C. Wright. The Committee was afterwards enlarged by the addition of President Edmund Stanley, Esther Pugh, Peter W. Raidabaugh and Robert E. Pretlow.

HOWARD M. JENKINS: I have received, in my capacity as Secretary of the General and also the Local Committee, a number of communications. Some of them are resolutions, or minutes, expressing sympathy with the object of the meeting, and others are names of delegates. I take this opportunity of handing these to the Chairman, to give to the two committees that have just been appointed.

THE CHAIRMAN: One more matter of business. The Local Committee of Arrangements have asked me to say that it is their judgment that the proceedings of this Conference will have such permanent value that they should be published. It is suggested that the Business Committee take the subject under consideration, both as to style of publication, if it shall seem expedient to publish the proceedings, and the size of the edition. Those questions can be best answered after the Committee have had communication with those in attendance and have learned what the desires of individuals or of peace associations may be. The question is largely one of means. Funds have already been provided, through the generous contributions of Friends, for paying all the other expenses of the Conference, but the question of publication was not taken into consideration. It will be left, therefore, with the Business Committee.

BENJAMIN F. TRUEBLOOD: If any who are present would like to subscribe for a number of copies of the Report for their own personal use, and will communicate with us, the Business Committee will know much better how to proceed in the matter.

THE CHAIRMAN: The time has come for the reading of the papers prepared for this session. The first on the program is on "The New Testament Grounds of Peace," by Professor Elbert Russell. Owing to ill health Elbert Russell has found himself unable to be present. He has entrusted his paper to his personal friend, Robert E. Pretlow, of Wilmington, Ohio, who will read it to us.

THE NEW TESTAMENT GROUNDS OF PEACE.

BY PROFESSOR ELBERT RUSSELL, CHICAGO.

The grounds of peace in the New Testament are found in the teaching of Jesus as it is exemplified in his life and interpreted by the apostles. We must take Jesus's example as the standard by which to interpret his teaching. Otherwise it is possible to deduce from isolated sayings of the Master the most divergent and contradictory ideas of right and wrong.

From the Gospels we learn that Jesus explicitly refused the sword or any other violent means to propagate his doctrines or to found his kingdom, relying only on the power of truth, love and self-sacrifice to overthrow evil and secure the triumph of righteousness. From his character and plans the military virtues and ideals were conspicuously absent. The pacific virtues of the prophet and sage characterized his life and determined his career. At the time of his great temptation, he was compelled to decide by what means he would seek to make the kingdoms of the world his own. Jewish expectancy said the Messiah would secure his dominion by military power. Universal experience said there was no way to world dominion except by the sword. On the mount of temptation Satan offered Jesus the sovereignty of the world on the same evil terms on which others had before held it—by military force. But Jesus refused to be a military king. Again, in Gethsemane, Peter offered Jesus the service of his sword, but Jesus declined both Peter's sword and that of the angelic legions that were at his call. Standing before Pilate Jesus acknowledged himself a king—a king whose power rested on truth, not on might.

Such was Jesus in a world organized politically, socially and religiously on a basis of military force; in which military prowess and conquest were regarded as the sign of greatness for the individual and the nation. In that world the disappointing, incomprehensible, maddening thing about him was his pretence to kingship without an army to back him—his claim to a kingdom which was not of that world. To the Jews who were expecting a military Messiah he was a stumbling-block. To the Romans, who knew no power but law enforced by the sword, he was an enigma. To the Greeks whose wisdom did not transcend a military society he was a fool. The world of that day could have understood the Christ with a sword, but the cross of Christ was an offence.

If there is in the life of Jesus a real incarnation of God (and there is), his whole life is an example for us to follow, and in this example is found the surest ground of peace in the New Testament, for the ways he trod are paths of peace.

The grounds of peace in the teachings of Jesus and His apostles are threefold: (1) Jesus removed the distinction between fellow-countryman and foreigner, so far as men's moral obligations to each are concerned, thus removing any pretext for international war which would not also furnish a justification for intestine war. (2) Jesus forbade the use of violence to promote righteousness or root out evil. (3) Jesus instructs his disciples to follow his example in seeking to extend his kingdom by relying exclusively on spiritual rather than physical force, the forces of peace and not those of war. Let us consider briefly each of these points.

I. The Jewish people had been trained to feel their peculiarity among the nations, and had been encouraged to keep aloof from them during their formative period, lest they should become polluted morally and religiously by intercourse with their heathen neighbors. This attitude, which had become very pronounced in Christ's time, was expressed in the saying: " Thou shalt love thy neighbor and hate thine enemy;" in which expression "neighbor" means "fellow-countryman" and "enemy" means "foreigner." But this spirit of clannishness and of hatred to foreigners could not be part of the world religion which Christ came to establish. Christ extended to all men the privileges and obligations of fellow-countrymen. "But I say unto you, love your enemies (foreigners with whom you have dealings) and pray for them that persecute you (the Romans) that ye may be sons of your Father who is in Heaven; for he maketh his sun to rise on the evil and the good, and sendeth rain on the just and the unjust. For if ye love them that love you (your compatriots) what reward have ye? Do not even the publicans (Roman tax-collectors) the same? And if ye salute your *brethren* only, what do ye more than others? Do not even the *Gentiles* the same? Ye therefore shall be perfect (in impartial love) even as your heavenly Father is perfect."

This is likewise the lesson of the parable of the Good Samaritan. The young man would accept Christ's summary of the law, "Thou shalt love thy neighbor as thyself," and yet justify his Jewish exclusiveness by the word "neighbor." Jesus tells him how one of the most hated of foreigners, the Samaritan, proved neighbor to a Jew whom his selfish fellow-countrymen had neglected. The love due a neighbor knows no national bounds. How is war between different countries possible, even for so-called patriotic reasons, if one is to treat the foreigner as though he were a compatriot?

II. In the parable of the Tares, Jesus teaches that no violence is to be used to remove evil men from the world and to promote the cause of righteousness. Jesus's first parable, on that day of parables by the sea—the parable of the Sower—had dispelled whatever hopes the disciples may have had of the easy and immediate triumph of the kingdom of God. It showed them that the preached word was not always to be fruitful. We know something of the character and thought of these men. James and John afterward wished to call down fire upon a hostile Samaritan village. Peter was quick with his sword when his Master was arrested in Gethsemane. Simon belonged to the "zealot" party, which had inspired some of the bloodiest insurrections against the Roman rule.

All the disciples shared the current Jewish notion that the Messiah would crush the Roman power, conquer the nations, restore the kingdom of David, and make it universal by military force. On hearing that Jesus's kingdom was not to triumph at once, and by the mere preaching of the word, the question would naturally arise in their hearts, "What are we to do to destroy the evil that opposes and secure the triumph of the kingdom after the word shall have been tried and found inadequate? Shall we take the sword to destroy the sinners and hostile Gentiles?" This natural question Jesus anticipated and answered in the parable of the tares of the field. The kingdom of God is not to triumph through military force nor is violence to be used to keep the world good. Christ's servants are to carry on the contest with evil by the means and methods which he himself used. Beyond that the removal of evil from the world must be left to the Son of man to whom the work of judgment has been committed by the Father.

Paul and Peter were only making an application of this teaching of Jesus when they charged the early Christians not to attempt physical resistance but to be in subjection to existing governments.

III. Jesus trained a body of disciples and sent them to carry on a contest against the devil and his works. He gave them full instructions for the work, but said nothing of military power. They were to preach the gospel, heal the sick, to bear witness of him, and suffer for their testimony, and to do these things with impartial love for all men. In the beatitudes given at the time he chose the twelve apostles, he promised them that the meek, the peacemakers, and those who bore persecution unresistingly, should inherit the earth, be known as God's sons, and possess the kingdom of heaven. The military virtues had no beatitude from Jesus. His disciples, as he described, commissioned and blessed them, are men of peace.

These, in brief, are the grounds of peace in the New Testament. They are fundamental in it. Christian peace is not a precarious inference from isolated texts in the New Testament, nor an appendix to Christian ethics, but it inheres in the very nature of the kingdom of God which Christ came to establish on earth.

THE CHAIRMAN: I will now call upon Dr. George A. Barton, of Bryn Mawr College, who will read a paper upon the "Elements of Peace Doctrine in the Old Testament."

ELEMENTS OF PEACE DOCTRINE IN THE OLD TESTAMENT.

BY GEORGE A. BARTON, PH.D., BRYN MAWR COLLEGE.

With reference to the relation which the Old Testament bears to the doctrine of international peace there are four possible attitudes of mind:

1. We may take the ground that the Old Testament is a record of a divine revelation, that it exhibits war as a part of the divine plan, and that, therefore, it justifies warfare among Christians. This attitude has been generally taken by Christians in many different centuries. It has its advocates yet. It has served to flood the Christian world with wave upon wave of barbarism. Although it is still advocated by some Christian teachers, it is too superficial to merit refutation in a company like this.

2. The second possible position is in part identical with the preceding and in part the antithesis of it. It holds that the Old Testament reeks with un-Christian barbarism, that it is a millstone about the neck of the Church, and that no advance can be made in the realization of the Christian ideal of peace until this unwieldy impediment is cast aside. This attitude of mind is as superficial as the preceding. It is produced naturally by reaction from the extravagant claims of those who advocate the first position.

3. A third attitude is sometimes taken. It is said that the victories gained by Israel, which were of real advantage to the nation, were not the result of war, but of divine interposition, and that large military establishments were not only contrary to the commands of God, but disastrous to the political prosperity of the nation.

This position would be comforting, if true, but unfortunately it rests upon a method of Old Testament study, which can no longer be regarded as thorough. Our Old Testament historical books were compiled and edited by men who lived just at the period when the Hebrews were passing from a nation to a church. These narratives were collected, not so much for the sake of history, as for the religious lesson which they might be made to enforce. Without doubt, too, the nation had suffered from the military ambitions of its greatest leaders. Equally undoubted is the fact that there was a large Providential element in the military victories won by their ancestors; but in retelling the stories of these to enforce a religious point of view the Providential element was heightened, the warlike element, which in the early time was very real, fell into the background, and the whole perspective was innocently and unconsciously changed.

Let me give an illustration. In the sixth chapter of Joshua two different accounts of the taking of Jericho are woven together. In the older of these we are told how the Hebrews captured the city by a ruse. They quietly marched about the city for seven days, in such a manner as to appear unable to attack it, thus throwing the inhabitants off their guard, and when the garrison least expected it raised a great shout, and, rushing upon it, captured the city. The deed was really a military stratagem, but the victory was, like all victories, ascribed to Jehovah, the God of battles. The victory was won so easily, however, that it was ascribed in an especial manner to the interposition of God, and it was only natural that in later times it should give rise to traditions in which the Providential element overshadowed the other entirely. Indeed it is not impossible for such a point of view to be taken in modern times about modern events. I have heard of a Friend, who regards the signal victories of the American fleets over the Spaniards, in the war of 1898, accomplished as they were with almost no loss of life, as evidence that America was as much the chosen instrument for the overthrow of Spanish despotism as Israel was for the extermination of the Canaanites, and that God fought for the American fleets as he did for Israel of old. If this were not an age of books and of critical historical study, there might easily grow up in America a very unreal tradition about that war—a tradition in which the actual military element, which we so much regretted, would sink out of sight altogether, and an impression prevail that it was determined wholly by Providential interpositions. Obviously, then, if we would find in Israel's history valid principles which may be applied to real international life in this world, we must adopt a less superficial method of study.

4. A fourth attitude is possible. We may recognize that the religion of Israel was the Providential preparation for Christianity, that in the beginning the Hebrews differed little from their neighbors and kinsmen either in religion or in the arts of life, but that as time advanced they saw more clearly the nature of God and their proper relation to their neighbors. If we proceed thus we shall expect their religion and morals to be crude in the early period, but we shall expect, as we approach the time of the coming of the Prince of Peace, to discover a clearer apprehension of those great principles which should make war forever impossible.

This last is the point of view which this essay is an endeavor to set forth, though obviously in the time at my disposal the proper treatment of the subject can only be hinted at.

In the animal world warfare and struggle seem to be perfectly natural. Biologists teach us that it is by means of these that animal life has been pushed forward to its present degree of perfection. Man is from one standpoint a member of the animal kingdom. In the earlier stages of his development he has necessarily been pushed forward by the same processes which have moulded all animal life. He cannot be led forward by the lofty ideals which inspire by their brightness and purity until he can appreciate something of their beauty and sublimity. Until then, like his fellows in the animal realm, he must be pushed forward by the blind forces of struggle and survival. To discover the elements of a peace doctrine in the Old Testament, we must discover the power to appreciate the great religious truths on which it rests. Those truths are the Fatherhood of God, and the brotherhood of man. Until men have clearly understood that God is the God of all men, and that it is as wrong to injure a stranger as a brother, because both are the children of the same Father, no peace doctrine is possible to them.

Now, in the early days of Israel's national life the necessary religious foundation for this truth had not been laid. Each tribe, or, at the most, each nation, had its god. Each nation thought it must worship its own god, but it in no wise denied the reality of the gods of other nations. These gods were conceived as larger men, ready to fight with one another, or to over-reach one another in all the ways which men would do. This applies to the early history of Israel as truly as to that of other ancient peoples. When David was temporarily driven from his native land, and had to take refuge in Moab, we hear him complaining: "They have driven me out this day that I should not cleave unto the inheritance of Jehovah, saying, Go serve other gods" (1 Samuel 26: 19). Jehovah's power was, he seemed to think, limited to Palestine, and, when on foreign soil, David naturally supposed he must worship a foreign god. This accounts for the fact that David practiced such barbarities upon conquered enemies (2 Samuel 12: 31). From his religious point of view these enemies had no rights. Obviously in such an age the peace doctrine could find no root.

In Amos, the first of the literary prophets, we find a broader outlook, both as regards the extent of God's rule over the nations, and as regards the barbarities of war. He perceived that Jehovah controlled all nations; Jehovah brought the Philistines from Caphtor and the Aramæans from Kir, as well as Israel from Egypt (Amos 9: 7). It was Amos, too, the possessor of this breadth of religious vision, who condemned that violation of treaties, that barbarity to women, and that disregard of the sacredness of death, which are so characteristic of war (see Amos 1: 9; 1: 13; 2: 1).

It takes, in any age, a long time for a higher ideal to win its way, and that was true of Israel as well as of others. Isaiah sang of the birth of the "Prince of peace," in language which is much obscured in our common versions of the Bible, but which is so enshrined in the affections of the Christian world that one hesitates to disturb it, even in the interest of truth. When Isaiah's language is really understood, however, it differs but little from the hard standards of the age of war. That Prince, as Isaiah conceived him, was to be a "wonderful plotter, a very god of a warrior, and a father of booty" before he was "Prince of peace." In other words Isaiah's conception is still the conception of a conqueror; the peace which this passage pictures was such as Kitchener is making in South Africa.

Many years later Isaiah had a more attractive vision. In the eleventh chapter of his prophecy, when describing the Messianic kingdom, he sang of a time when—

> "The wolf will lodge with the lamb,
> The leopard lie down with the kid,
> The calf and the young lion will graze together,
> And a little child will lead them."

This language is no doubt figurative. The prophet pictured under these animal forms the way in which human passion was to become harmelss. It is not clear, however, whether his thought embraced the world in this Utopia of peace, or whether he confined it to the kingdom of Israel. The words which immediately follow favor the latter view.

Such religious conceptions as those of Amos were, nevertheless, bound to bear fruit. Under the influence of the prophets the old laws were recast and king Josiah instituted a reform on their basis. We now possess this work in our book of Deuteronomy. It is characterized by a large humanitarian element. It sought to soften the rugged features of the hard life of ancient times. It instituted laws in behalf of the poor, in behalf of slaves, who were usually the captives taken in war, and even in behalf of animals.* In its treatment of war itself there is a milder, more human and reasonable note than one is accustomed to find in antiquity (see Deuteronomy 20, and cf. Goldwin Smith in *Independent* of August 22d, 1901, p. 1959 ff.). Of the Levitical code which came into its present form even later, though many of its laws are old, the same may also be said.† If that code seems to limit the sympathies of Israel at times by enforcing kindness towards members of that race particularly, it also commanded the Hebrew to love the resident alien as himself (Leviticus 19: 17, 18). When we remember that the resident alien was usually a captive of war, we can see how beneficently the teaching of prophets like Amos was taking effect. The idea that there was but one God and He the God of all men, was producing a new conception of humanity fatal to the spirit of war.

In no book of the Old Testament does this leavening doctrine, that God cares for all men, and its corollary, that mercy is due to all, shine out more clearly than in the book of Jonah, but we have been so occupied in quarreling about Jonah's whale that the significance of the message of the book has escaped us. The book was written to enforce the great truths that God's care extends to all men, that he chose Israel not for her own sake merely, but to bear his message of warning, of righteousness, and of mercy to all men,

---

* See Kent's "Humanitarian Element in the Old Testament Legislation," *Biblical World*, October, 1901.

† See Kent, in *Biblical World* for November, 1901.

and that even the worst of Israel's enemies may find mercy with God and become his people. The book of Jonah is a missionary tract. The kindliness of God extends to all nations; the spirit of helpful sympathy should prevail toward them in the hearts of his worshipers—this is the message of this unique book, and it is a message calculated to extirpate the spirit of selfishness and narrowness from which all war springs.

The climax of Old Testament thought in this respect is reached in that little prophecy, found both in the second chapter of Isaiah and in the fourth chapter of Micah, the origin of which is a puzzle. Was it composed by Isaiah, by Micah, or by some unknown prophet? Perhaps the latter is the correct view. From this unknown seer it may have been introduced by editors into the positions in the books of Isaiah and Micah, where it now stands. Be that as it may, in its inspired utterance we have for the first time an adequate expression of what a real monotheism means for the world. "The mountain of the Lord's house shall be established in the top of the mountain and exalted above the hills. Many nations shall give him their allegiance; his word shall rule them; he shall judge between many peoples and decide concerning strong nations afar off; and they shall beat their swords into plowshares, and their spears into pruning hooks; nation shall not lift up sword against nation, neither shall they learn war any more." One God for all nations, hence one brotherhood among men, and a universal peace on earth. This is the only logical view for a monotheist, and is the inevitable result of a belief in one God. Such is the strength of old custom, especially of custom consecrated by religious sanction and rooted in human passion, that this prophetic vision did not make a deep impression on the prophets' contemporaries; but nevertheless the beautiful picture of international amity, clearly drawn against the dark background of a savage antiquity, anticipated by two millenniums the vision of our Whittier, who sang:

"Evil shall cease and Violence pass away,
And the tired world breathe free through a long Sabbath day."

Viewed in the manner here indicated, the Old Testament neither sanctions war nor is a millstone about the neck of Christianity, nor is it the record of a people who lived in a world so unreal that it can teach us no practical lesson. It affords a basis for the peace doctrine, both because it exhibits the fact that war springs from the animal side of human nature, and is fostered only by a conception of God so limited as to be but little removed from heathenism; and also because it reveals the fact that the doctrine of monotheism cannot be really held without creating in men's minds an abhorrence of the barbarities of war, and without inspiring visions of a universal peace. The former element, though painfully apparent, is a waning or diminishing element; the latter, as revelation in its progress nears the Central Figure in human history, clearly appears as the increasing and triumphant element.

The Chairman: The next paper, entitled "The Failure of the Christian Church in Regard to Peace Principles," is by Mary Chawner Woody, of Winston-Salem, N. C., who will now read it.

THE FAILURE OF THE CHRISTIAN CHURCH IN THE PAST IN REGARD TO PEACE PRINCIPLES.

BY MARY CHAWNER WOODY, WINSTON-SALEM, N. C.

It needs no argument or incident to show the great blessing which the church has been to the world—even in time of war; but the signal failure of the church to fill its mission of peace is harrowing in the extreme.

The Prince of Peace came in an era of peace to establish a kingdom of peace under the reign of love. There had been in the Roman Empire alone 644 years of constant war—from Tullius Hostilius to Augustus Cæsar—with only six years of peace. But now the temple of Janus was closed, and at the advent of Jesus the shepherds heard the anthem of the angels, " On earth peace, goodwill to men."

The blessed Saviour taught his philosophy of love to his chosen followers, established his kingdom in the midst of the nations, and plainly stated the practical application of his principles. His disciples were slow to comprehend the force of love, and on slight provocation desired to call down fire from heaven on their enemies. Even at the last of the three years of constant teaching they misunderstood the figurative language and thought to rule by physical force. Then Jesus gave to the leader the plain words, " Put up thy sword, for all they that take the sword shall perish with the sword "; and then an example of tenderness before the eyes of the little church should have taught his followers for all time that the human body was not to be mutilated and mangled with implements of war. As the soldiers were binding him, at his words, " Suffer ye thus far," the restoring hand was loosed a moment until it could reach the wounded ear of Malchus and touch it back to health. Previously that evening, as Jesus closed his instruction to his followers on close fellowship with himself, he left the legacy of peace—forgotten in his very presence.

This peace is first in the child of God. " It is a triple peace "— peace with God, peace with our neighbor, peace with ourselves. " It has a wider scope than the individual." It is the effect of righteousness that shall be peace. Cardinal Gibbons very truly interprets the gospel when he says: " God is the God of peace to the individual, the Father of peace to the family, and the Prince of Peace to society."

The very force of the law of love will lead into the kingdom of peace. The coals of fire will melt the stony heart. Love is the most potent killing agency ever applied—cold steel and " reeking tube " are not to be compared with it.

If the Church was not to affect society why did Jesus say to that little company, " Ye are the light of the world " ?   Why did he use that closer metaphor, " Ye are the salt of the earth " ?

This was a prophecy that his chosen followers were to modify the whole world, that the principles enunciated by him would affect every institution they reached.

It has been wonderfully fulfilled. Though under the light of the gospel there are many thousands who have not accepted its truth, yet their whole character is modified by it. There can be little comparison between the unbeliever who has been brought up among Christian people and the heathen who has never come in touch with the salt of the earth. But it is to be shown here wherein the salt in this kingdom of peace has failed and so been trodden under foot of men.

The principles of the Prince and the anthem of the angels and the legacy left have not been utilized in the church, and so it has lost its pacific element. It has yielded to a lower law, and thus broken a higher and more effectual.

If an ear of the enemy could not be cut off in defence of the Son of God, where is a sufficient cause for Christians ever to assume the defensive? But the Christian Church has brought over from the old dispensation an eye for an eye and a tooth for a tooth, and has attempted to engraft into the broad spreading tree of the gospel the seclusive, exclusive exotic of the Jewish religion. This has wrought untold mischief.

The Church seems never ready, when a crisis comes, to meet it, because it has failed previously in not teaching the precepts of the gospel, " line upon line." " In time of peace prepare for war " has been faithfully observed, and so a Christian nation, filled with Christian churches, rushes into war on the slightest pretext, and the dove of peace cannot then be heard above the roaring artillery. If the salt of the earth would keep its savor, every Christian nation would be so saved by it that the folly of war would be impossible. It is the business of the Church to make people kind and just and wise, so that " kings would not play at the game of war."

Dr. Chalmers says it is only by the extension of Christian principles among the people of the earth that the atrocities of war will at length be swept away. If this is true the failure is apparent; the Bible has not been sufficiently taught, the Sermon on the Mount has been hid as out of date. The gospel of love has been pushed aside as impracticable.

A leaflet issued by the Howard Association says: " The regicides perpetrated by Italian and other anarchists, the assassinations and conspiracies of nihilists, the vendettas of Southern Europe, and the gross municipal disorders and corruptions of some of our American cities have all been especially characteristic of sections of people who, even if in some cases making a profession of religion, have really never been habituated or inclined to an acquaintance with the supreme truths of God and eternity as revealed in the Holy Scriptures." Professor Huxley is quoted as saying: " By the study of what other book could children be so humanized? . . . Nowhere else is the fundamental truth as strongly laid down that the welfare of the state depends upon the righteousness of the citizen." " The Bible is the most democratic book in the world." That many grow up in our Christian country utterly ignorant of the Bible lies at the door of the Church. All quarters where there are disturbing elements, or likely to be, the Bible should be applied by all possible means more bountifully than would the health officer throw salt into a cesspool that breeds diphtheria. Take the late assassin, for instance. The Christian Church is responsible for such a character being developed in our midst. The assassin had strong convictions and a courage equal to his convictions. But that his convictions were wrong is a stigma on our instruction. If the penetrating gospel of love had been as faithfully applied to his mind as were anarchistic views it is altogether probable that right principles would have been maintained with even greater tenacity. But behold the attitude of the church; it is vividly given in a cartoon of a minister and an anarchist side by side, the same spirit in both. The anarchist exclaims, " Kill all rulers " ; the minister exclaims, " Lynch all anarchists." When will these bewildered people believe the gospel of love?

A modified form of Christianity has been taught and not the gospel pure and simple. The Church has so often given man's idea of christianity and not God's thought.

The fundamental doctrine of love to God and faith in man has not its full application. From the beginning the Church has continued daily to say " Our Father," but has not yet learned that if we say " Our Father " we must say also " My brother." For " He hath made of one blood all the nations of men to dwell upon the face of the earth." Until the Church teaches the brotherhood of man there can never be the federation of the world. The beloved disciple gives the gauge by which every Christian is to be measured. " If a man say, I love God, and hateth his brother, he is a liar; for he that loveth not his brother whom he hath seen, how can he love God whom he hath not seen? " How can he say, " Our Father " if he does not say " My brother " ? But the writer continues: " This commandment have we from him, that he that loveth God love his brother also." This means the Filipinos, the Boers, the negroes, the Indians and the Chinese.

The Church was to be a light to the world, but it has wasted much of its force in controversy. " Ye are the light of the world." But how could the Church throw light upon the world when quarreling about the light itself? How could the Church win the darkminded when it did not recognize him as a brother?

When the Dutch made their settlement in South Africa it is said that over their church door was this mongrel legend: " Dogs and Hottentots keep out." In these diminutive people they could see no trace of kinship. But under the brotherly care of the Moravian missionaries these same Hottentots received the gospel, and two years ago, at the Moravian Synod in Herrn Hutt, this same Hottentot mission was transferred to the list of self-supporting churches. We admire the piety and persistence of the Boers, but lament their forgetting that the grace of God which bringeth salvation to all men hath appeared.

How could the Church invite the world to a peace meeting when at strife within itself over possible renderings and interpretations and modifications? Filled with this enmity the Church is shorn of its strength. If the prayer of Jesus "that they may be one" were fulfilled, what power the united Church would now have in averting any storm cloud that might be gathering in all Christendom. She might also be an arbiter for heathen countries. Instead, the responsibility of many wars lies at the door of the Church. For instance, our own Civil War came only after the Church had carried the strife so far as to split in two itself; then it was easy for the state to follow. The Church had failed to maintain the conditions of peace. Though the Catholic Church has as one of its principles, "The church shuns the shedding of blood," yet the New York *Journal* is authority for these words from the Pope to the Queen of Spain during the conflict in Cuba: "We repeat with all our heart, it is our wish that God may give victory to the Spanish arms in favor of your throne and the Catholic nation." The proper whole-hearted wish for the highest dignitary in the Church should have been for the success f God and humanity.

When matters came to a crisis the salutation from the Protestant Church in America was in the same spirit as that of the Pope; so war with Spain was inevitable. If vessels laden with supplies to relieve suffering from the hand of Christian people of the United States had waited in Cuban waters instead of a man-of-war, it would not have been a menace to Spain.

By inflammatory sermons and bloodthirsty journalism both church and state were carried off their base, though Fitzhugh Lee, our consul, sent a cablegram that it would not do to send a man-of-war to the scene of conflict; but the Maine went and slipped into Havana harbor, and what has followed? And who can see the end of mangled forms and garments rolled in blood? The gospel of love is shut out by stronger walls than heathen superstitions from the drink-maddened Filipino.

What is a little shout of glory for some name and the questionable honor of a rear-admiral? The mother of Worth Bagley gave the true sentiment when the news of the slaughter of the young ensign reached her Raleigh home, and she exclaimed, "Tell them to stop fighting! I want no Spanish mother's heart to bleed as mine does to-day."

At the close of the eighteenth century, under the leadership of the head of the Greek Church, Russia, Catholic Austria and Protestant Prussia partitioned out Poland. The freedom-loving Polanders, with no country to defend, have come to look upon all rulers as tyrants. The failure of the Church at the close of the eighteenth century has borne its legitimate fruit at the close of the nineteenth. What a century plant, with its deadly bloom in every civilized country on the globe! Because the Church has blessed and shouted over the armies, God's law, " he appointed to the nations their bounds," has been broken, and a people without a country have lost their confidence in the Church and have become a deadly foe to every ruler. In the American Revolution Kosciuszko drew his sword for the freedom of America. In 1901 a Polander takes the life of its President.

The Christian Church quotes with joy the prophecies of Isaiah, but thinks them only ideal and impracticable. The great failure of the Church in the past has been that it has not recognized that under the leadership of the Head of the Church men are to work out the fulfillment of prophecy. The mere existence of these prophecies upon the inspired page is a condemnation of war and a command to the Christian Church to work for their *fulfillment*.

A recent example of the success of the gospel plan has been given us from the far-away New Hebrides, whose four thousand men were only lately turned from cannibalism. The converted chief went with Frank Paton, the son of the veteran missionary, to establish a mission in one of the villages. He was met with loaded rifles, and was shot in protecting Mr. Paton. In his beautiful Christian death the chief insisted that no revenge should be taken for his mortal wound. What was the result? The evangelist says that this kind of a revenge opened the way for a band of the followers of their martyred chief to go two days of each week to preach Christ in the villages. What a contrast to the bands sent by Christian America to Christianize the Filipinos!

Cardinal Gibbons, in a sermon at the beginning of the century, said, " The teachings of the gospel form the only basis of peace for the rulers of the earth. All the arts and resources of diplomacy will be in vain; all the courts of arbitration and peace conferences that ever shall assemble will avail but little . . . unless their decisions are guided and framed under the invocation of the Lord of Peace, who sits enthroned on the cross."

" God grant that the new century may inaugurate a new era of people fulfilling the prophecy of Isaiah." In a recent sermon, Pastor Sailliens, of Paris, said: " To bring back the church at once to apostolic simplicity, humility and spirituality seems an impossible task. . . . As long as the churches adorn the arms of warriors with consecrated laurels and sing *Te Deums* in honor of their victories, war will continue and men will kill each other in good conscience, thinking they have the approbation of heaven."

THE CHAIRMAN: We have three-quarters of an hour now in which to discuss the three most interesting and valuable papers you have heard. I shall first introduce Dr. Rufus M. Jones, of Haverford College, who will open the discussion.

RUFUS M. JONES: I suppose most of us are too old to remember how it feels to grow up, and how hard and slow it is to get over certain things that are in the grain to start with. We don't remember, perhaps, how easy it is for the child to have the spirit of fight spring up, and how slow the process is of getting rid of it entirely. Well, now, being from observation familiar with the growth of life from childhood to maturity, and the changes which it brings, we ought to expect that some such thing would appear in the progress of the race from childhood to maturity, and that is what we find.

There is, perhaps, no sadder note coming from the early period in the history of the race than that almost earliest note in the Old Testament. You remember a man named Lamech, who invented a weapon. He is the first man, or among the first, who used his head to invent something. The inventive power of man is one of the greatest which God placed in the world. Well, this man Lamech, as soon as he invents his weapon, as soon as he gets an instrument through the exercise of this inventive power, begins to glory in it. He does not glory because he can thereby advance the world's interests and make it better. Here is what he says to his two wives, in the little poem—one of the earliest notes of song—imbedded there in the early part of the Book of Genesis:

> Adah and Zillah, hear my voice;
> Ye wives of Lamech, hearken unto my speech:
> For I have slain a man for wounding me,
> And a young man for bruising me;
> If Cain shall be avenged sevenfold,
> Truly Lamech seventy and sevenfold.

That is the sort of man you have to start with. There are a good many pages in the Book we read and love, through which we have come to the great truths of God and of human life, and you have this seventy-times-seven repeated later in another strain. "How many times shall I forgive the man who hurts me?" a disciple asked. "Seven times? That is what we have been told." "I say unto you, not seven times, but seventy times seven," was the answer. There you have the forgiving spirit lifted to an indefinite height, because the words are indefinite words. Thus you pass along from the spirit of revenge, the spirit that breathes through the man who invents his first weapon, along to the spirit of that Personality who came to show us what life really means and what spirit should prevail in a human being. When two of his pupils came to the Master and called His attention to the fact that when Elijah had difficulties with some people, he called down fire from heaven and got rid of them, and said: "Is not this a similar case? Shall we not call down fire?" he replied: "You know not what spirit you have. We are not living under the spirit of Elijah; we have passed away from that. You do not seem to know what time you are living in; you do not seem to realize at all the new idea of life."

We have learned in our every-day life and in what we read, and this last paper this morning has recalled it to us, how continuously the spirit of the old time, the spirit of Lamech and of Elijah, keeps its hold on men, and goes on, in spite of the fact that the warmer waters of the Gulf Stream are slowly flooding the world.

Two great figures of the seventeenth century, Oliver Cromwell and George Fox, were diametrically opposite characters. You see one of them going into great battles. Shouting the Psalms, he and his men called on God to destroy enemies. You find the other going up and down among men taking the buffets, the scorn and the abuse of men and saying, "I am living in the virtue of that life and power which does away with the occasion for all war." That is the other spirit. That very idea, however, is most beautifully brought out in those very Psalms that Cromwell used to shout as he went to battle. This old poet, when he was lifting up the type of life that ought to prevail, said about it: "Righteousness and peace have kissed each other." There never will be any permanent peace in the world until just that dream of the old Hebrew poet is realized; just as fast as righteousness prevails peace prevails; they are linked together; they are bound forever in one whole. We must learn that we have to treat men as brothers; that every man is to be treated as though he were our other self. We must lift every man up to our own plane, and whenever we come to the point where that sort of righteousness permeates society peace will come with it. Righteousness and peace always will kiss each other. They belong together.

THE CHAIRMAN: The subject is now open for general discussion by the Conference.

DAVIS FURNAS: I have been interested in the papers that have been read, and have enjoyed them. I fear, however, that you will set me down as one of the ignorant old fogies. I was educated to believe that Friends had no place in military organizations, nor among military men. Now, I have been discouraged sometimes when I have heard of ministers of the Gospel of Jesus Christ, ministers in the Society of Friends, making war speeches on Decoration Day. We may make all the profession we please; it is not the profession that brings about an object, but it is the doing of the thing that we profess. When we profess to be members of Christ's kingdom of peace and go around making war speeches for popularity's sake, we shall not accomplish much in the promotion of peace. Our ministers ought to stand forth in the love of Christ and proclaim nothing but peace on earth and goodwill to men.

WILLIAM G. HUBBARD: If the Chair please, I wish just to set my testimony to the last paper that we listened to. While the others were good, it seems to me that probably that is one of the most important that we shall have.

I have had a good deal of contact with the ministers of different denominations, and with churches, and I feel very keenly the force of the charges of inconsistency brought against ministers of the Gospel of Christ. When I was a student in college I listened to a man that I had learned to love for his devoutness. On one occasion, when he was making a public address, I was thoroughly shocked to hear him say: "A rebel has no right except the right to six feet of earth with a bullet in his heart." We know how many editorials have been written in some of the leading papers, and often in religious papers, speaking in the most approving terms of war. Now it seems to me—and I have felt this a great many times in my work—that we have not done our full duty as believers in the doctrine of peace, not to have brought this doctrine more to the attention of the various denominations throughout the country. When I addressed at one time a great educational institution in one of the Western States, the president of the institution and the president of the board of directors both came on to the platform, at the close of the meeting, and said: "That is the first address on peace I have ever heard." I have heard that remark made by educators in Western institutions probably a score of times. The pastor of one of the large churches in Cleveland said to his congregation, at the close of one of my addresses, "I think you must have been deeply interested in this presentation. It is the first time I have ever heard a sermon on peace." The man had been preaching the Gospel of the Prince of Peace for thirty years and yet had never heard a discourse on that subject before! I presume there are a thousand schools of higher grade in the United States where no address has ever been given along this line. I simply want to raise this question, not to discuss it: Are we doing our duty? A hundred thousand Friends, probably, are represented here. Ought it to be possible that a man of general intelligence and reading should be able to say, "I have never heard an address on peace?" Will this Conference plan to disseminate more generally these arguments that are being produced here, and bring the matter more strikingly and more thoroughly to the attention of the Christian people of the United States?

ALLEN FLITCRAFT: I have been interested in each of the papers, and also in the discussion. With the first paper we all agree. All true, vital Christians, it seems to me, must endorse what is in it. In reference to the second, I know that those who are not really in the spirit of the Gospel, and are disposed to encourage war, will try to support their views by the use of the Old Testament; but as I read the Old Testament, and get into the spirit of the inspired writers who produced it, I find that it is in favor of peace. I have risen merely to say this: Jesus Christ had not anything directly to do with philosophy, science or government; neither, I believe, had His apostles. Their mission was of a spiritual character. If the professing Christians of to-day were living in the spirit and advocating the kingdom of Christ more than the kingdoms of this world, as did the early Christians, our governments would be far in advance of what they are. While we are reflecting upon the church and the ministers of other denominations—and perhaps we can truthfully do it—how are we living ourselves? The principles of Christ will keep others as well as ministers in the spirit of the Gospel. While we look to ministers and expect their light to shine more brightly if possible than that of others, who of us are entirely clear? Are we doing our duty as individual members of the Society of Friends?

Again, a word in reference to our government. Our government is, unfortunately, not founded upon the principles of peace, upon the Gospel of Jesus Christ. In the present condition of people, it would probably not succeed, if it were so founded. It is not our business to endeavor to tie the hands of those that may be in authority at the head of the nation, but to do our part in having the condition of our hearts right. Then we shall be instrumental in leading others to Christ, and in hastening the day when the knowledge of the glory of the Lord shall fill the earth as the waters cover the sea. Then it will not be necessary to have governments founded upon force.

ANNA BRAITHWAITE THOMAS: Why is it that the church has failed to grasp these principles of peace? Why is it that good men to-day support war? I do not think it is from bad principles. The ministers who have preached and written in favor of war in South Africa and in the Philippine Islands have not done so, I think, from a desire of glory, or for punishing enemies, or for aggrandizement. They have done it because they thought that the cause of righteousness and truth would through these wars be advanced in the world; that the victory of England in South Africa and the victory of America in the Philippine Islands would be for the advancement of the Gospel of Christ.

One reason why they have believed thus is, I think, because we have not done our part in the propagation of the Gospel message of peace. We peace people have been, at least we have been looked upon as, negative. We have not had an aggressive spirit. If we want to overcome these erroneous beliefs, if we want to carry others with us, we must show that evil can be overcome with good. We must actually overcome evil. We must carry out in pacific ways what they think is to be done by the sword. We must let them see that we are actually getting things done in Christ's way.

Another thing: I think we ought to enlist the sympathies of the young people. The peace movement has a hold on the older men and women, but it fails to attract the young people. Why is it? Just the want of this aggressive spirit. The young generation's hearts are enlisted in the cause of Christ and of His kingdom, but they do not comprehend the slow way of non-resistance. The peace-at-any-price policy, as it is called, does not enlist their sympathies. We must go forward aggressively in the name of the Lord, and show them that we are overcoming evil with good, and that Christ means to conquer the world. Christ was a young man (I say it reverently); He understood the feelings, the emotions and the ambitions of youth; He spoke to the young people; He still has a word for them, and I believe that we ought to enlist them in this warfare.

The church *has* failed; I have seen so many proofs of it. I have almost wept to see the representatives of the peace societies of the continent of Europe stand up one after another, as they did a short time ago at the Peace Congress in Glasgow, and say, "I am an unbeliever; I am a freethinker; I have no use for the Gospel of Christ." Evidently the church has failed. We have failed to make our principles a power. But we must do it. We must give energy and time to presenting the Gospel of Jesus Christ, the Gospel of peace. We must make people understand that Jesus Christ is the Prince of Peace. If we can do that we shall be able to take away one of the greatest obstacles in the world to the progress of the Gospel. Many people are being kept away from Jesus Christ by this one stumbling block: that the church endorses war. It is our business to change that and to let people understand that the Gospel is a Gospel of peace.

JOHN CHAWNER: There are two thoughts that I want to express in connection with two different sides of the subject that has been presented this morning. With regard to the teaching of the Old Testament history, we know there are some points in it that are seemingly not consistent with Christian principles. I am glad that the address we have had to-day has dwelt on the points that are consistent, and has pointed out the Christian principle, the real Christ thread in the Old Testament, leading up to Christianity as presented in the life of Christ.

In regard to the failure of Christians, I remember what I once saw in a railroad train in Indiana. I took from the rack a Bible that had been placed there by some Bible Association, and on the fly-leaf some one had written, "Christianity has produced more wars than all other causes." The answer that occurred to me was the remark of the Apostle: "Whence come wars and fightings?" etc., and I wrote the reference to James beside the statement on the fly-leaf. We know, as we look back over the history of the Christian Church, that there is truth in the statement that it has been the cause of much war—has undertaken at times to disseminate the principles of peace by war. We must do what we can to have it different in the future.

HOWARD M. JENKINS: I only want to take one moment to say that I enjoyed very much all the papers of this morning, but particularly the presentation by Professor Russell, and by our friend, Dr. Barton. They appear to me in both cases to have gone to the marrow of the subject, and to have presented it to us very admirably.

WILLIAM W. BIRDSALL: I have profited this morning particularly by the presentation of the "Elements of Peace Doctrine in the Old Testament." I have long found in the Old Testament the finest expression of aspiration after peace. I believe we ought to come more and more to see in it what Dr. Barton has pointed out to us, namely, the developing expression of the mind of God through the errors of men, rising more and more nearly to perfection as time went on and men grew more and more able to see and realize the light.

JAMES B. UNTHANK: I have enjoyed very much all that has been said. It has been very instructive and edifying. I wish to make a suggestion: I hope that nothing which seems to reflect upon our fellow Christians of other denominations will go out as the voice of this Convention that is not thoroughly authorized in fact. We ought not to make statements that may be offensive to other Christian people, if they are not strictly true.

THE CHAIRMAN: It will certainly be understood by all that the contents of these papers are the expressions of individual opinion. We have already entrusted to a Business Committee the duty of gathering up the threads of discussion and of determining the proper form which the Declaration of the Conference shall take. This suggestion they will of course take into account.

After making announcement of meetings of the Business Committee, the Committee on Credentials, and the readiness of the Entertainment Committee to provide all visiting members of the Conference with homes, the Chairman continued:

I wanted to say before leaving this place that I personally have been more than gratified, and that my heart is profoundly thankful for the response which Friends have given to the invitation to meet in Conference on this subject. We have in this room at this time representatives of those who claim, and rightly claim, the name of Friends, from Maine to California, and from Carolina to Oregon; at least one Friend has crossed the continent from the borders of the Pacific to this City of Brotherly Love on the Delaare, for the single purpose of being with us here and sharing the benefit of a Conference like this. Surely we who dwell near by ought to appreciate such a sacrifice on the part of even a single individual; and we ought to draw inspiration from it for the work that we have in hand. I personally have felt that inspiration as I have looked over this audience to-day; and I could only wish that every one of you could, in turn, take a seat upon this platform and look into the face of such an audience. It is a rare company of rare men and rare women. It is a gifted company, able to respond to the invitation to discuss the most important and profound topics that are to come before us from hour to hour. I shall vacate this chair on declaring the meeting adjourned; and when we come together at half-past three o'clock this afternoon the place will be taken by my friend, Howard M. Jenkins, of Philadelphia. The meeting now is adjourned until that hour.

Second Session.

Fifth-day Afternoon, Twelfth Month 12th.

The Conference reassembled in Witherspoon Hall at 3.30 p.m., with Howard M. Jenkins, editor of the *Friends' Intelligencer*, presiding. A few moments were given to silent devotion before entering upon the exercises of the session.

The Chairman: We have had sent us several communications expressing sympathy with the objects of the Conference. Some of these, or at least their substance, will be presented at this time by the Chairman of the Business Committee.

Benjamin F. Trueblood: The W. C. T. U., of Hoopeston, Ill., sends the following message: "'The Lord will give strength unto His people; the Lord will bless His people with peace.' We most earnestly pray that this meeting may be productive of much good, believing that it will mould public sentiment in the right direction, and that you, with us, may hasten the advance of Christian love, and henceforth every effort may be made to settle all difficulties by means of that love which the Christ principle sets forth. Mary G. Smith, President; Etta K. Smith, Secretary." Similar communications, conveying sympathy and desiring the success of the Conference, have been received (one or two of these came at a later session) from "Trenton Friends' Association," Trenton, N. J., signed by Louisa H. Dunn, Secretary; from the "Association for the Promotion of First-Day Schools within the Limits of Philadelphia Yearly Meeting of Friends," signed by John L. Carver and Mary H. F. Merillat, Clerks; from Burlington Quarterly Meeting of Friends, Trenton, N. J., signed by Franklin S. Zelley, Clerk; from Lobo Monthly Meeting, Coldstream, Canada, signed by Samuel P. Zavitz and others; from the "General Conference of Friends' Associations," held at Moorestown, N. J., signed by William C. Coles, Chairman; from White Water Quarterly Meeting, held at Fall Creek, near Pendleton, Indiana, signed by T. Morris Hardy, Clerk.

James Wood: If the Chair please, I have a proposition that I wish to present, and I ask for its reference to the Business Committee without reading it.

The Chairman: James Wood submits a proposition which he asks to have referred to the Business Committee. That course will be taken.

The Chairman then spoke as follows on the subject, "The American Ideal":

THE AMERICAN IDEAL.

BY HOWARD M. JENKINS.

In conversation, a good many years ago, with the late James H. Campbell, of Pennsylvania, sometime representative in Congress, and later, by appointment of President Lincoln, minister to Sweden, he described, not without emotion, an incident which had occurred to him while in the service abroad. He was making an excursion far up the coast of Norway, when in one of the deep and grand bays there—the fiords—he met a plain peasant of the country. It was near the close of our Civil War—perhaps after that event—and the Norwegian, finding that the visitor was an American, questioned him with pathetic eagerness. "Tell me, sir," he said, "tell me, does that great republic yet live?"

Shall we, to-day, ask that question? Does the great republic yet live?

It was, prior to the year 1898, perhaps we may say prior to the year 1899, the name of the United States of America which, amongst all nations, most and best moved the hearts of men. It stood to them as the symbol of hope. Whether it was a plain peasant of Scandinavia, far up toward the Arctic snows, or whether it was a brown islander of the far Pacific, under tropic heats, their admiration went out to the nation which seemed to stand, and in large measure did stand, for the elevation of mankind. Doubtless, across the seas' breadth the scars and seams upon our national edifice were hardly seen; it was the broad features, the lofty and striking outline, which compelled respect. Our more sordid, our less generous, qualities were obscured by the great principles which we declared—those of human rights and of humane endeavor.

Let us reflect that our republic, in the year 1898, was almost a century and a quarter old. Never in all that time, but once—when Mexico was attacked in the interest of slavery, and by its order—had we waged an aggressive war upon another nation. On the contrary, those peoples who had struggled for better conditions, the world over, looked always to us. It was the United States who promptly recognized the republics of South America when they rose against Spain; who gave moral support to Greece when she defied the Turk; who did not conceal her sympathy for the Hungarians when they were in revolt against Austria; who gave the order which freed Mexico finally of European control. Not, the world over, did any people, anywhere, contending for the common, the inherent, the natural rights of men, fail to look to the United States for at least a sympathetic and encouraging word.

There was every reason for this. The United States was

founded upon principles which aroused the world's hope. In its declaration of the reasons for claiming an independent life, it appealed not to any narrow and technical reasoning, not to selfish and mean motives, not to considerations of mere statecraft, not to military ardor or personal ambition, but first and above all to doctrines of civil liberty which applied to every nation and people, and which roused them all to look for a better day.

Justice, then, freedom, goodwill, the humane and generous conservation of life, the elevation of the individual man, was the charter principle of the United States, and signified its Ideal. It was an inspired choice. No power in human government can be so great. No influence can be so enduring. It is this ideal which the world needs. It is this that the world longs for. We do not doubt, surely, as we survey the wide field of human experiences, that all too much there is injustice, and oppression, and hardship, that men sink, and women faint, and children die, because of their burdens. Whether it is in the Old World or the New, whether the system of government is ancient and decayed, or modern and corrupted, whether the sun shines hot there or the winds blow cold, whether the mountains rise high or the plains are wide, in many lands people long for emancipation, and have—or did have—to incite and support their hopes the example of this great republic.

What is it, let us ask more particularly, that gives vitality to this Ideal? What is its animating principle? Not the methods of Force. They have been exploited, amid blood and tears, for ages. It is not the " prestige " of armies or navies. Cæsar and Napoleon, all the generals and the admirals, greater and less, have drained dry that turbid stream. It is not the tinsel of " glory," the glitter of rank, the pride and luxury of privileged classes. None of these. The Old World, which has looked so longingly to the New, groans under them all. To support armies, to build navies, to carry on " campaigns," to work destruction, to maintain luxury and pride, it has taxes that exhaust the strength of labor, and exactions that grind poverty into degradation. Lands like Germany, in which we are told free institutions had their birth, suffer as well as Spain and Italy; Teuton as well as Latin is in bondage; Russia, Turkey, India, are all staggering to-day under systems which the American Ideal rejects.

Our system was the opposite of theirs. It was the antithesis of Force, of Oppression, of Inequality, of Caste. And it was still more. It had the note of generosity, of kindliness, of comradeship. This made our ideal distinctive, and awakened the world's response. It was because we declared Goodwill that goodwill returned to us. That was the sign and the secret of our power. No guns we ever made, no armor we ever forged, no apparatus of destruction we ever contrived, brought us nearer to the heart of other nations. But every sign we made of regard for their rights, every help we gave them to continue their struggle upward and forward, made them our friends, firmly and faithfully—tied them to us with better than "hooks of steel."

Such was and is the true American Ideal. Not one great name in American history is associated with anything that contravenes it. Whether we go back to the first president of the republic, or farther, to those who planted the colonies, we shall find the one impulse of those who enjoy a righteous fame in our annals was to raise men, not to depress them; to help them on, not to grind them down; to enlighten their minds and elevate their characters, not to treat them as "dumb, driven cattle." The spirit of the land, the great intent of its people, that out of which hopes sprang and fresh efforts rose, that which faced hardships, which bore trials, which contended with difficulties, was a generous, a hopeful, a magnanimous one.

It is not new to say this. O, no! The true grandeur of nations was long since nobly defined and splendidly proclaimed. But old truth must be ever freshly learned and continually repeated. We must drink again at the pure fountains of our national life. Our duty—"plain duty," indeed—is to preserve to ourselves and to the nations the Ideal which is so honorable, and has been so honored. We must keep our beacon burning. Its rays of hope are needed. We must keep our true place in the world. Our work is not to threaten, not to oppress, not to plunder, not to slay; it is to do in the community of nations such work as a good and upright man does in the community about him. This will make us truly a "world power." Then we shall be able to answer joyfully to any challenge, in the remotest corner of the world, "Yes, brother, the great republic still lives!"

THE CHAIRMAN: The first paper this afternoon will be read by our friend, William G. Hubbard, of Lansing, Michigan.

EARLY FRIENDS' VIEW OF PEACE SUSTAINED BY SCRIPTURE, BY REASON AND BY HIGHER CIVILIZATION.

BY WILLIAM G. HUBBARD, LANSING, MICH.

When George Fox was offered the captaincy of a military company he said, "I have come into that experience which destroys the root and cause of war."

This expression, which has become classic among Friends, contains the very substance of their views on the peace question. More fully stated it is this: The Christian experience is one wherein the "love of God is shed abroad in the heart by the Holy Ghost which is given us." The heart and life become controlled by the love which Christ manifested. Love takes out all malice, covetousness and revenge; hence destroys the very "root of war." If the Apostle James was right in concluding that " wars and fightings come from the lusts that war in your members," then if you introduce that which destroys those lusts you destroy " the root and cause of war."

This is a simple proposition, but it contains the most irresistible logic. Man with sin in him is a warring creature. He is ferocious, unkind, unjust, inhuman, cruel. Jacob Riis takes the ground that every child born since the fall of man is by nature a savage, and needs to be civilized by some refining process. Whether Jacob Riis is right or not, we all know there is much of savagery in man's unregenerate nature. But the reconstruction that he gets in his inner nature when he is regenerated by Christ takes out or supplants that savage nature.

When Oliver Cromwell asked George Fox, the founder of Friends' Society, if he would " promise not to take up a carnal sword or weapon against him or the government as it then was," George Fox replied: " I deny the wearing or drawing of a carnal sword or any other outward weapon against him or any man. And that I was sent of God to stand a witness against all violence and against the works of darkness; and to turn people from darkness to the light and to bring them from the occasion of war and fighting to the peaceful gospel, and from being evil-doers, which the magistrates' sword should be a terror to."

This was written by George Fox to Cromwell in 1649, and for more than 250 years every true follower of George Fox has believed and taught that no Christian could take up the sword " against the King or any man."

" Or any man," with George Fox, covered the whole human race, in all nations, heathen or civilized. All to him were children of our Heavenly Father. Hence, all must be loved and cared for.

The " experience " into which George Fox had come " destroyed " not merely " the root and cause " of some wars, but of " war," of all carnal war.

Early Friends believed and practiced this doctrine. They would not go to war *against* the government or *for* the government. They took this position, not from what George Fox had said or done, but from what Christ had taught on the subject, and from what he had wrought in them.

In the year 1675 Robert Barclay in his "Apology " (page 514) declares " revenge and war an evil as opposite and contrary to the Spirit and doctrine of Christ as light to darkness." He thinks all the evils of war come from opposition to Christ. He says: " Through contempt of Christ's law the whole world is filled with violence, oppression, murders, ravishing of women and virgins, spoilings, depredations, burnings, devastations, and all manner of lascivious cruelty. So that it is strange that men, made after the image of God, should have so much degenerated that they rather bear the image and nature of roaring lions, tearing tigers, devouring wolves, and raging boars than of rational creatures endued with reason."

This is a graphic picture of what war produces in men when they reject the " law of Christ."

William Penn's treaty and dealings with the Indians on the Christian principles of brotherhood, justice and love constitute one of the brightest pages in the history of America. In that treaty William Penn asked that Christians and Indians should be bound with " a firm chain of friendship made between them, and that this chain of friendship should always be made stronger and stronger, and be kept bright and clean, without rust or spot, between our children and children's children while the creeks and rivers run, and the sun, moon and stars endure." Is there anything more beautiful and Christlike in man's relationship with man than that? Is it not astonishing that statesmen and rulers have not long since seen the wisdom of Penn's policy, and formed treaties of good fellowship and love and arbitration all over the world? Will it not be well for this Conference to appoint a delegation to wait on the President of the United States and ask him to take the initiative in forming treaties with all nations to bind them to " good fellowship " and arbitration?

SUSTAINED BY SCRIPTURE.

The attitude taken by George Fox and the early Friends is in beautiful harmony with the teaching of Christ. The great Galilean laid down general principles. He did not give specific laws. He legislated to control conditions of life rather than the acts of men. Men try to control the stream of life, but Jesus struck at the fountain. Men make laws to control men's conduct; Jesus sought to control their purposes. Men decide a certain action to be wrong, then make a law forbidding it. And men of evil purpose find new ways of doing wrong; hence there is no end of legislation. But Jesus legislated for the unborn thought. The law-books of men are too multitudinous to be counted; they would fill many large buildings. The laws of Jesus Christ are few and can be read in an hour. In what is generally called the Sermon on the Mount Jesus announces his platform of principles. The great central thought is the law of love. The most striking expression of this law is found in the last ten verses of the 5th chapter of Matthew. Here he declares what Erasmus called the new philosophy. This " new philosophy," this " diviner law," is that *love* should govern the lives of men. The old régime of revenge, of " an eye for an eye and a tooth for a tooth," was ended. His followers were to " resist not evil," they were to " love their enemies," to pray for them, show kindness to them, clothe them, feed them, bind up their wounds, suffer wrong at their hands rather than do them harm.

" Love your enemies," said the great Galilean. Why should we do this? He explains in his next utterance. " That ye may be the children of your father in heaven." Ah, indeed! must one love his enemies in order to be a child of God? That is the teaching of the Son of God. He emphasizes it. "If ye love them which love you, what reward have you?" "If ye forgive not men their trespasses, neither will your Father forgive you your trespasses." Nothing could be more definite. It leaves us without choice; it is this or nothing.

The standard is high, but Christ himself makes ability to "love your enemies" the very basis of Sonship. Do this "that ye may be children of your father in heaven."

But cannot a man love his enemies and kill them with Mauser rifles and Krupp guns sometimes? If you think you can govern your neighbor's household better than he is governing it, is it not your duty to institute your superior rule of family government over his household at whatever cost? The father of the neighboring household will no doubt object to your interference. He may resist you with force. He will doubtless call to his aid his hired hands and older sons. And you may have to kill him and some other members of his family. But would you not better kill off half his tribe than not to have his children brought up under your superior gospel rule? A military general said to a conference of preachers in California: "We will make way for the Gospel in the Philippines if we have to kill half of the inhabitants to do it." The papers said many of the preachers cheered the expression. Now if that is consistent with loving your enemies, then heaven is in harmony with hell, murder is a virtue, hatred is love, darkness is light.

But we insist that love is beneficence, it is kindness, it is helpfulness. We insist that Paul was right when he said, " Love worketh no ill to one's neighbor." We insist that you Englishmen cannot love your neighbors, the Boers, and go on slaughtering them about the kind of government they should have in their household, the Transvaal. They offered to arbitrate, and after that, it seems to the writer, every man killed was a man murdered.

"Love worketh no ill," and it is not love that says, "We will conquer the Boers if we have to kill all the population to do it."

We make the above remark, not through desire to oppose the British, but to give concreteness to our argument. The law of love is in opposition to all war. It was not love that drove the Indians from their lands and slaughtered them to get possession. Love said, "Nay; but we will buy their lands of them"; we will treat them as friends, as brethren; we will deal justly with them. The King said, "But you have already bought their lands of me, Friend William." But love insisted that usurpation of ownership gave no right to their lands. Which was the Christian way? Let the peace propaganda keep that question before all men: "Which is the Christian way?"

If the Englishman cannot love the Boer by killing him, neither can the American love the Filipino by chasing him through swamps and burning his villages and destroying life till whole districts are depopulated. The Filipino made a constitution and planned his own government. But King Greed said: " We bought of Spain the right to rule the Filipinos." But Spain, the usurper, had no more right to transfer rule to America than King George had a right to transfer the land of the Indians. We should have treated the Filipinos as we did Cuba, and assisted them in forming a government and invited them to become a part of our government, if they wished. But war tramples down rights, and constitutions, and sets at naught all commandments of God.

WAR IS IRRATIONAL.

There is no sense of right in men's fists. If two men dispute, and each contends he is right, how are they to prove which is right? Certainly not by pounding each other's faces. No matter which comes off best in such a conflict, it does not prove that he is right. If two men cannot prove which is right by a physical contest, two thousand cannot do so nor two millions. There is no sense of right in muscle, nor in powder and lead, nor in cannon, nor in ships of war. But the human mind *can* weigh problems of equity, and reason alone can find the right. Hence Dr. Franklin was correct when he said: " War is the maddest human folly." No acts of men so completely override reason as war. War is insanity.

HIGHER IDEAS OF CIVILIZATION.

Everything that civilizes man refines his nature, makes him more sensitive and kind in his feelings, more considerate towards his fellow-beings, more careful not to hurt or oppress or to wrong them? The more highly one is civilized the more he revolts at cruelty, oppression, wrong and bloodshed. Hence as civilization advances by a thousand processes of culture, education, refinement, the opposition to war grows stronger, and the greater is the demand that nations shall settle their disputes by arbitration.

The greatest teacher the world has yet received set up a standard of life, which, when followed, will lift men above all war, bloodshed, cruelty and oppression. That standard is in the words, " Thou shalt love thy neighbor as thyself."

Love means beneficence, kindness. When you love you want to help, to happify, to show goodwill. Love him as yourself, and you will no more think of taking his life than of taking your own life.

Thy neighbor may be African living in heathen cruelties. Love him into a better life. Show him a better way. Don't shoot him about boundary lines, nor to get his lands, nor his diamond mines, nor for any other purpose. Treat him justly, educate him, civilize him, not with New England rum nor Milwaukee beer, nor with

Mauser bullets, nor with Krupp guns; but civilize him with Bibles, missionaries, school teachers, printing presses. Teach him to " do justly and love mercy," not by robbery and murder, but by doing justly before him. Teach him righteousness by being righteous, not by despoiling him of his land and murdering him. In other words, don't try to teach him the ways of peace with implements of war.

It may be true, and doubtless is, that some are growing worse in spite of good opportunities and good environments, but much more is it true that the church, the school house, the printing press, the court of justice, the reign of law, are lifting the race up into a refinement where it revolts at the idea of slaughtering men by machinery and blowing them to pieces with giant powder.

War is concentrated cruelty. Look at those two vessels yonder at sea. They have begun a tremendous cannonading of each other. The roar of the cannon, the screeching of the shells and the deafening explosions of bombs make one feel as though all the magazines of pandemonium were going off. A gunner gives the range to his gun and his own head is taken off by a cannon ball, but his aim sends a shell crashing into the machinery of the other vessel. It explodes and sets the great battleship on fire; but men fight and fight until the deck is strewn with mangled bodies, and the flame has heated the iron deck so hot that it is roasting the flesh of the wounded. Some are jumping into the sea to drown rather than be roasted to death. Look! Yonder a great cannon ball goes plowing its way through the bodies along that deck and scatters the flesh and bones of soldiers into the air and into the sea! The great vessel that cost millions is sunk by an enemy in an hour; and hundreds of men, with dear ones at home, are dying in the flames or drowning in the sea.

What does it all mean? Had the men on the victorious vessel been injured by the men on the other vessel? Not the least. The victors and vanquished had never looked into each other's faces. They did not even speak the same language. Why, then, this awful slaughter of strangers? It is war. And war sets at naught all laws of humanity and all requirements of mercy. In the language of Sherman, " War is cruelty and you cannot refine it. War is hell."

Now there is but one conclusion possible from the above considerations. The position of the early Friends in rejecting war is abundantly sustained by the New Testament Scriptures. These Scriptures being given forth by divine wisdom, it follows that whatever position is consistent with them must comport with highest reason and wisdom. Any other attitude would make the author of them an unwise and irrational being.

It follows that as these divine teachings are better understood in the light of higher civilization, it will be seen that they can be applied to the affairs of nations. The fact that the United States, the nation most nearly up to the Gospel plane, has had 52 disagreements with other nations, such as usually lead to war, and has settled 48 of them by arbitration, shows that George Fox, Robert Barclay and William Penn took a position 250 years ago that is just now dawning upon the most advanced thinkers as true—true to God, true to statesmanship, and true to higher civilization.

THE CHAIRMAN: We will next have a paper by Mariana W. Chapman, of Brooklyn, New York, on " The Inherent Immorality of War."

THE INHERENT IMMORALITY OF WAR.

BY MARIANA W. CHAPMAN, BROOKLYN.

Immorality is a mild term when one can hardly think of a command in the decalogue that is not violated in war. Crime changes its aspect when it is held up in the dazzling light of that kind of conflict. Our moral sense is instantly destroyed; manslaughter becomes virtue, and yet makes, none the less, fatherless children, widows, and parents with broken hearts. The cruelty that runs a man through with the point of a bayonet becomes honor and bravery and courage, but the man bleeds and suffers and dies. We have the charge of the six hundred, and it is so much greater and finer and more thrilling because they do not arrive—the six hundred.

What is the glamor that is cast over our eyes that so perverts their vision? It is the lurid light of war, the perversion of morality. Think how nations look at their great Gatling guns, and consider them valuable in the ratio of the number of men they will sweep off of the face of the earth, the same men whom, in the perspective of peace, they would consider it incumbent to treat with all respect and consideration. And then revenge! It cannot be more strikingly set forth in character than in Rudyard Kipling's ghastly poem of " The Grave of the Hundred Head." It was after—

" . . . . the men of the First Shikaris
Picked up their Subaltern dead
With a big blue mark in his forehead
And the back blown out of his head."

And in their vengeance upon the enemy

" Five score heads were taken,
Five score heads and twain.
. . . .
And the drip, drip, drip from the baskets
Reddened the grass by the way."

All of these heads were piled up on the grave of their young lieutenant, and he concludes:

> " Thus was the lesson plain
> Of the wrath of the First Shikaris,
> The price of a white man slain."

He was slain by a treacherous foe; but even treachery has its advocates when it is practiced upon the enemy. It is the attribute of a skillful general to surprise the opposing army.

We chronicle with exultation the simulation and cunning that leads the enemy astray and makes him an easier victim. It belongs to this perverted standard. And then, the impoverishment of the nation to compass this killing of men! All these great armies must be maintained by the labor behind them, labor that could be turned to so much better purpose. And what the army does not get for its necessities lawfully, it must take unlawfully as it goes through the country—which puts robbery at a premium. Let us give everything its plain name! Horses, cattle, hogs, chickens, corn, supplies of all kinds, carefully garnered by hard-working farmers, the fruits and harvests of the year, are seized by ordinarily honest men. All these things go on from camps, and there is no sense of moral obliquity; and gambling—shall we speak of the increased temptation to squander the little that belongs to the soldier's life? and drunkenness—a temptation so prominent that reams of paper have been covered with arguments for the greatest safeguard against its peril! All tend to poverty, then and thereafter—the poverty that is the handmaiden of woe to the third and fourth generation—individual poverty and the poverty of the nation.

Some years ago the Chancellor of the Exchequer in London announced that 40,000,000 pounds sterling must be raised for war expenses, and that was before the war in South Africa. That money must come out of the people at home.

There is another immorality, one of the gravest of evils, that goes with camp life. Wherever there are camps come fallen women, and the sequence is fallen men. Not long ago a letter was published from an army officer in India, asking for a fresh importation of young girls for these dens of infamy. Where were they to come from? Out of the homes of the poor! Add to this wickedness, then, the sacrifice of young girls. And these men in high office have called it a necessary evil. It is nothing of the kind, because there is no such thing. The words do not belong together.

There is an immorality in forcing men into abnormal, unsanitary conditions, conditions that fill the hospitals with disease and pestilence and mow down more men than powder and shot. Military necessity, so called, not only imposes these conditions, but has with it a red tape that often prevents an alleviation of much suffering that otherwise could be accomplished. We are too familiar with recent details of hospital service during the Spanish war not to understand this feature.

War is a violation of the entire code of morals as it has stood for the last two thousand years. It is the crime against civilization, against all that makes life worth living, that separates husbands and wives, mothers and sons, sisters and brothers. All who are dearest the soldier leaves behind him for what is called the national honor; another perversion of mind, the same perversion that existed in the past about personal honor when Aaron Burr shot Alexander Hamilton. Hundreds of others had done the like before; but it needed that illustration to kill dueling in this country.

Now, as we look back upon our civil and fratricidal war, is not the perspective bloody enough at this distance to make us know that it was the grossest of immoralities, and that the North should have been willing to allow, and the South to accept, indemnity for every slave within its borders? It would have cost less in money if they had been paid for twice over. How much less in agony and suffering and privation can never be estimated.

If we have an individual morality about homicide, why can we not have a collective morality about collective homicide, a collective conscience? It is because the ascent of man in ideals is not complete. Large bodies move slowly, but the powers of light are always struggling with the powers of darkness, and each time we come out on a higher plane. Virtually, all nations agree that war is the worst manner of settling disputes, and that really only shows which nation is the strongest, not in the least which is right. That kind of settlement is an immorality in itself. The world is surely reaching this point of intelligence, and will soon be able to see the greater morality in an international court of arbitration. That is the acme of present ideals; but when it is accomplished we shall not, as some may fancy, have arrived at the millennium, but we shall have a basis of greater justice and morality in the settlement of national difficulties.

We have, then, inherent in war, injustice, manslaughter, cruelty, revenge, cunning, deceit, treachery, robbery, gambling, intemperance, oppressive taxation, poverty, impurity of life, a transgression of sanitary laws more fatal than battles, and the terrible sorrow that comes to the hearts of the people.

One can easily say these sins are not confined to war. The world is full of them outside. Yes, but none of them are required in the line of duty. They bring no honor to the man who promotes them. He is society's outcast, and all the forces of law are against him. Public opinion does not laud one man for outgeneraling another. He may grow rich on the proceeds, but his cunning is at a discount. He cannot rob, he cannot gamble, and he cannot drink with the same impunity. Society, at least, looks askance at his career.

While it is hard for the average man to touch pitch without

defilement, we must acknowledge that many do come out of war unscathed, and lead upright and honorable lives; but such acknowledge freely the evil that is inherent. The Grand Army of the Republic said of General Grant: "He was profoundly convinced that war as an arbiter of national differences was a terrible crime against humanity, civilization, and the age. It supplants statesmanship, law and principle, and enthrones passion, brute force and disorder, to determine right and justice."

Shall we not go one step higher in our consideration, the step that lies next to morality, where the power of the Divine touches the human soul? Is it so long ago that it has lost its force that the Master said: "All things whatsoever ye would that men should do to you, do ye even so to them"? That is, at least, one with some of the last words of our lamented President: " Let us remember that our interest is in concord, not conflict, and that our real eminence rests in the victories of peace, not those of war." So let him pass into history.

THE CHAIRMAN: We have passed over in the program the title of the paper of President Rosenberger, of Penn College, because it seems that he is not here. It was not known to those in charge of the program until we began the session this afternoon that he was not here; but we have a letter from him, which Dr. Trueblood will read.

The letter from President Rosenberger was read, in which he expressed his deep regret at not being able to be present, his great interest in the Conference, and explained that his absence and inability to prepare the paper were due to sickness in the College Faculty.

THE CHAIRMAN: We will take up at once the discussion of the two papers that we have had; and to open the discussion we will call upon our friend, President Sharpless, of Haverford College.

ISAAC SHARPLESS: It seems to me that the ground of objection to war on the part of the early Friends was something a little deeper than the immorality of the custom. George Fox said, in a quotation which has been made here, that he was led into that spirit which took away the occasion of war. It seems to me that one might argue in a fervid way that wars were immoral and yet be in a spirit which would permit him to go into war if any little turn of the argument should suggest to him that this particular war was moral. That, I believe, is what is happening all the time in the case of a great number of Christian people. Abstractly they admit the immorality of war; but when the particular war arises they always find some reason to consider that it is an exception to all the wars that have preceded it, and that in this particular case, war—this war—is moral.

I suppose that if a man could be possessed of the spirit which George Fox said he had, and could go into battle and stab his enemies with bayonets and shoot them down with bullets, and could undertake all the concentrated wickedness and agony which accompany war from beginning to end, and still maintain the spirit which he had when he went into a solid, religious meeting, he would think, and perhaps we would think, war was right. If he held the inner consciousness of rectitude when he was going through these operations, then I believe that he would not object to war unless argument could be framed which proved war to be inconsistent with the teachings of the New Testament.

So I should like to suggest that we must go a little deeper than simple moral argument in order to justify the position of Friends with regard to war. We must bring people into the experience in which war to them becomes impossible because it is so foreign to their deep personal, spiritual conviction. That state of mind is not usually reached, perhaps, yet a very little distance into the real experience of Christianity will make a man feel more and more that the occasions of war become impossible to him.

As to the moral side of the question, I perfectly agree with the writer of the last paper that the moral considerations utterly condemn war; that its inherent immorality is so manifest that a person cannot engage in it if he is conscious of the fact of its immorality and also is obedient to the precepts of the New Testament. But I would suggest that there is a kind of inherent morality in the human race, which is, in a certain way, distinct from the morality of the New Testament. I do not mean that it is contradictory to it. I mean it would have arisen if the New Testament had never been written. Things are not right, or wrong, simply because they are enjoined or forbidden by the Bible. The injunctions of the Sermon on the Mount and the prohibitions of the Decalogue would have existed in a measure in human society, constituted as it is, if there had never been any Old or New Testament. It is impossible for society to arise and grow up without certain fundamental laws lying at the basis of it which must evolve and develop in the course of the process; and these laws are just as immutable and certain, though they are perhaps a little more difficult to find out, as the physical laws governing the universe. When, therefore, we argue against war, from the moral point of view, we simply say that war does violence to human nature or to human society. It is impossible for the highest ideal of civilization to exist and at the same time for war to exist.

War is prohibited in the Bible. As to the New Testament there does not seem to be any doubt about it. Indeed, most Christian writers will say so to a greater or less extent. A writer in this afternoon's *Bulletin*, who has a very interesting article upon this present

Conference, practically says as much. Almost any one in the position of this writer, who has looked into the subject carefully, will admit that with the growing sense of morality of the human race there will come a gradual abolition of warfare.

I do not think that the early Friends had worked out the moral and economic arguments and thus reached their opposition to war. That has been a work of the time since theirs. War can, from these points of view, be pronounced inexpedient and wrong; but these Friends were not profound philosophers, and they had not at that time all the moral and economic arguments at their command. The early Quakers were idealists. It did not make any particular difference to them what were going to be the results of their theories. This is something in which we make so great a mistake. People nowadays say wars have produced beneficent results. They say this particular war looks as though it were going to produce beneficent results, and therefore that it is right. But that was not at all the way the early Friends proceeded. I think that is really the difference between the way in which Friends have approached this subject and that of some other Christian people. The early Friends were not utilitarian. They did not feel that any amount of good results would prove the rightfulness of war.

We hear that argument again and again: "Did not the Revolutionary War produce independence? Did not the Civil War destroy slavery? Have not good things come from all war? Did not our late war free Cuba?" We shall have to give an affirmative answer to these inquiries. But that is not the question. We must go to the root of the matter. We as Friends will have to abandon such arguments as our main stock in trade. We shall have to go back to the position of George Fox, that war is of a spirit which is not in acordance with the best, most sanctified, human spirits—human spirits illuminated and transformed by the Spirit of God; that there is deep down in the human heart a spirit of eternal justice and right which renders war unhallowed, whatever its causes and occasions.

From this point of view war is seen to be wrong, not because it produces bad results, not because in certain cases it produces suffering, but because it is in violation of the eternal principles of right, because the spirit of God says to the spirit of man that the spirit of war is entirely incongruous with it. When George Fox said that he had come into the spirit which took away the occasion of war, he gave us the root principle on which we must build our fundamental argument against war. Let us buttress it around as much as we can with all these economic considerations, these arguments about the immorality of war as contrasted with the New Testament standards; but let us hold fast to this central principle of Quakerism with regard to war, a principle which is going to outlive all these other arguments and which is going to carry the Society of Friends on to victory, on this subject, at least.

51

THE CHAIRMAN: Our friend James Wood has with him a copy of the address which the Friends presented to President Washington at the opening of his administration. It is an extremely good statement of the Friends' ground upon the subject of war, and it seems altogether appropriate to read it now.

JAMES WOOD: This address was presented on the 10th day of Third month, 1789, to the President of the United States:

ADDRESS OF THE FRIENDS TO PRESIDENT WASHINGTON IN 1789.

To the President of the United States:

The address of the religious Society called Quakers, from their Yearly Meeting for Pennsylvania, New Jersey, Delaware and the western parts of Maryland and Virginia:

Being met in this our annual Assembly, for the well ordering of the affairs of our Religious Society, and the promotion of universal righteousness, our minds have been drawn to consider that the Almighty, who ruleth in Heaven, and in the kingdoms of men, having permitted a great revolution to take place in the government of this country, we are fervently concerned that the rulers of the people may be favored with the counsel of God, the only sure means of enabling them to fulfill the important trust committed to their charge, and in an especial manner, that divine wisdom and grace, vouched from above, may qualify thee to fill all the duties of the exalted station to which thou art appointed.

We are sensible thou hast attained great place in the esteem and affections of people of all denominations over whom thou presidest, and many eminent talents being committed to thy trust, we much desire they may be fully devoted to the Lord's honor and service, that thus thou mayest be a happy instrument in His hand, for the suppression of vice, infidelity and irreligion, and every species of oppression on the persons or consciences of men, so that righteousness and peace, which truly exalt a nation, may prevail throughout the land, as the only solid foundation of this or any country.

The free toleration which the citizens of these States enjoy in the public worship of the Almighty, agreeable to the dictates of their consciences, we esteem among the choicest of blessings, and, as we desire to be filled with fervent charity for those who differ from us in matters of faith and practice, believing that the general assembly of saints is composed of the sincere and upright hearted of all nations, kingdoms and people, so, we trust, we may justly claim it from others, and in a full persuasion that the divine principle we profess leads unto harmony and concord, we can take no part in carrying on war, on any occasion, or under any power, but are bound in conscience to live quiet and peaceable lives, in godliness and honesty, amongst men, contributing freely our portion to the indigencies of the poor, and the necessary support of civil government, acknowledging those that rule well to be worthy of double honor; and if any professing with us are or have been of a contrary disposition and conduct, we own them not therein, having never been chargeable from our first establishment as a Religious Society, with fomenting or countenancing tumults, or conspiracies, or disrespect to those who are placed in authority over us.

We wish not improperly to intrude on thy time or patience, nor is it our practice to offer adulation to any, but, as we are a people whose principles and conduct have been misrepresented and traduced, we take the liberty to assure thee that we feel our hearts affectionately drawn toward thee and those in authority over us, with prayers that thy presidency may, under the blessing of Heaven, be happy to thyself, and to the people, that through the increase of morality and true religion, divine providence may condescend to look down upon our land with a propitious eye, and bless the inhabitants with the continuance of peace, the dew of heaven, and the fatness of the earth, and enable us gratefully to acknowledge his manifold mercies, and it is our earnest concern that he may be pleased to grant thee every necessary qualification to fill thy weighty and important station to his glory, and that finally, when all terrestrial honors shall fail and pass away, thou and thy respectable consort may be found worthy to receive a crown of unfading righteousness in the mansions of peace and joy forever.

Signed in and on behalf of the said Meeting, held in Philadelphia by adjournments from the 28th of the Ninth month to the 3d day of the Tenth month, inclusive, 1789.

NICHOLAS WALN, Clerk.

You will bear in mind that this was immediately after the Revolutionary War, when Friends had the most trying experience; and this was the first official statement of the position of the Friends that had been made. It is certainly an admirable document, and contains as complete a statement of the conception of the early Friends in regard to war, which we are discussing this afternoon, as I have seen.

Perhaps it may not be amiss to read George Washington's reply.

The answer of the President of the United States, to the address of the Religious Society called Quakers, from their Yearly Meeting for Pennsylvania, New Jersey, Delaware and the western parts of Maryland and Virginia.

Gentlemen:

I receive with pleasure your affectionate address, and thank you for the friendly sentiments and good wishes which you express for the success of my administration and for my personal happiness.

We have reason to rejoice in the prospect that the national government, which, by the favor of divine providence, was formed by the common councils and peaceably established with the common consent of the people, will prove a blessing to every denomination of them; to render it such my best endeavors shall not be wanting. Government being, among other purposes, instituted to protect the persons and consciences of men from oppression, it certainly is the duty of rulers not only to abstain from it themselves, but according to their station to prevent it in others.

The liberty enjoyed by the people of these States of worshipping Almighty God agreeably to their consciences is not only among the choicest of their blessings, but also of their rights, while men performing social duties faithfully do all that society or the State can with propriety expect or demand, and remain responsible only to their Maker for the religion or mode of faith which they may prefer or profess. Your principles and conduct are well known to me, and it is doing the people called Quakers no more than justice to say that (except their declining to share with others the burden of the common defence) there is no denomination among us who are more exemplary and useful citizens. I assure you very explicitly that in my opinion the conscientious scruples of all men should be treated with great delicacy and tenderness, and it is my wish and desire that the laws may always be as extensively accommodated to them as a due regard to the protection and essential interests of the nation may justify and permit.

[Signed]   GEORGE WASHINGTON.

I will state that the manuscript of this address, with the reply, was found among old papers at the Twentieth Street Friends' Meeting House, New York, on First-day of this week, by David S. Tabor. The reply of George Washington purports to have the genuine signature of our first President.

THE CHAIRMAN: We will take up now the discussion of the papers that have been read. Our friend, ex-President Magill, of Swarthmore, will occupy the time for a few minutes.

EDWARD H. MAGILL: Among the many excellent things which we have heard this afternoon, nothing impresses me more deeply than the remark of our friend Mrs. Chapman, when she said, in regard to the common saying, "War is a necessary evil": "There are no necessary evils. Evils are not necessary." War is necessarily an evil; that is the way it should read. I was reminded of an address that I listened to with great satisfaction in this city, a few years ago, on "Evolution versus Revolution," in which the speaker took the ground that our two wars—our War of the Rebellion and our Revolutionary War—were both of them avoidable. The speaker was Andrew D. White. He said in regard to those two cases something like this: "The Rebellion—the War of the Rebellion—was a political blunder. It had been proposed to buy the slaves, but the objection was made that it would cost many millions to buy them. Yet the war cost far more, besides the enormous loss of life. "It could," he said, "all have been avoided by taking the advice of those moderate men in that early day."

Then the case of the Revolution, which I, in common with all the rest of you, have always been taught, Friends as we are, in our schools, in our histories—everywhere—to consider a necessary war. Dr. White argued that it was not so. He said that Washington and his associates were men raised up, no doubt, for the special purpose, and who accomplished that purpose as no other body of men, perhaps, could have accomplished it so well. But they had to begin at the end of the Revolutionary War and labor for years to get the thirteen States to unite. If that labor—that labor of diplomacy—had been begun in 1775, instead of 1783, it might have secured the separation of this country from England in peace. They would have accomplished it quite as easily as they brought the thirteen States together after the war was over. Wars never settle anything; they only put the contestants in a state of mind so that they will be willing to try to settle their controversies. If they had only been willing beforehand, in the beginning, it could have been settled without war.

THE CHAIRMAN: The subject now is open for general discussion.

ANTHONY M. KIMBER: Many men preach the thirteenth chapter of 1 Corinthians; but may we comprehend this wonderful chapter, the wonderful saying in it: "Charity suffereth long, and is kind." May the Lord help us to be faithful in this ministry of suffering. Respecting the second essay, I remember that General Armstrong, a Christian soldier, many years ago was lecturing to his class about the same subject, and one of the colored men asked him how it could be reconciled with the customs and rules of war, and General Armstrong frankly admitted that in time of war all the moral law had to be suspended.

JOSEPH POWELL: I want to say to members of the Society of Friends, in particular, that I do not feel so proud as some appear to be of the stand we have taken in this cause. When I heard what was said a little while ago about buying the slaves instead of fighting a war, I remembered that it was not a Friend, but Elihu Burritt who advocated that. A view which I have was expressed by President Sharpless so clearly and so exactly that I want us to remember what he said and take it to heart. I know Friends who say, "I am a member, and I am considered as good a member as any we have, probably." They think so, I know. But they say, "Prepare for war," although they profess to be opposed to it. They cannot understand, seemingly, the condition of spirit and mind that President Sharpless has spoken of. But this is the only thing that will do. We may say what we please in the way of opposition to war, but it amounts to little unless we are willing to bear all the suffering and all that is unpleasant that may come upon us if we are loyal to that profession.

SAMUEL S. ASH: I have just a word in harmony with the exercises of the afternoon. We do not get all of our peace doctrine from the ministers of the Gospel; we get some of it from soldiers and military men. I recall an incident which took place in my boyhood, when I was making a visit with my father, who was a physician of the court. We visited and dined with a captain, and at the dinner table my father remarked that the only excuse he could make for the captain's occupation was that sometimes, perhaps, war was a necessary evil. The captain was not a moment in responding: "Why," he said, "Doctor, I am a better Quaker than you are. War is always evil, and never necessary."

DAVIS FURNAS: I was very much interested in the address by President Sharpless, in his statement that there is in every soul something that teaches him what is right about war as about other things. I believe this is the foundation principle of Quakerism. I believe that the Almighty Creator so ordered that every man should have that which, if he would follow it, would teach him the right. I once had an interview with a Hindoo, and found that he had—

contrary to the views I had held about the Hindoos—just as clear views about many things that are wrong—about drunkenness and other sins—as those who have been educated in Christian communities. There was a spark of divinity in him. There is in every man that which is sufficient to guide him—about war as about other evils—if he is only obedient to it.

RICHARD H. THOMAS: I have been very much interested in what I have heard this afternoon, and especially agree with what Isaac Sharpless has said about the secondary character of the suffering and the expense of war. The fact of suffering is no good argument at all. It is a very noble thing to suffer for a righteous cause. If all that war implied was suffering and expense on the part of those who suffered willingly, there would be a great deal to be said in favor of it. Of course, the fact that there is suffering would make it a very serious matter and a thing not to be entered upon without thought; but the mere fact of suffering may be an argument in favor of a thing, rather than against it. If a cause is worthy, every one of us ought to be willing to suffer for it. If I thought that the peace principle meant that I was to hesitate to suffer, if suffering was called for, I should despise myself and cease to be a peace man. Peace principles ought to be based not on objection to suffering, but on objection to sin.

When it comes to the question of the inherent immorality of war, it does seem to me that it is not a secondary matter. What do we know of war? War is not a mere name. What does it consist of? If there is immorality in connection with it, that does not necessarily make it evil. There is, possibly, immorality connected with every business. There is a possibility of disobeying the laws of God in every possible line of activity that we may follow, and yet we have no objection to these lines of activity. But when anything that people do is inherently immoral, then the immorality becomes an essential feature in it. Why was it that George Fox had this experience which took away from him the occasion of all wars? It was because something had happened to him; because he had yielded himself up to the power of God, to let that power into his heart which had made him able to be strong against all that was contrary to the will of God. Why is war contrary to the will of God if it be not inherently immoral? If it were inherently moral it would be in accordance with the law of God. It seems to me that if we can once show to Christian people that it is inherently immoral, as the paper pointed out so clearly, we have made a very great step forward. This is not a side consideration; it is an essential element in the question. It is because war arouses the passions that make earth hell; it is because it is contrary to the law of God,—which is the highest immorality,—that we are opposed to it. It seems to me, therefore, that it is a matter of very great importance that we should see the clear-cut lines of argument, and that one of the important and necessary ones is that war is inherently immoral.

THE CHAIRMAN: We have now very fairly discussed these important questions, and the Chair, therefore, proposes to bring this session to a close in a very few minutes.

The Committee on Entertainment will be glad to see any who are not yet provided with homes. The Business Committee, which has been increased by the addition of President Edmund Stanley, of Kansas; Esther Pugh, of Indiana; Robert E. Pretlow, of Ohio, and P. W. Raidabaugh, of Indiana, will hold a meeting immediately at the close of the session. This evening the meeting will convene in this hall at 8 o'clock promptly. President Unthank, of Wilmington College, Ohio, will preside, and the program as published will be carried out.

One of the newspapers of the city has asked the privilege of taking a photograph of the Conference, and, as there seems to be no objection, it is hoped that you will all be willing to assist the newspaper people to get a satisfactory picture.

BENJAMIN F. TRUEBLOOD: While the photographer is getting his machine ready I should like to call the attention of the Conference to what seems to me one of the most hopeful things connected with the peace cause—the first announcement of the Nobel peace prize.

Alfred Nobel, of Norway, was the inventor of dynamite. He did not invent dynamite for war purposes, and he was very much troubled that it had been turned so exclusively to war ends. He was a strong peace man; in his will he left millions of money, the income of which he provided should be annually distributed in five prizes. One of these prizes was to be given each year to the individual, or society, who had during the year done the most for the promotion of international arbitration and peace. A committee of the Norwegian Parliament was organized, which has charge of the distribution of the prizes. The first prizes were announced day before yesterday. They amount to something over $40,000 each. The peace prize this year was given to two men, instead of one. One of these men, Henri Dunant, was the founder of the Red Cross work. He spent his whole fortune in the organization and development of this work. He is now a very old man, living in a private hospital near Geneva, Switzerland. The Norwegian Committee, in consideration of his eminent services to the cause of humanity and peace, voted that he should have half of the first peace price, something over $20,000. The other half was awarded to the veteran of the peace movement in France, our friend, Frederic Passy, who has spent more than thirty years in developing the peace propaganda in his country. He well deserves this recognition of his eminent and long-continued services to the cause. The awarding at this time of this valuable prize is certainly a most encouraging proof of the progress which the peace movement has made, and of the public confidence which it has won and now holds.

The meeting then adjourned.

Third Session.

Fifth-day Evening, Twelfth Month 12th.

The Conference reassembled at 8 p.m. with James B. Unthank, president of Wilmington College, Ohio, in the Chair.

The Chairman: I shall not, on taking the chair this evening, make any extended remarks. I wish only to call attention to one matter. I have been very much surprised in the last few weeks to learn something about the Friends that I never knew before; and that is, that they are in a certain sense Anarchists. I do not know whether you knew that or not; but it was a piece of information to me. It comes, also, from very high authority that we Quakers are Anarchists. I thought we had always been, for the whole period of our existence, a law-abiding people; that we had been credited with even too much loyalty to government. We have been criticized because we do not object to things in a forcible way; but we have never before, to my knowledge, been charged with disbelieving in government. Now comes a great metropolitan weekly and says that Friends are to a certain extent Anarchists; and, upon having the matter called in question and denied, it reiterates the assertion, and says that we are Anarchists because we do not believe in participating in war when the government is in a struggle. I do not give the name of this religious paper, because it would be invidious; but this paper believes in war, and I do not know what war does but suspend all the functions of peaceable government and introduce a state of anarchy. I cannot understand how it is that Friends are Anarchists and the believers in war are so thoroughly loyal to government and so much opposed to anarchy, when war itself introduces into the country and into the community a state of anarchy. The objection, at least, is not very consistent. I recommend this matter to the Business Committee, that they may consider whether it will not be wise for us, in our resolutions, to declare, for the information of those who know nothing of our history, that we believe in human government.

We will now proceed with the program of the evening. The first exercise is a paper upon "Early Christianity and War," by James Wood, of Mount Kisco, N. Y.

EARLY CHRISTIANITY AND WAR.

BY JAMES WOOD, MT. KISCO, N. Y.

The battle of Actium, followed by the death of Antonius, 31 B. C., closed the long series of conflicts in the Roman empire by which Caius Julius Cæsar Octavianus gained his supreme position, and led to his receiving the name of Augustus, never before borne by any one. From that date the empire continued to enjoy profound internal tranquillity until Augustus died in the seventy-fifth year of his age and the fourteenth of the Christian era. Thus the Prince of Peace entered upon his mission when the temple of Janus was closed, as it had been since 29 B. C., when Augustus performed the ceremony of closing it for the third time in all Roman history.

> "No war, or battle's sound
> Was heard the world around;
> The idle spear and shield were high up hung;
> The hookèd chariot stood
> Unstain'd with hostile blood;
> The trumpet spake not to the armèd throng;
> And kings sat still with awful eye,
> As if they surely knew their sov'reign Lord was by."

For a century and a half the policy inaugurated by Augustus secured the peace and prosperity of the empire. Even the follies and excesses of Gaius, Claudius, and Nero did little harm beyond Italy itself, while the rule of Vespasian repaired the damages inflicted by the wars of the rival emperors after Nero's death, and the abilities of Trajan, Hadrian and Antoninus secured tranquillity and good government, and spread the beneficent influences of Roman law and civilization. Thus Christianity was established under remarkably favorable conditions of peace and prosperity, and its early adherents were spared the fiery trials that an earlier century would inevitably have placed before them. Parthians and Medes, and Elamites, and the dwellers in Mesopotamia, and in Judea and Cappadocia, in Pontus, and Asia, Phrygia and Pamphylia, in Egypt and in the parts of Libya about Cyrene, and strangers of Rome, Jews and proselytes, Cretes and Arabians returned from Jerusalem to their various homes after the day of Pentecost in peace and safety, with the glad tidings of what they had seen and heard. Subsequently apostles and teachers went whither they would in unaccustomed security. While garrisons were maintained throughout the empire the people were not subjected to that stress of pressure for military service that was always inseparable from a time of war, and the doctrine of peace and goodwill could be promulgated with a freedom and earnestness that the ordinary conditions of the empire would not have permitted. It was doubtless owing to this that in the earliest period of Christianity we learn of its followers' position in regard to war only in the statement of principles.

Marcus Aurelius died in 180, and his death was followed by a century of war and disorder. Throughout the third century the Roman world witnessed a series of desperate conflicts between rival claimants for the imperial purple, so that, between the death of Servius in 211 and the accession of Diocletian in 284, twenty-three emperors sat in the seat of Augustus, and all of these but one died violent deaths in battle or at the hands of the mutinous soldiery, and this one died of pestilence. Beside all this, the vigor of the north had begun its assaults upon the decaying strength of Rome. The favorable conditions for the establishment and growth of the early church during the Augustan age, and the period that immediately followed it, were succeeded by new conditions which severely tried the patience and the faith of the followers of Christ, and called upon them to stand firm in their devotion to the principles of the cause they had espoused. Like other periods of sore trial the weak were sifted out from the strong, and left the body steadfast in the heroic courage of a transforming faith.

It is of interest to note that the early Christians' opposition to war was based primarily upon the teachings of the gospel, and after that upon the fact that the military oath was distinctly pagan and many military practices were mixed with idolatrous rites.

Justin Martyr, who suffered martyrdom at Rome under Marcus Aurelius about the year 165, says in his Dialogue with Trypho: " We, who were once full of war and mutual slaughter, have every one through the whole earth changed our swords into ploughshares, and our spears into implements of tillage, and now cultivate piety, righteousness, charity, faith and hope, which we have from the Father Himself through Him who was crucified." It is quite probable that Justin's words—" every one through the whole earth "—must not be taken too literally, but should be understood to mean that every one who has truly learned the gospel knows that these things should be. The same early Father in the Church in his first Apology, chapter 39, after quoting the prophecy of Isaiah respecting the going forth of the word of God from Jerusalem, and the consequent prevalence of a state of peace, says: " That these things have come to pass you may be readily convinced; for twelve men, destitute both of instruction and of eloquence, went forth from Jerusalem into the world, and by the power of God gave evidence to every description of persons that they were sent by Christ to teach all men the divine word; and we, who were once slayers of one another, do not fight against our enemies."

Irenæus, the disciple of Polycarp, also one of the earliest Fathers, discusses the same prophecy, and proves its relation to our Saviour by the fact that the followers of Jesus had abandoned the weapons of war and no longer knew how to fight.

The early Church soon found that schools or sects were formed among its members. The Gnostics were the earliest of these, of whom Gibbon says: " They were the most polite, the most learned and the most wealthy of the Christian name." Very different from this was the body of Montanists. They have too frequently been judged by the testimony of their opponents who disliked the sound and simple views which the Montanists held of the priestly dignity of all Christians, and that the gifts of the Spirit are not confined to one order in the Church, or even to one sex, and that the true successors of the apostles are those who receive the spirit of prophecy from the Holy Ghost himself. The teachings of the Montanists had a marked influence upon the great Tertullian, who himself so shaped the form and policy of the Western Church. In his earlier writings he seems to have thought that military service might be recognized, since in his "Apology," a pre-Montanist work, he says, in Chapter XXX.: " We pray for protection to the imperial house for brave armies." Subsequently Tertullian was very clear and explicit. In the " Soldiers' Chaplet " he says: " We must first inquire whether warfare is proper for Christians. Shall it be held lawful to make an occupation of the sword, when the Lord proclaims that he who uses the sword shall perish by the sword? Shall the son of peace take part in the battle, when it does not become him even to sue at law? " Again, when writing " On Idolatry," he says: " You inquire whether a believer may enter the military service, and whether soldiers are to be admitted into the faith. How will a Christian man war without a sword which the Lord has taken away? In disarming Peter he unbelted every soldier."

We have evidence of the position of the early Christians concerning war by the writings of their opponents and persecutors. Prominent among these was Celsus, an Epicurean, who wrote his " Word of Truth " about 160 during the reign of Marcus Aurelius. He objects that the state received no help from the Christians either in civil government or war, and that if all men were to follow their example, the sovereign would be deserted, and the world would fall into the hands of barbarians. We know of the writings of Celsus only through those of Origen, who, nearly a century later, wrote a refutation of the former's criticisms. Origen replied: " The question is what would happen if the Romans should be persuaded to adopt the principles of the Christians, to renounce the service now rendered the gods and magistrates, and to worship the Most High. This is my answer. We say that if two of us shall agree on earth as touching anything that they shall ask, it shall be done for them of the Father of the just, who is in heaven. What, then, are we to expect, if not only a very few should agree, as at present, but the whole empire of Rome? They would pray to the Word, who of old said to the Hebrews, when pursued by the Egyptians, ' The Lord shall fight for you and ye shall hold your peace,' and if all should unite in prayer with one accord, they would put to flight enemies far more numerous than were discomfited by the prayer of Moses and of those who prayed with him. If all the

Romans should embrace the Christian faith they would overcome their enemies by prayer; or, rather, they would not go to war at all, being guarded by that divine power which promised to save five whole cities for the sake of fifty just persons."

Surely the doctrine of peace is here placed upon lofty ground. In this work against Celsus, Origen says of himself and his brethren: "We no longer take up the sword against any nation, nor do we learn any more to make war. We have become, for the sake of Jesus, the children of peace." Again, alluding to the efficacy of prayer, he says: "By such means we fight for our King abundantly, but we take no part in his wars, even though he urge us."

This general position continued to be maintained a century later. During the reign of Diocletian, at the beginning of the fourth century, Lactantius insisted upon the absolute inviolability of human life and the unlawfulness of war. He adds: "To engage in war cannot be lawful for the righteous man, whose warfare is that of righteousness itself." The edition of the "Canons of Alexandria" used by the Ethiopian Christians stated: "It is not meet for Christians to bear arms."

Many citations might be made from Eusebius, the father of ecclesiastical history, to further prove the position of the early Christians concerning war, but the chain we have given from Justin Martyr to the fourth century is sufficient. It is a matter of great interest that in the time of Constantine, while the church, recognizing that its practice had violated its old-time doctrines and many professed Christians served in the army, there yet was an expectation that it would return to the true ground. The twelfth canon of the Council of Nice over which Constantine himself presided, provided a long period of excommunication for those who in the ardor of their early faith renounced the military calling, but afterward were bribed to return to it. Alas, during that reign of Constantine, Christian virtue so weakened that it surrendered to the world, and the many evils entered the church which have so long undermined its power.

Among numerous instances where individual Christians refused to engage in military service because of the teachings of Christ, one will suffice. The account is given in Ruinart's "Acta Sincera," and has good historic proof. In A. D. 295, at Teveste, an episcopal city in Numidia, the recruiting sergeant brought before Dion, the Proconsul, a young man of twenty-two years, one Maximilian, as fit for military duty. As he was about to be measured, he said: "I cannot engage in military service; I am a Christian." He repeated: "I cannot fight; I am a Christian." Again he said: "I will not serve. You may cut off my head if you will. I cannot engage in earthly warfare; I am God's soldier." Every argument was used to persuade him to yield, but without avail, and every threat was made, and he triumphantly gave up his life for the testimony of him whom he loved.

Eusebius gives a number of instances where Christians refused to serve in the army because of pagan and idolatrous requirements. One of these was a centurion named Marcellus. The legion to which he belonged was holding a sacrificial feast in honor of one of the Cæsars. Marcellus rose from the mess-table, and, unclasping his military belt, threw it down, exclaiming: " From this moment I cease to serve your empire as a soldier. I am resolved to obey none but Jesus Christ, the eternal King. I despise the worship of your gods. Since the service involves the obligations of sacrificing to the gods and emperors, I renounce the standards, and am a soldier no longer." He was condemned to death and beheaded.

Another instance was that of Marinus, a Christian soldier of Cæsarea, who was about to receive promotion to centurion rank, but would not sacrifice to the emperor.

There is a legend familiar to readers of church history that purports to show the determination of Christian soldiers not to violate their consciences, nor to aid in the persecution of their brethren. The story of the Theban Legion, consisting of 6,600 men, all Christians, has often been told, but its authenticity is very questionable. It is said they were summoned from the East for the service of Maximian in Gaul. When in the valley of the upper Rhone they found they were to be used in the persecution of the Christians, and they refused to obey the emperor's commands. Their commander, Mauricius, and all the legion were put to death. The story is referred to A. D. 286. At that time Maximian was associated with Diocletian, and there was then no persecution nor was there any in Gaul during his reign. The documentary evidence in favor of the legend is very weak. There was no recorded mention of it until two hundred and fifty years afterward. The story is similar to one in Syria, where a Greek martyr of the same name suffered the same fate. Again, it is alleged that the Theban Legion suffered in that year at the spot where is now the City of Cologne on the Rhine, and where the Church of St. Gereon, named for the commander, commemorates their martyrdom. It may be that the Theban Legion, and their suffering on the Rhine and on the Rhone, belong to the same historic classification with St. Ursula and her ten thousand virgins, whose bones we see in another church in Cologne.

But we must not suppose that there was equal faithfulness on the part of all who made profession of Christianity. Passages in Tertullian show there were professing Christians in the army in the second century, and Eusebius shows there were others at a later period, but there seems to be no reliable evidence that these were in any considerable numbers at any time. The story of the Thundering Legion has often been used as furnishing conclusive evidence that the Christians of the second century united with their fellow subjects in serving the emperor in the field. We are told that during the war with the Germans and Sarmatians in the year

174, Marcus Aurelius and his army were in a situation of great peril. The soldiers were without water and were tortured with intolerable thirst, and at the same time were threatened by an attack from the enemy. In this extremity the Twelfth Legion, composed entirely of Christians, fell upon their knees, and their prayer was followed by a shower of rain which allayed the thirst of the Roman soldiers, while the thunder terrified the barbarians so that a complete victory was gained over them. The emperor, to commemorate the event, gave the name of " Thundering " to the legion. But the narrative will not bear critical examination. The legion had been called " Thundering " from the time of Augustus. It was claimed that the emperor, in gratitude for the signal deliverance, ordered the persecution of the Christians to cease. That there was a remarkable deliverance of the Roman army is a historic fact, but the persecutions alleged did not begin until three years after the victory. Pagan writers attributed the deliverance to Jupiter, to whom the emperor and the whole pagan army prayed, and also to the incantations of an Egyptian magician. It is probable that some unscrupulous person started a similar claim for the efficacy of Christian prayer.

This brief examination into the subject of early Christianity and war shows that in the first two centuries of the Christian era the followers of Christ very generally practiced the spirit of His teachings, and were obedient to His commands concerning war, and that this continued with a modified completeness during the third century. If the examination was continued further we would find that the occupation of the throne of the Roman empire by a professing Christian in the person of Constantine so united the Church with the world, that the rank and pomp and wealth and fashion of the latter demoralized the Church so that its sacred principles were violated, its testimonies were neglected or trampled under foot, pagan rites and usages were introduced into its worship, and an era of decadence was inaugurated, which heroic efforts in various periods have in some measure stayed, but which still continue to mar the Church's efforts and to hinder her sure conquest of the world.

THE CHAIRMAN: We will next have an address on the " Attitude of Christians as to War and Peace," by Dr. Jesse H. Holmes. of Swarthmore College.

THE ATTITUDE OF CHRISTIANS AS TO PEACE AND WAR.

BY JESSE H. HOLMES, PH.D., SWARTHMORE COLLEGE.

Christianity met with a great disaster early in its career—a disaster largely made possible by its rapid spread—in that it came to be officially recognized as a state religion. In its inception Christianity was particularly marked by its strong appeal to the individual. We cannot in our day fully grasp the originality displayed by its founders in turning their backs upon gods who dealt with mankind by the wholesale, as races or nations, and turning to God who speaks to the individual soul, and for whom not the nation, but the man, is the unit. Such conception is not, of course, a new one as presented by Jesus and his followers; it was present in the minds of many of the prophets, and was not unknown among ancient philosophies.

But such idea of God was fundamental in Christianity. It was not to Jews, not to Gentiles, not to rich or poor, not to great or small, but to individual men that was preached the gospel of the kingdom within us. For three centuries it made its way amid persecution and against opposition, passing on from soul to soul, uplifting the slave and humbling the master, illuminating the wrecks of old philosophies, and bringing back to life a zest and interest which it had in large measure lost. In those three centuries it had honeycombed the Empire. Slave had whispered the gospel to his fellow-slave, or perhaps timidly to a kindly master. It circulated in the arteries of trade, it was talked in the streets, it grew even when hunted into the catacombs. In all this it was taught only as man to man. It was backed by no great official power, but represented in all that it accomplished its own native force and energy. Where it won its way it was by mastering the consciences of men. It had no prizes to offer by which to tempt the time-server. Only a fervent conviction of truth, only a deadly (or, rather, a truly living) earnestness could induce men to ally themselves with a proscribed sect. We may hardly doubt that the Christian Church of this time was made up of real Christians; they had stood the test of fire, and with only a natural human alloy of baser metal, they had been proved sterling.

It was under such circumstances that disaster fell upon it in the form of an unhoped-for and dazzling success—the Empire became officially Christian. The old and well-worn temptation rejected by Jesus himself was now offered to his Church, and it fell. "All the kingdoms of the earth will I give thee" might have been the language of Constantine when he made the Roman empire Christian in name. And what great things might not the Church of the Christ do with all the kingdoms of the earth? The vision of a new heaven and a new earth so dazzled the bishops of the fourth century that they forgot to notice the small and apparently insignificant condition annexed, "If thou wilt bow down and worship me." Not for the first time was a distinctive price unnoticed in the glory of immediate possession. Christianity received the kingdoms of the earth, and bowed down before Satan. Thenceforth there were princes in the household of him who was "meek and lowly;" thenceforth Christianity went forth, sword in hand, to conquer heathendom, not for the Christ-spirit, but for a nominal Christianity. The Church turned from men to man. It baptized nations, indeed, after it had conquered them—baptizing with water —and, indeed, with fire also—but neglecting the baptism of the Holy Spirit. Only incidentally, and in small measure, did it spread abroad the spirit of the Master. Those methods which had made Christianity so great a power that the Empire was forced to adopt its name were neglected for those which had produced the very weakness under which the Empire suffered. The Church chose the way of the devil to reach the ends of God, taking no warning, as it might for the very ease of the journey, that it had left the straight and narrow for the broad and easy way.

Christianity broke up into warring sects. It dealt with principalities and powers; its eye became keen for estates, and it dealt in souls mainly by wholesale. Almost every generation, indeed, has seen small groups of individuals breaking away from the evil of official religion, and striving for a return to the spirit of Christianity —to a direct walk with God, a direct communing with his self-revealings. But, seeing the supreme success of the Master's failure, the crown of martyrdom is no longer offered beyond a certain point. So soon as Christianity becomes strong enough to be dangerous the kingdoms of the earth are offered again, and still this bait is taken. Protestantism, Calvinism, Puritanism, have in turn denied God in spirit while defining and explaining Him in words.

I would not be understood as indicating that Christianity has been altogether lost, altogether a failure—so far from it that it has always been and is to-day the leaven of human life. Its representatives have been, and are, few and weak, in worldly power, but they have been, and are, the hope of the world. And the long look over the centuries since Christianity was Romanized by a pretense of Christianizing Rome does not tend to discouragement. More and more, century by century, men have caught at God's personal fatherhood and man's brotherhood as the great facts of the divine message—at love, as the fulfilling of the law. "Not by might or by power, but by my Spirit" is now more than ever a triumphant note.

I wish to use this opportunity to make a distinct plea for the individual—the separate person—as the indivisible and indestructible unit in all matters of righteousness; that we shall undo the wrong of centuries and stand responsible to God alone. Christian churches and Christian nations are made of Christian men—are nothing apart from them or in addition to them. The whole is not greater than the sum of its parts. Nothing is right for us as Friends, as Christians, as citizens, which is wrong for us as individuals. There is no mysterious entity to be called a nation or a church which may cancel our duties as sons of God, and substitute another standard of right and wrong. If individuals making up a church represent a spirit of force, of violence, the church cannot represent a spirit of peace and goodwill. If missionaries are backed by gunboats, if they collect indemnities under threat of the bayonet, they are missionaries of that power which promised the kingdoms of earth in order secretly to destroy the kingdom of heaven. If citizens go forth to slay and destroy they may carry the name of civilization on their lips, but they are simply homicides and barbarians.

Men salve their consciences, yea, even benumb their consciences, by shifting the responsibilities of their deeds to a mythical something called a government, a church; but no power can release a man from the burden of his deeds. Not that all homicide and destruction is alike evil, not that men may not deceive themselves so that the worse appears the better. But this is only possible by avoiding the Christian attitude and shirking the Christian responsibility. I do not even say that all homicide and destruction are necessarily culpable; but only that what is wrong for each of us as a man cannot be right for each as a citizen, as a Christian. The righteous laws of nations are superadded to the moral law, not substituted for it. All our duties as members of churches, as citizens of nations, are based upon our duties as members of the human family, and stand for those higher duties consequent upon closer relations. They can never release us from the fundamental duty of a sense of universal brotherhood. We can no more, without violation of Christian principle, build our gain, our greatness, our exaltation, upon the loss of the Hindoo or the Hottentot, the Spaniard or the Filipino, than upon that of our fellow-Quaker, or our fellow-American. And it is a neglect of this principle fundamental in Christianity; it is this placing metes and bounds upon our Christian charity, that marks the barbarizing of Christianity during sixteen centuries.

Some phases of this essential falsehood are these:

1. That Christianity is for peace, indeed; but that because of human weakness Christians must excuse war;

2. That peace tends to make cowards of us, and that we must have war in order to support the virility of the race;

3. That while violence for selfish ends is wrong, it is lawful to do evil that good may come;

4. That experience shows that many evils could not have been overcome without war.

(1) Christianity is for peace among men, but must defer to the weakness of humanity. Christianity must indeed stoop to the weakness of humanity, not to excuse that weakness, but to cure it. We must pardon the sinner—must we also accept the sin? Jesus, indeed, refused to punish the sinner; did he at the same time make light of the sin? Shall Christianity trail its white robe in the mire of sin to show its fellowship with sinners? Shall it do evil that it may draw near to evil-doers? Not so do I understand the teaching of the Master or the teaching of the Spirit. The Christian is not called upon to be stupid, selfish, and sinful in order to reach those who are immersed in stupidity, selfishness and sin. Such doctrine could never have obtained except for the pagan idea that we are fractional parts of a nation or of a church, and must therefore assimilate ourselves to its average quality. But the Christian attitude is that of an independent unit, a partner with God in the work of subduing his earth. His duty to God transcends all temporary human relations. And, indeed, the conclusion at its best is a reversal of common sense. Because men are weak, let us be strong; because they are ignorant and violent, let us be wise and gentle. If they exalt force, let us show them how much more powerful is love. Of course, if our plea is that we are too weak to stand against the crowd, or that we believe the voice of the mob is the voice of God and to be obeyed—that is frankly an avowal of disbelief in Christianity, and should serve as an appeal to those who are Christians to convert us.

(2) Does peace make cowards of us? If it does, then Christian teaching is falsehood, and we should turn to a new and true gospel. It is the worst of hypocrisy to proclaim a gospel of peace as a theory and a gospel of war as a practice. And this is largely the attitude of a nominal Christianity to-day. Numerous pseudo-Christian ministers have exalted the value of war as necessary to make men brave and self-sacrificing. In other words, they do not believe that the gospel they preach ex-officio tends to produce brave, true men. Occasional wars are necessary to serve as an antidote to the effects of periods in which Christian practices prevail. If for years we have been at peace—the condition longed for by prophet and Messiah—therefore, lest our manhood decline, let us burn cities; let us starve women and children, and kill men by thousands to avert the degeneration due to peace and the preaching of peace. Either Christianity is a mistake and a failure, and should be given up wholly or in part, or it is true and right, and should be applied in times of difficulty and danger as well as in times of ease and comfort. Indeed, unless it is a total failure, Christianity is needed especially at times when men differ and when passion tends to take the place of reason.

But, does peace make cowards of us? Let us turn first to war itself for answer. Peace made the men called heroes by the newspapers, who made up our armies in the Spanish war. Practically, all of them were born, educated and matured in a period of profound peace. But the courage of a soldier is not a very high type of courage. He is drilled beforehand, so that his own will shall have the smallest possible activity in the time of crisis. He risks being killed, indeed; but when did taking risks come to be a high type of courage? If it is so, truly, then, the gambler is somewhat of a hero too. I am not arguing against the courage of the American. I fully believe in his courage; but the taking of risks, even heavy risks, is not the best evidence of it. It is the motive, not the danger, that shows a hero. We have vastly better evidence in the heroes of peace, who never fail to appear in accidents, in wrecks at sea, in fires on land. These are they who take risks, often far greater than those of the soldier, to save life, not to destroy it. We have greater heroes than those of war, again, in those who face unflinchingly long years of monotonous labor, giving their strength ungrudgingly to win comfort and happiness for their families. We have heroes in our physicians, who so devote themselves to healing the sick and alleviating suffering that they deny themselves even the vacations which are their due. We have heroes in the pioneers who conquer the wilderness, in the explorers who expand the domain of human knowledge, in all those whose lives are self-dedicated to the good of others. We mistake deeply, we do injustice to our race, to our religion and to our civilization, when we grant our chief applause to the showy, organized national destroyers rather than to the unnoticed, miscellaneous saviours, who do their work, demanding no meed of praise, who never claim to be heroes, but who support upon their bent shoulders the hope of the world. Glory to the builder, not to the destroyer.

(3) But shall we not do evil that good may come? If good come on the whole, then what we do is not evil. It is in the consequences of an act that exists its quality, whether good or evil. If an act has no consequences it has no moral element. But the flaw in the proposition that we may make war for a good purpose lies in its short view. The experience of the race and the teaching of our highest instincts unite in making clear that the total result of war is evil, and only evil continually. It is cheap and common to assert that war freed our nation from English domination, and that it struck the shackles from four millions of slaves. We leave out of account the heritage of bitterness and hatred not yet outlived that followed after the Revolution, to say nothing of the thousands of lives thrown away or made miserable. We skillfully avoid the question, which is a vital one, whether greater self-control, greater patience might not have accomplished more with less of evil. And we leave out of account the evident fact that the slavery question is not settled—that, indeed, it is perhaps less soluble as a race question embittered by the brutal years of violence and by sectional discord, than it was as a slavery question. Again, we fail to consider what self-restraint and patience might have done. And

our fourth difficulty is involved in our third. War is sometimes necessary for the sake of others. The strong must be violent to help the weak—or, as before, the end justifies the means. Even so, friends, if what we look upon were the end—but there is no end. In a wave of nation-wide enthusiasm we went to war with Spain where men were governed badly and against their will, and where starvation and torture were used to enforce submission. After a harvest of suffering, disease, and crime had been reaped, we now look to a Cuba free from Spain, and we find ourselves immeshed in a war with a people whom we govern badly and against their will, and where starvation and torture are used to enforce submission. Good may, indeed, come in spite of evil, for of unmixed evil there are few examples in the affairs of men, but good does not come because of it. If so much good has come in spite of all the evil, what would not the world be if it could be brought to Christianity?

There is no more fundamental atheism than is involved in a proclamation that God is too weak to win His way without calling in the devil to His help. There is no deeper infidelity than that which so distrusts the strength of righteousness that it must lean upon the arm of unrighteousness. It is from this attitude of apology that I would earnestly call Christians to-day. " Let us have faith that right makes might," and in that faith let us fare forward courageously in the path we are in. Let us no more evade and pretend. Are we ashamed of the Christ and his message? If not, let us speak it, and live it in spirit and in truth. May we not have in clear unmistakable tones the outspoken, uncompromising demand for righteousness on the part of each individual before God; the selfless plea for self-conquest; for the ruling of our own spirits? May we not have a definite rejection of compromise with evil, of deals with iniquity, a courageous and confident stand upon the power of the spirit of love to solve the hard problems of the world?

THE CHAIRMAN:—The next paper is on " The Christian Idea of Force," by Dr. Richard H. Thomas, of Baltimore, president of the Peace Association of Friends in America.

THE CHRISTIAN IDEA OF FORCE.

BY DR. RICHARD HENRY THOMAS, BALTIMORE, MD.

For our present purpose force may be briefly defined as power made effective for use. Thus we speak of spiritual, mental and physical force, and of the various forces of nature. Without force no results are accomplished. Therefore, when a man of peace says, " I do not believe in using force," however praiseworthy his meaning may be, his words are incorrect, and he lays himself open to the charge of being a mere visionary. When he explains: " I believe not in the use of physical, but of spiritual and moral force," his opponent answers: " Your child is about to cut himself with a sharp knife; will you not snatch it from him ? " " Certainly." " He is running toward a precipice. You shout to him to stop. Either he does not hear, or will not obey. Will you not run and catch him, and save him ? "

" Would you never, for any reason, punish your child in other ways than by word or look? If so, you do believe, under certain circumstances, in the use of physical force." But you reply, " That is different. It is right to do these things." Yes, it is right, but you cannot do them without physical force. Your real contention, then, is not against physical force, as such, but against the wrong use of it.

We cannot even say that under all circumstances the use of brute force is wrong. A Samson might hold a lunatic or a criminal, to restrain him from violence, in his strong embrace, not brutally, but by brute force, and receive from the most ardent peace advocate nothing but praise. Then even brute force is not always wrong, so it be not brutally used.

Further, if physical force may sometimes be well used, spiritual and moral force may be wrongly used. The assassin of our late President, for instance, claimed his deed to be morally right, and if, as the Bible says, there be such a thing as spiritual wickedness, there must also be a wrong use of spiritual power.

From the simple human standpoint, which is, after all, hardly removed from the divine, we may therefore conclude that of all the great divisions of force, spiritual and moral, physical and mechanical, none are in themselves either right or wrong, but that the moral element lies in the manner in which they are used and the object to be gained.

What, then, is the teaching of the New Testament on the subject? First, I find no distinction made between physical and spiritual force in the sense that one is set off as being necessarily right and the other as always wrong. Paul on one occasion missed a splendid opportunity for making such a distinction. The only explanation I can think of why he did not make it is that he did not believe it existed. He says, indeed, " The weapons of our warfare are not carnal." How many of us would say, and have said, " But spiritual." But Paul misses his opportunity and says, " Not carnal, but mighty." The position is stronger. He discards carnal weapons for something better. To-day, many assume that weapons not carnal are necessarily weak. Paul thought otherwise. Writing to Rome, the very center and symbol of power in the civilized world, he says that he is not ashamed of the Gospel of Christ, for it is the power of God unto salvation to everyone that believeth. To the men of force he brings something more forceful. This is no jelly-fish sentimentalism, but the utterance of a man glorying in the Source of his strength. The Christian ideal of life is a manly ideal, and includes struggle and conquest, not with carnal weapons—for carnal means human nature, rising up against the rule of God—not, I say, with carnal weapons, that is with force acting under the direction of the lower impulses of our nature, but with weapons fashioned and used in accordance with the mightiest force in the universe.

That the idea of force is very prominent in the minds of the New Testament writers is clear even to a superficial reader. Their belief in the resurrection of Jesus Christ supplied them with their unit of available power. This was the standard by which they estimated the possibilities of their life and work. Paul prays that the Ephesians may know that this is indeed the measure of the power of God in them. This estimate gave them manifest advantages. It rendered it impossible for them to be discouraged at any rebuff or defeat. Why? Christ had, humanly-speaking, suffered the most humiliating of defeats, and yet through that very defeat he had conquered. They knew that he had sounded depths of sorrow and darkness they could never know, and that every difficulty they could meet would always lie well within this unit of force, which became practically available for everyone as the result of the power of God working within him, as he lived in conscious submission to it.

This did not make them unnatural men and women. They did not count upon God as savages do upon a fetich. They saw that his power works through means, and they never hesitated to use means properly adapted for their purpose. Paul, when his health broke down on his first missionary journey, did not say, "The power of God is sufficient," and so disregarded the danger. He changed his course, and went to the mountains of northern Galatia to recruit, and so came to preach the Gospel there. When he knew that there was a plot against his life, he took pains to have the governor who was responsible for his safety informed, so that he might not be needlessly exposed to an attack by his enemies. He repeatedly claimed his civil privileges as a Roman citizen. But he refused to respond to the pointed intimations of Felix that he should offer him a bribe, although he knew that the power of money would secure his liberty. He promised his comrades in danger during the terrible storm that, although the ship would be lost, all lives should be saved, yet he also said that unless the sailors were prevented from leaving the ship in the boats the others could not be rescued. The faith of the first Church was that God had power to deliver them from all danger, and therefore when they were living in the will of God, and death or suffering came upon them, they realized fully that this also was the will of God. The death of Stephen did not dim their faith, nor did the exile that most of them had to suffer afterwards. The death of James did not discourage them from praying for Peter. Why should not they be put to death as their Lord had been?

The whole atmosphere that they breathed was different from what they had known before, and from what those about them knew. It was their mission to bring others into this same relation to God. They proclaimed neither a well-worked out system of morality nor of doctrine. Both these were to a certain degree in a state of fluidity. What was prominent in their experience and in their message was that through Jesus Christ they had come to know their true relation to God and how to attain it, and live in it with the power of the risen Saviour. They did not themselves fully grasp all that this implies. Paul, for instance, seems to have failed to understand that God has much concern for the lower animals, and asks, " Does God care for oxen ? " He does not seem to have seen that Christian love bars out slavery. Cornelius is allowed, so far as we know, to remain a Roman soldier centurion, although there must have been duties that he had to perform in heathen practices essentially connected with the army, that to our minds, apart from the necessity of fighting, would be wholly out of harmony with Christianity. His example can as well be cited to support the theory that idolatry is consistent with Christ as that war is.

But all these things did not affect the everlasting principle under which the first Christians lived. It was not for them to see to the end of that which shall forever be opening out fresh glories and fresh avenues for love and service. The seed of Christian thought and experience that they planted is still growing and developing. But it was theirs to learn the secret of true power, and how it is known as we live in harmony with the source of it, that is with the spirit of the life and teaching of Jesus Christ and in confidence in him. What, then, is the spirit of his life and teaching?

First, let us recognize that he used all the great divisions of force that I have mentioned, and set us the example that we should use them also. That he made use of what is known as spiritual and moral power is too clear to need exposition. In his words, " Be ye wise as serpents, and harmless as doves," we have his endorsement of intellectual activity as applied to practical matters. In his scourge of small cords we have his endorsement of physical force. Why should we try to deny it? With Christ, what he did and what he taught are not in contrast. They mutually complete each other, and this act is not out of harmony with his teaching. True, small cords do small injury. But, explain it as you will, whether he used the scourge on men or not, the act was an exercise of physical force, used to protest against an abuse, and we lose much and gain nothing by trying to explain it away. But let those who gloat over this fact, and who think that it endorses the war method, remember how weak small cords are, and not attempt to support by them the wars of Christendom, with their thousands slain, and whole districts devastated. Such a burden is too great for small cords to sustain, and, after all, it is a poor argument that urges that because a certain degree of physical force is justifiable, therefore every degree of physical force is justifiable. To protest against an abuse, not even sufficiently to do away with it, but only enough to make the protest understood, is one thing, and is wholly unlike doing men to death either individually or on the battlefield. I think these small cords would never have been used to support war had not war advocates been so hard put to it to find New Testament arguments for their contention, and had not peace advocates weakened their cause by attempting to maintain that all physical force is in itself condemned by Christ. Before leaving this incident let us remember that what Christ was doing was simply as a protest and not as a punishment, and that his choice of small cords shows his care to injure no one. As to his overturning the tables of the money changers and driving out the animals, this only gave their owners the trouble of collecting them again, as it was all within the Temple inclosure, and there was no danger of theft or loss.

Physical force, therefore, if it be used in a Christlike spirit, is supported by Christ's example. Apart from this spirit no force of any kind can be justified on the Christian idea. It is the same, therefore, with Christ's teaching as we found in respect to the simple human point of view, that the true distinction is not between spiritual and physical force, but between the use of any force for worthy ends in the Christian spirit, and force not so used.

To discover the Christian idea of force we must understand the purpose and method of Jesus Christ. Does any one doubt that the purpose is truly expressed in the words, "The Son of Man is not come to destroy men's lives, but to save them"? There is also a general agreement that in his method he trusted to the sweet reasonableness of his teaching and to the divine power within him, shown through his life and sufferings, to reach and convince men. Some, however, claim that what he says about not bringing peace but a sword, and his direction to the twelve to sell their garments and buy swords, show that he had other methods also in his mind. But the context in neither case bears this out. The sword he says he was come to send refers simply to the family strife certain to be engendered when the anger of those who do not accept his message is aroused against those who do. He explains that he is speaking of the mother and father being arrayed against the son and daughter. Therefore, unless we are prepared to maintain that Christ approves of family quarrels, we must understand he is not expressing approval of strife, but pictorially referring to feuds that must arise in the nature of the case. That his command to buy swords is purely figurative is shown by his reply, when the disciples said, "Here are two swords." "It is enough," as though two could be enough for twelve men. Later on, when Peter used one of these very swords, Christ rebuked him, and soon afterwards explained that the reason his servants did not fight was that his kingdom is not of this world.

We are justified, therefore, in maintaining that Christ's method is wholly in accord with truth and justice, and that he consistently employed force on this principle, and that sooner than depart from it he allowed the worst evils to come upon him.

But some say that Christ was carrying out the design of God in our salvation, and that therefore he suffered, but that we, who are not the saviours of men, are on a totally different plane. Much in this assertion seems to add to the glory of Christ, but, certainly, so far as it teaches that we are to live on a different plane from Christ, it lacks any support from the words of Christ, or of any New Testament writer. In his prayer he says: "As thou hast sent me into the world, even so have I sent them into the world." Again, "As I am, so are ye in the world." "The servant is not above his Master . . . It is enough for the servant to be as his Master." Paul even speaks of filling up that which is lacking in the sufferings of Christ. In the minds of our Lord and of His immediate followers, the adoption of the method and spirit of Christ were essential conditions of discipleship. Christ is more than an example. He demonstrated and made available for all men, as it had never been done before, the greatest force in the universe. Through it he won his great world-victory, and upon it his followers are to rely. It is the power that comes with such a surrender to God as enables us to love him and those about us with a love that will not fail under any provocation, a love that will cast out self-seeking and selfishness, and strengthen us for any sacrifice that is needed to obey God and to help our fellow men according to His will.

This is so contrary to the world's idea of force that it requires us to drink deep of the spirit of Jesus Christ to recognize and accept it. But it is only in doing so that we can have the faith that overcomes the world.

This is very different from a mere passive acceptance of ills and evil. Christ's force was not negative, but positive. Paul was anything but a negative character. Neither of them sat down before difficulties, waiting for all things to come right. They used this force to most effective purpose, and did not neglect the use of force in ordinary channels, so far as was consistent with the supremacy of this all-controlling force. We also, as they, have the same strength available for us, and through everything that may happen we are to be more than conquerors through him who loved us.

But we hear it objected: "Is peace safe?" Does any one ask: "Is war safe?" Are good causes never crushed in war? Do people whose defence is in firearms never have their houses broken into, and never kill their wives or children, as well as the intruder, or instead of him? From the point of view of safety of life and limb there is, humanly speaking, no absolute safety for any one. The Czar of Russia is probably in greater danger with all his guards than any one private citizen of his Empire. It is not a question of mere physical safety, but of what is the most effective method for the establishment of righteousness and the protection of the individual, and I maintain that the strongest method is Christ's method, and also that there has now been sufficient experience to make this assertion more than a mere matter of simple faith. The experience of the early colonists of Pennsylvania, as compared with other colonists, and of Pennsylvania itself when unpeaceful counsels prevailed, is a strong instance in point. The overcoming of the wild mountaineers of the Caucasus by the Doukhobors through persistent kindness is another example, and individual instances innumerable lead to the same conclusion. And yet, since our Master was ill treated and put to death, why should we complain that his followers may be called upon at times to serve the truth in similar ways?

On general principles, therefore, the Christian idea is that we trust this divine force and employ other forces only as they ring true to the method and purpose of our Lord's life upon earth. On this basis everything that contemplates success or victory through force brutally used, or through maiming and killing human beings, can never be justified according to Christ's idea of force. But this limitation, so far from lessening, strengthens us in preventing and reforming evil. I admit that it often works more slowly than our patience is quite ready for, but it is far more certain than other means. The real difficulty lies in this: first, that we hold the truth too much in theory, and have made it too little an essential part of our life; and, second, that we belong to a community only partially Christian, if indeed we may be sure that we are wholly Christian ourselves.

A broad difference between the first century and the nineteenth is that in the former the nation was nominally idolatrous, and the Christians in it, although without political influence, were a growing force leavening the whole, while we now, possessed of political influence, live in a nation nominally Christian, but largely pagan. The difference is apparently and really great, but among many advantages we have this difficulty, that there is a tendency to confusion of ideas, because methods and policies, from being called Christian, come to be regarded as such. In this way we have the consent of many professing Christians to things intrinsically heathen both in principle and application. Prominent among these is the war system. It cannot ring true to any just conception of the teaching of Jesus Christ. The weapons of its warfare are essentially carnal, the passions it arouses are the reverse of Christian, and the results of its work, after allowing for all the benefits that can honestly be claimed for it, are the reverse of what is characteristic of the work of Christ.

What then is the duty of one who believes that he has seen the true Christian idea of force? Certainly he is not to withdraw from those about him, as though he were holier than they. Moreover we have what the early Christians had not—political influence. This is something that no one, either man or woman, has a right to neglect. We cannot do so without being false to duty. Indifference means that we are exercising the wrong influence. We need not be always condemning those who do not see as we do, nor should we forget that so long as the majority of our countrymen believe that their great protection is in the force of arms, it is impossible to do more than limit the building of warships and appropriations for military purposes. We are to labor to render these things useless and out of date. Democracy means or at least should mean, the predominating influence of men out of office, and the fact that we may not consistently hold offices where in the judgment of those who would have elected us, it might become our official duty to call out the military, need not discourage us. There was practically no office whatever open to the first Christians, and we know what great influence they exerted.

Our position is not negative, but positive. We have, and we are to use, the mighty weapons of our warfare to the pulling down of strongholds, and the casting down of everything that exalts itself against the obedience of Christ. The Peace message is more than a theory or than a mere moral sentiment. It is not a weak assertion that we disbelieve in war and oppression, and believe in peace at any price.

It is, to begin with, an experience—an experience of union with the God of love and truth, such a union that we are taken possession of and held by that love. This will enable us to live in such a spirit as George Fox was in when, after he had been seriously injured, he looked at the disabled arm, not in anger or regret, but in the love of God. It is only in such an experience that we can truly test whether a given proceeding is right or wrong. The love of God in our hearts will then be the true decider. It is only by being in an experience that does away with wars and fightings and the causes of them in our own hearts, that we are able to know what it is to have the mighty weapons of God, and to be able truly to influence men. But if we are practically taking the same attitude that others are taking upon national and international questions, and simply drawing the line when it comes to actual fighting, we have given up our principle, and are holding a tradition.

Starting with the experience of union with Christ, we are where we can take a correct general view of things. We cannot expect men who have not recognized our principle to act in accordance with it. But when they do not do so, we shall not co-operate with them. We should be ready, however, as their brothers, in the providence of God, to suffer patiently with them in every way not inconsistent with our position. We can do what lies within us to bring them to see what is so true to us, and we can encourage everything that tends to promote justice and peace, everything that will help to bring in an era of true and permanent good feeling at home or abroad. We can endeavor to help those in official position to find ways of settling disputes peacefully, and we can show appreciation of their efforts in these directions. We can in times of excitement exert ourselves to allay it, and we can make the most of such movements as the Hague Convention, the Pan-American Congress, Boards of Arbitration, etc., between Labor and Capital. We can arouse the consciences of our fellow Christians, and, above all, continually live in the power of the peaceful conquering Saviour.

THE CHAIRMAN:—Before opening the general discussion, I will make the announcement that to-morrow the meeting will be opened at ten o'clock, and the doors will be closed during the devotional period with which the exercises begin. President M. Carey Thomas, of Bryn Mawr College, will preside at the session to-morrow forenoon, and the program, as you have it printed, will be carried out.

There will be some time now for a general discussion of the papers to which we have just listened, and this discussion will be opened by President Birdsall, of Swarthmore College.

WILLIAM W. BIRDSALL: I was particularly impressed this morning by that paragraph of Dr. Barton's paper in which he outlined the progress of the Hebrew idea of God and the effect of that idea upon their relations with each other. When their God was a God of the family, then each family considered itself to be under the protection and guidance of its own God; this belief permitted war with every family round about. It was a step of progress when the family God became a tribal God, and family war lost itself in the larger, still barbarous, idea of tribal war. So, when the idea came that Jehovah was a national God, it set free the tribe from war against tribe, but it set nation at war against nation. What an elevation of human life it was when they came at last to see that the God of their fathers was the God of men of every country and every clime, that all men were of one blood, and therefore brethren. It seemed to me that Dr. Barton had put his finger upon the vital point in this discussion, at least so far as the bearing of religion upon peace is concerned, when he said that the promulgation of the idea of the fatherhood of God made necessarily unlawful every act of war. But, as the idea of God became successively tribal, national, universal, was it not natural that in some degree at least the sense of individual responsibility should be lost, and was not the coming of a Messiah needed to call men back to their individual relation with the Most High, and to teach them to cease to think of Him as the God of nations or the God of battles, but to think of Him as the Father of the individual?

The method of Jesus was the individual method; He appealed

to multitudes, but always to multitudes as composed of individuals. If you wish to get typical instances of His method, where do you go? Not to His discourses to great concourses of people, but to His quiet talk with the woman at the well, or with one or two disciples, here and there. It was through His touch upon the individual heart that He gained His hold upon the mind and heart of His multitude of followers. How natural it was in the early stages of the Christian Church for it to gain its hold upon men's minds through the whispering of slave to slave, or slave to master, or friend to friend, through the preaching of evangelists and disciples; but it was no less natural, as numbers gathered, that the appeal should be to numbers and that it should be forgotten that it was the individual that was responsible, that it was through the individual that the church was to extend. How natural it was to reach out for numbers, for organization, for authority; and to yield to the temptation, as the Church did, to barter its birthright for the kingdoms of the world!

Dr. Holmes pointed out to us that something like this has happened in the history of every great religious movement. He omitted our own, but he need not have omitted it. Was not the appeal of George Fox to the individual? When he came into a neighborhood, did he not inquire what people there were tender? Did he not seek them out and minister to them as one mind and one heart to another mind and heart? All through his ministry was it not the individual to whom he preached; and did not those who followed him and who spread the Quaker faith through England and over the continent and into America pursue his method? When they grew in numbers and in power and in respectability, did not they, too, appeal to power—not indeed to the power of the State, but to the power of their own organization; and did not they, too, fail when they bartered their birthright of a living, individual religion for a religion hemmed in and bound by a narrow, a destructive, a disowning discipline?

Like early Christianity, the Quaker faith was propagated by mastering the consciences of individual men. That, it seems to me, the history of every great spiritual movement declares to be the true method. Organization is good; it brings together forces already in existence, arranges for their best applications, and provides for their greatest usefulness. So long as those forces live in the unities of which the organization is composed, so long is the organization vital, helpful, a force in the community. Just so soon as the unities of which the organization is composed lose their hold upon the vital force which first called it into being, just so soon is the organization a dead shell, hindering life, ready to be sloughed off and discarded.

If we will truly seize this idea of the individual responsibility, of the individual relation to the Source of light and truth, then, indeed, shall we be enabled to apply the Christian idea of force.

This will enable us to live in the world; to work with our fellows, though they see not with us; to do the work that is laid upon us without hindering the good work that is laid upon our brethren. It is right for us to come together in organization for definite work; it is right for us to protest as societies for every worthy cause and against every evil movement. But there is a deeper foundation for the culture and promotion of righteousness in the world. It is the appeal, which has never failed when made, to the individual mind, and its duties to the Father of Light. We do right to join ourselves together in every good work; but we do the essential thing when we turn to the voice of God in the soul, as George Fox called upon the great Protector to do. Much talk, he says, he had with Cromwell—much discourse about religion and about other things; and they came upon this subject of war. The Quaker apostle condemned him not, but called him to turn to the voice of God in his own heart, which he told him if he would hear would call him away from the occasions of wars and fightings and lead him into the peaceable spirit of Jesus.

JOSEPH ELKINTON: I think our friend Dr. Holmes has done us a great service in sounding the keynote of all true civilization, of all religion worthy the name of Christianity. It has been a question with me how we may approach those who do not hold the views that we do; and it has seemed to me he has given us a clue to the possibility of making men think it possible for them to be separated from perverted popular opinion, and, if need be, from their religious instructors, to have their views created by a higher Power than either of these.

I wish, also, to refer to Dr. Thomas's instance of the Doukhobors, who have given us perhaps the most striking illustration in recent times of what peace principles will do in practice. They were sent at one time into the heart of a country infested by the wildest-hearted men, sent there purposely to be annihilated by them. But they maintained their peace principles even to throwing away their arms, and they came out of that situation with very few deaths from the use of arms against them. It seems to me to be a most striking lesson. So does their recent deliverance from Russia. There are many other sects in that country pleading for freedom of thought, but the Doukhobors alone seem to have won. They have come to America by virtue, no doubt, of the sympathy and help of Friends in England and here, but also, there is not the least doubt, because they maintained their peace principles inviolate under circumstances the most trying in modern civilization.

THE CHAIRMAN: As no one else seems to wish to speak, the Conference is now adjourned till ten o'clock to-morrow morning.

Fourth Session.

FIFTH-DAY MORNING, TWELFTH MONTH 13TH.

The Conference re-assembled in Witherspoon Hall Fifth-day morning at 10 o'clock. M. Carey Thomas, president of Bryn Mawr College, occupied the Chair.

A few minutes at the opening of the session were given to devotion, during which prayer was offered by Mary Jane Weaver and Allen Flitcraft.

M. CAREY THOMAS: In the brief remarks I shall make from the chair, before calling on the speakers who have prepared formal papers, I thought it might be of interest to call your attention to the forces outside of the churches that are making for peace.

It is easy for us to let the warlike emotions of the past three years, which have swept over the United States in connection with our own war with Spain and England's war with the Boers, cause us to underestimate the force of the public sentiment in favor of peace and arbitration that has grown up during the preceding thirty years of almost unbroken European peace.

In looking back over the Nineteenth Century and reflecting on the great revolutions of thought and social feeling that will reach their culmination only in the Twentieth Century, we can discern, I think, two great movements making strongly for peace—the higher education of women, the immensity of whose results we cannot as yet fully foresee, and the socialistic organization of workingmen.

The Nineteenth Century has witnessed the abolishment of slavery in civilized Europe and her colonies, the reform of prisons and treatment of criminals, the humane care of the insane, the founding of reformatories of all kinds, and hospitals, systematic and wisely directed work among the poor in slums and tenements, the regulation of the employer in the interests of the employed, the vast spread of international commerce, with its trade unions. These mighty social and humanitarian movements, taking place simultaneously in all civilized countries, have created a consciousness of the human kinship which unites all the inhabitants of these different countries. The International Peace Conference at The Hague, in 1899, is one proof of this consciousness. The Pan-American Congress now meeting in Mexico has set before itself as its chief object the adoption by the South American delegates of the principle of arbitration. Yet a little more than two hundred years ago, in 1693, when William Penn drew up his scheme for a

European Council of Arbitration, it was regarded as a Quaker dream.

The general progress of popular sentiment will be greatly assisted and hastened, however, by two distinct and specific movements. The emergence of women as a sex into the life of affairs in the Twentieth Century, and the swiftly approaching political preponderance through universal suffrage and organization of the working man, and ultimately of the working woman, will be most important factors in bringing about peace in the Twentieth Century. No one who has known women that lived through the tragedies and agonies of our Civil War, or indeed of any war, can doubt that the suffering of war falls more heavily on women than on men, and that in consequence their influence as a sex will be exerted for peace, just as no one who follows the discussions of the workingmen's parties and the influence already exerted by socialists can fail to see that the time is approaching when the men who work with their hands in one country will refuse to fight the men who work with their hands in another country for any of the trivial causes for which nations have often declared war in the past.

Of all the great moral and religious principles and doctrines advocated by the Quaker Church, peace seems to be the only one that has not yet found universal acceptance. The other spiritual truths taught by George Fox and his followers, in 1650, are now accepted by all Christian Churches with more or less fulness. The spiritual interpretation of the Bible instead of the literal, the use of the Sabbath for man and not man for the Sabbath, the subordination of the symbol to the spiritual belief symbolized, the comparative unimportance of creeds and dogmas, the abhorrence of slavery, conviction of temperance, recognition of women's responsibility and share in the work of the church, are now taught by all Christians.

This is not, however, equivalent to saying that these changes in the thought and practices of the Christian Church have come about in consequence of Quaker teaching. Quakers in the past have separated themselves too much from other Christians by useless peculiarities of dress and language which ceased to have any real significance over one hundred and fifty years ago; and these superficial and unnecessary differences have made them a peculiar people and isolated them from other Christians.

But whatever mistakes may have been made in the past, the Quaker Church is now ready to stand shoulder to shoulder with the other churches in the support and dissemination of peace. It is almost impossible for any Friend of the older generation to believe in war; his ancestors have suffered too much for their peace principles in the past. But this is not true of the younger generation of Friends; they, and indeed all of the young people of to-day, seem to me warlike in spirit. For the past three years they have listened to and read in the papers stirring military speeches delivered in praise of war by our leading public men. We have a gallant warrior

President in the White House, and we must remember that our late Spanish War has been the first great patriotic emotion of their youth. I am usually able to carry the students of Bryn Mawr College with me when I speak to them on public questions, but I am not able to command their sympathy when I speak in favor of peace. Those of us who believe in peace and arbitration must remember that it is necessary for us to supply the antidote of an uncompromising and insistent expression of contrary opinion, unless we wish the younger generation to grow up far more warlike in spirit than our own.

Peace and temperance are, I believe, the next great moral victories to be won, and they will surely be won in the present century; but it is not enough to recognize this intellectually. The outcome of this Conference should be an aggressive peace propaganda, not carried on separately by the Quaker Church, but in concerted effort with all believers in peace and arbitration. Friends, with their profound belief in peace, bred in their inmost fiber, as it were, by their continuous and consistent church inheritance, stretching back for over two hundred and fifty years, should become the backbone of such a propaganda.

Bacon says somewhere that "men must not turn bees and leave their lives in the wound," and I am confident that the time is close at hand when it will be generally recognized that the nation that goes to war except in the last extremity, and perhaps even then, like a colony of bees, loses in the war, whether it be victorious or not, many things which constitute the true life of its people, and among them sympathy, justice, tenderness for others and righteousness.

THE CHAIRMAN: I will now call on the first speaker on the morning's program, Peter W. Raidabaugh, of Plainfield, Indiana.

THE IMPORTANCE OF TEACHING PEACE PRINCIPLES IN THE BIBLE SCHOOLS.

BY P. W. RAIDABAUGH, PLAINFIELD, INDIANA.

The Bible School could have no more dangerous enemy than one who would separate it from the established work of the Church —the organized body. The Bible School is considered and spoken of as belonging to some particular branch of the Church, just as a boy or girl is thought of as having a father and mother and belonging to some particular family. The Bible School is a child of the Church, and should be considered as the Church assembled for Bible study; its highest usefulness is reached when the youth are taught the principles of the Gospel of Christ in such a way as to lead them to accept Christ as a personal Saviour and to dedicate their lives to his service.

The majority of those enrolled in our Bible Schools have not reached maturity and need the help of mature minds in their study of the Scriptures. They are largely passive beings, mere receivers of influence, and are in the period of preparation for the active responsibilities of life. They are like buds that must be unfolded before the beauty of the flower can be seen, or like gems hidden in a casket which must be uncovered before they can reflect the rays of light. Their pupilage will soon end, and they will enter upon the activities of life, and give to the next generation the influence the Bible School has thrown around them in this period of development. During this time the child must be assisted by wise and pious leadership that a correct foundation for the future building be laid. As you teach a child so you impress him. His mind is a rich garden spot, ready to receive and respond to the seed sown.

The whole creed of a child may be summed up in a single sentence, " I believe in God, my parents and my teacher." He cannot get beyond this and untangle the theories of learned theologians; but he does believe what is taught him by parent or teacher, because he believes in them. The truths taught in the Bible School class are to him the whole of the Gospel. The whole compass of truth is in what his teacher says. A Jesuit priest said, " Give me a child until he is eight years of age, and you may have him after that." By this he meant to say that during the first eight years of the child's life he would so impress upon his mind the tenets of the Roman Catholic Church that he would forever remain true to the teachings of that church. It is a well-known fact that a child seldom wanders from the path in which he starts—in childhood he starts for a goal and usually reaches it.

One who would use an intricate machine needs to understand what it is designed for and how to use it. The mind of the child is such a machine. It cannot be expected to work accurately except for the purpose and in the manner its Maker has designed. The work of the Bible School teacher has so much to do with the child's mind that it is necessary that he should have some understanding of its nature and its modes of operation. He must not only study the Scriptures so as to teach them correctly, but he must study the child so as to impress the truth taught. He should know that the action of all the faculties, except the will, is mechanical and acts on the suggestions of another, and that there can be no choice or freedom only as it exists in the will. The order in which the child-mind operates is, first, to perceive—grasp the truth; second, to judge; third, to feel; and fourth, to choose. The faculties thus brought into exercise are Perception, Judgment, the Sensibilities and the Will.

Success or failure in teaching and impressing truth so as to reach the will depends on whether we do or do not follow this order. All the ideas or truths which are presented to the child-mind are taken up and passed through the process of thinking, and from the thought, or truth, presented it turns out the actions of life, much like a machine taking in the raw material and turning out the finished product. The mind grows only by receiving. Some minds receive slower than others; some think slower than others; some cannot be hurried beyond their own speed without great danger; some minds demand greater care as to statement of truths than others; some demand greater care as to explanation and illustration than others; and some depend more on repetition than others, but all reach the same end.

Some one has said: "Sow a thought and reap an act; sow an act and reap a habit; sow a habit and reap a character; sow character and reap destiny." The child begins the development of a good or bad character in thoughts, and these are followed by acts which develop into habits that become fixed and unchanging. Mohammed says a mountain may change its base, but not a man his disposition. No one can be better than his best thoughts. High ideals are incentives to high living. The most of us can think a great deal higher than we live. Hence the importance of correct teaching on all lines of Gospel truth in our Bible Schools. I have to do with but one truth in this paper—peace principles.

False standards are raised; brute force is often held up as heroic. "The man behind the gun" is lauded, and he who can practice the greatest deceit or slay the most is considered patriotic and worthy of homage from his fellows. The newspapers are full of commendation for acts of heroism on the battlefield. The pulpit joins in the praise of war and calls for a manifestation of patriotism on fields of blood. The air is full of this thought. There is a glamour thrown around the soldier's life. The young man in uniform and brass buttons is the envy of other young men, and admired by the ladies. He walks the street with a sense of superiority. If he is killed in battle, no matter how sinful his life has been, he is looked upon as a crowned hero. This thought has descended to us from barbarous tribes whose greatest warriors gained the highest heaven. The trend of thought is along this false standard of heroism and patriotism. The literature for our children is filled with it. Books in our Bible School libraries have for their heroes a blood-stained villain. The comments in lesson helps associate heroism and patriotism with deeds of warfare. Our children are taught, in the period of early and lasting impressions, that heroism and patriotism are only found in deeds of valor on battlefields, and that it is honorable to slay an enemy of one's country.

The remedy for this evil is to teach the child the true spirit of Christianity as seen in the teachings of Christ and throughout the New Testament. We must teach that impurity of thought is back of impure language, that falsehood in the heart is back of the untrue word, that character is the hidden life known to our conscience and open before God; that reputation is not the real life of the man, that reputation is what men say we are, character what we are; that reputation is in the hands of our fellow men, character in our own hands. Teach the child that a true hero is one not ashamed of honest toil; that labor, whether of hand or brain, is heaven's ordinance for human improvement; that the hand of the son of toil is made hard in a service a thousand times more honorable than war; that heroism is found bending in the fields under heavy burdens; sweating in the workshops of the land; that heroines are found in the factories, clothed in calico, blanching brow and cheek to preserve the whiteness of the soul; that a true heroic character is that which does right.

There can be but one logical course for all writers for the young and all teachers in our Bible Schools to take, and that is to present the true spirit of the Gospel of Christ, and impress on the young mind the brotherhood of man, that right thinking may beget right acts and lead to right habits, working in them a pure character. Impress the sacredness of human life, that murder is murder, whether in times of peace or war. Teach the spirit of the Master in dealing with enemies; that love is to be the controlling spirit of the Christian's life; that the new birth means the implanting of a new force in the life, a power contrary to the flesh. Instead of presenting a picture of Napoleon or Wellington or Grant leading armies on to victory, make Florence Nightingale, Clara Barton, Grace Darling, John Howard or Livingstone the central thought for illustration, or give a picture of that great and godly man as he sailed up the Delaware Bay, and for the first time stepped on the American soil with his heart beating immortal with its pulsations of love for man and God. Tell how he planted the seed of a mighty nation on the shores of the Delaware, and never wronged the Indian. So that to this day the story of William Penn is told in legend to the Indian children of the West, and all who belong to the "Broad Brims" are hailed as friends of the despised children of the plains.

By so doing the army of bright boys and girls in our Bible Schools will have the advantage of a right start in life, and the principle of peace and good will toward men will be so impressed on the coming generation that there will be a great forward movement resulting in all differences between nations, between capital and labor, between man and man, being settled on the broad principle of human brotherhood.

THE CHAIRMAN: The next speaker on the program is President Edmund Stanley, of Friends' University, Kansas, who will speak on "The Principal Influences Making for Peace, and How They May be Strengthened."

PRINCIPAL INFLUENCES MAKING FOR PEACE AND HOW THEY MAY BE STRENGTHENED.

BY PRESIDENT EDMUND STANLEY, WICHITA, KAN.

To study the slow progress of great reforms as interested observers, impressed with the need of radical changes in the affairs of men, conscious of the wrongs endured by society, and convinced that relief can be had simply by the accepting, calls for a degree of patience not easily exercised.

Surprising beyond measure is it that nations and peoples continue to refuse the greatest boon that in the providences of national experience and human life is attainable.

It took the devastation of all the nations of the earth who laid claim to any achievements in skill, learning and literature, to make an Alexander; the sacrifice of two million of the best of Europe's people to make a Cæsar; an upheaval of governments that left all Europe a seething mass of political ruin to make a Napoleon. These wars made heroes, but evolved them through the sacrifice of nations and of national honor.

Yet in the face of history, with all its lurid facts touching the horrors, waste and injustice of war, sane men, men of critical judgment, Christian men, persist in the advocacy of rapine and murder as the only feasible means of settling differences among nations.

The trend of human events—socially, economically, morally, religiously—is in the direction of a purer philosophy, of more intelligent and humane economic laws, of higher and better methods of preserving and cultivating moral precepts, of a Christian civilization world-wide in its scope, embracing all human interests, and imbued with the real, living spirit of the Master.

Apparently the economic phase of this reformation is to-day giving to the world the most conspicuous evidences of real progress. We could not admit, however, that the results coming in this way are the greatest, important as they may seem, since much of the work being done along these lines is based upon an uncertain foundation and has nothing for defence save the advantages that come through business relations and commercial transactions. It is but an armistice for gain.

As the wants of man increase—and they do with every upward step in civilization—a wider and continually growing field of production becomes a necessity. Once, in the home, in the family, nearly the entire supply of materials needful for the comforts of life was produced. A house could be built with less than a half dozen tools, and little variety of materials.

Intellectual growth and refined tastes demand a change in manner of living, and buildings, furniture, provisions, clothing, transportation—in fact, everything with which we have to do—must submit to transformation.

Such have been the changes in the progress of civilization that to-day the commonly accepted necessities of life can scarcely be supplied by a score of peoples under as many different climatic conditions. The production and exchange of that which our higher civilization terms necessities is cultivating and fostering a spirit of dependence, a common commercial interest, a friendly spirit. A touch of material interests as well as a touch of pathos may make the world kin, and unquestionably it is doing so to-day.

The wants of man have been the cause of the development of great commercial interests; and the warp of these stupendous enterprises is interwoven with the woof of the surplus of every people under the sun.

To make the case stronger still in the interest of universal peace, the operation of this intricate machinery is dependent upon a universal system of credit. A structure in which the wealth of nations is involved must be operated upon economic principles; and disturbances that hinder progress, that interfere with exchange, that reverse fortunes, that threaten national existence itself, cannot hope for encouragement from this commercial scheme now being unified and brought to system with astonishing rapidity.

It needs no prophetic vision to reveal the fact that in the near future the financial and commercial interests of the world will be arrayed on the side of universal peace. No one questions the fact that the Turkish Empire has escaped the perils of more than one war because of the financial interests that would have been jeopardized by military conflict. Nations as well as men are debtors and creditors, and as such must operate upon business principles; and the uncertain turns of military campaigns can hardly recommend an appeal to arms as a businesslike method of dealing with controverted questions of national import.

Again, the limitations to conquest now thrown about civilized warfare will tend to discourage war as a means for settlement of differences. In former times the additions of territory, the increase of revenue from subjugated peoples and the spoils of war, including not only stolen treasure and confiscated property, but the lives and services of the subdued people—these made war a profitable employment, a means for the accumulation of wealth.

But economic interests, humane principles, and the higher light that has touched the human conscience have placed a hedge about modern warfare, and the restrictive measures that have been and are being thrown about it have deprived nations of the opportunities once enjoyed of making the vanquished people a prey to the greed of the conqueror.

While much financial gain may still come to a country through conquest, it is a fact that there is much uncertainty connected with an enterprise dependent wholly on military success, and the immediate support of the undertaking must come from the people, the business interests, the resources of the country that chooses to engage in war.

In the face of modern civilization a nation must have some powerful excuse for engaging in war, stronger at least than those which are given by historians for many of the great struggles of the past centuries. True it is that excuses given to-day are of little real force; but, if compared with those of earlier periods, we must admit that there are evidences of real progress.

A war in the interest of humanity is a step in advance. We would condemn it as wrong, unnecessary and unwise; and yet there is back of it evidence of a development of principle that will assert itself against all wars that the masses would call unjust, and against many of the wrongs which accompany military operations.

The world will demand justice and equity in the administration of warfare before it will accept the higher and broader truth, a peaceable adjustment of differences in accord with wisdom and equity. Nations may continue to wage war for just (?) causes; but more and more will they come to see the lack of wisdom in the choice of method for settlement of differences. In fact, I am constrained to say that no nation to-day, that has a *just claim* against another nation, need hesitate a moment to refer that claim to the honored tribunal that the best governments of the world have provided for the adjustment of international questions of dispute; and, further, that when a strong nation makes war on a weaker one, in the face of the opportunities now provided for relief, for obtaining justice, it is an admission of an unjust demand on the part of the stronger. The weaker nations make war upon the stronger only when forced to do so.

Our own nation could have obtained more than justice and equity would have given her in the trouble with Mexico, and she could have had it for the asking. War became necessary because we asked too largely. Our demands were exorbitant. Mexico would have given us more than was ours by right rather than risk her fortunes in war. If England's claim is just and the demands of the Boers unjust, could not England with safety entrust the case with the International Court?

Our own sad experience in the Orient is but another example of a great power making demands of a weaker people and yet failing to submit its policy to a court of arbitration to determine the justice of the demand. There was a question in the minds of the American people, and, no doubt, in the minds of the people of other nations, as to our real status in the matter of the Philippine Archipelago. Had we waited and inquired; had an international tribunal passed upon the question, it is probable that the native tribes would have accepted the consensus of opinion given by disinterested nations, and there would have been little or no war necessary to establish the authority of our government over the islands, if the ruling of the court had been in our favor.

We have a right to hope that there is a growth in national conscience; that our civilization is producing men who are honest not only in individual affairs, but in national affairs as well. In every school, in every home, in every church, the great principles of justice, honesty and truth should be inculcated, and the instruction should be broad enough and comprehensive enough to reach beyond the limits of any country or any government.

The development under such teaching (and we have much of it) is already a powerful barrier in the way of war policies. One will say, if we fight for a just cause, " God is on the side of right, and right will prevail." Right may prevail, but not because of the wrong-doer. Victory does not come as a special favor to those who make war to establish right. I am persuaded that the soldier on the battlefield is the least to be censured for the wrongs of human warfare. It is his " but to do and die "; but the greater wrong lies with those responsible for his deeds, his suffering, his death. He obeys the mandates of government, the law under which he lives, and fills as best he knows, possibly, the place to which his environments have assigned him. Not so with the teacher, the clergyman, the politician, the legislator, the author in the public press. These are moulders of public conscience that is given expression in law and put into action by the representatives of government.

To make these factors in government right in heart, in life, in service, is reaching the root of the evil. If it is true that " The headship of the English-speaking people passed with the opening of the Twentieth Century from England to America," then it behooves us to assume the new responsibility not only with the dignity that becomes a great nation, but thoughtfully and prayerfully; for there comes a charge to our hands that demands consideration and bears large responsibility. The English-speaking people must have a part in the progress of the new century. The questions that are interesting this convention are facing the world, and their solution will determine in a large measure the growth and character of human society. If Epicurean philosophy could work moral ruin in Greek and Roman society, what may we expect from equipage and conflict of arms with the intelligence and inventive genius of this portentous era! May we not reasonably anticipate all the moral degradation of the past with multiplied exhibitions of destruction, devastation and death that follow in the wake of the military campaign?

We are led to believe that the outlook is more hopeful. The signs of the times certainly indicate an awakening of the public conscience, a growth in sentiment against war as a factor in human government.

Again, immediate contact with the realities of military life takes from it many of its attractions and much of its glory. The soldiers of the civil war were not the most active in advising the nation to enter into a military contest with Spain when our diplomatic relations became strained. They had seen and experienced the realities of war. There are multitudes of people who would cease to advocate an appeal to arms if they could but witness the horrors of the battlefield for a day, could understand the depths of its moral degradation. The illustrated story of the battle, the telegraphic report, the daily and almost hourly paper that tells of the suffering, not of the past, but of to-day—these things are bringing the realities of war in touch with the daily life of those at home, in business circles, in legislative halls, and a whole people can feel the real burden as though a part of the actors in the conflict.

Society will not long endure this suffering, this sadness; and men's consciences will cry out against the wholesale slaughter of noble men, and demand that more humane methods be devised for determining and settling national disputes.

Much as we may desire it, we can no longer keep away from the sad view of carnage. Our ears can no longer be closed to the cry of distress, the wail of sorrow. It is at your door and mine. We read to-day the story of suffering in South Africa, and know it is a living picture, the incident of the hour. We are not listening to recitals of incidents and experiences of last week or of last year; but the story, the picture, is a thing of the present.

A people intelligent, cultured, educated, God-fearing, cannot and will not remain long under such pressure and in living touch with such scenes of distress and suffering, such evidence of moral corruption, and not cry out for relief from this universal curse.

The *Christian head* may, it is possible, accept a belief that war is a necessity among nations, and therefore must be defended; but the *Christian heart*, with its love, its sympathy, its compassion, its self-sacrifice and devotion, cannot long stand and face the fortunes of war without experiencing a conviction that it is wholly wrong and its very existence inexcusable. Modern inventions are bringing us face to face with what has hitherto been the far-off side of human warfare. Heretofore we have seen the pageantry of military parade, and thought to applaud. The curtain has lifted, and with the echo of the applause comes the sad sigh of distress, the moan of anguish and of death; and we instinctively shrink from the pageantry so grand, for we know it is but a covering to hide a monster of hideous mien.

These ideas, by some, may be called unpatriotic. Rather, international arbitration, universal peace, the abandonment of war as a policy in government, are in the interest of a higher patriotism. Love of country implies love of its people, its institutions, its laws. It is this love for humanity that prompts the advocacy of measures that promote the general good, that relieve society of its grievous burdens, that lessen suffering and sorrow, that ennoble character.

A government has nothing to fear from a citizenship that would refer all questions of dispute to a court of justice and equity, and that abides by decisions of arbitrators in personal or national questions of controversy.

But what of the Church? Where has she been, and what her position in the great struggle for relief from this greatest curse to mankind through all the records of history? The pulpit has resounded with the eloquence of learned and renowned teachers in spiritual things, who have tried to justify and sanctify human warfare. They have called the thing righteous, when they must know that it has been the means of destroying the fruits of years of missionary labor. It has blocked the way to missionary success, and has caused the uprisings and revolts which have resulted in the massacre of multitudes of faithful missionaries and untold thousands of the people that have accepted the gospel through their teaching and labors.

One could scarcely believe the story of the Church. The picture is too dark to dwell upon, and we stand mute and condemned. There is no excuse to offer. May we not hope that those who profess the name of Christ are learning more and more of the real spirit of the Master, and that the professing Christian world is coming into a better understanding of his precepts and his life.

I am constrained to believe that there is a very marked growth of sentiment in the churches; that the followers of the Christ are learning this lesson as never before; and that we may confidently expect a much more general acceptance of this great gospel precept, as found in the Golden Rule, than has been known in the ages past.

On this, as well as on every other great social and moral question, there must be a side consistent with the Christian profession. Trickery and intrigue, deception and falsehood, secret conniving and open dishonesty, inhuman cruelty and wholesale slaughter—these are acknowledged requisites for successful campaigning. Christ condemns them all; and in place of these he establishes for his followers the precepts embodied in the Golden Rule. The world accepts the one side and conforms to its teachings. There is no place for the Church unless it be on the other side.

The Christian is not different from the world so long as he follows in the footsteps of the world; and the kingdom of our Christ can never grow strong by and through the services of men who profess loyalty to him, but in life continue to conform to the precepts of the world.

From every pulpit should this truth be declared, for truth it is: "There can be no war among the Christian nations of the world to-day if the Church as a united force will stand opposed to it." Many of the wars of history could have been averted if the Church had fully comprehended the teaching of the Master on this important question; and at no time has the Church been more powerful than it is to-day in shaping the course of government and in moulding public opinion.

After all, the Church is, must be, the most effective force in this reformation. And on every hand we see evidences of a change of sentiment, a growth of opinion in favor of humane and reasonable methods of dealing with questions heretofore submitted to the arbitrament of war. The work of various Christian organizations of modern times has tended to unify the Church, and with this unification of interest comes the conviction that only through a deeper spirituality can we hope to enjoy the full benefit of the real power of the Church, as a united body working for the establishment of the kingdom of Christ. It is the spirit of the Christ that the Church must understand, must teach, must exemplify in human life, that her benign influences may be felt, her better precepts understood, and her laws recognized and embodied in the governments devised and operated for the welfare and happiness of humanity.

I am constrained to believe that the advocates of peace are becoming more practical in their views and in their teaching. It is not ours merely to stand steadfast for a principle and to suffer for a testimony. It is ours to meet the great and perplexing questions of government and help to solve them. Convince the nations of the world that there is a more just and more economic way of settling questions of dispute, a way more in harmony with the age, more helpful to society, more humane, more reasonable, and right will prevail, war will be relegated to the past; justice will rule in the affairs of nations, and the social, financial, moral and spiritual progress of mankind that will follow will be without parallel in the history of the world.

THE CHAIRMAN: The last formal paper of this morning will be on "Woman's Responsibility and Opportunities for Promoting Peace Principles," by Mary Jane Weaver, of Batavia, New York.

WOMAN'S RESPONSIBILITY AND OPPORTUNITIES FOR PROMOTING PEACE PRINCIPLES.

BY MARY JANE WEAVER, BATAVIA, N. Y.

In a few days we shall have come up to the first Christmas of this new century, to the day set apart to commemorate the birth of him whose advent was heralded by a multitude of the heavenly host, praising God and saying, " Glory to God in the highest, and on earth peace, goodwill toward men." On that day a multitude of the earthly host of his professed followers will take up this same anthem, proclaiming it far and wide. If only a deeper comprehension of this wonderful proclamation and the responsibility resting upon us for its fulfillment could come to all God's children this Christmastide than they have ever known before, this gospel of peace would have a voice every day in the year, and would soon be published everywhere in all its fulness and blessedness.

Certainly the time has come when there should be concerted, persistent effort on the part of peace-loving Christians to get the ear and reach the heart, particularly of the Church at large. Ministers of the gospel of the Prince of Peace are in the main silent on this subject. With them an arrest of thought on this line is absolutely necessary, and I hope that some means may be devised at this Conference, having this end in view. Somehow this leaven should be worked into the masses also.

Friends from the first have believed that war is entirely contrary to the teachings of Christ and the spirit of the gospel; hence the promulgation of the principles of peace in an earnest, forceful way is entirely consistent with our attitude. This is a message God would have us bear to the world. How can we be true to Him, or consistent with our profession except we are doing all we can to bring this great truth to bear on the minds and consciences of all we can reach? Being right ourselves is not sufficient. We must agitate and educate.

While I rejoice in all peace societies the world over, I believe the Religious Society of Friends ought to be the strongest, the most pronounced and the most aggressive of them all. Our responsibilities are measured by our opportunities, and in our Society women have large opportunities and privileges, such as are not accorded in any other branch of the Church. Within our wide field of service the way is open for them as for men. Some one has said: "When Christian womanhood is aroused she will make war upon war with weapons that are mighty, for the great forge in which her weapons will be cast is the forge of God Almighty himself."

It would seem that women who pay the first cost of human life, who go down into the jaws of death to become the mothers of men, would naturally protest against the destruction, in the awful carnage of war, of a treasure so precious; that mother-love would rebel against a system which takes from her the son in whom she has invested so much from infancy to manhood, and, if occasion requires, places him where he must do his best to destroy the life of others, or give up his own life in the attempt, and this in the face of God's command, "Thou shalt not kill."

Those of us whose eyes are open to the great crime and wrong of war must not fail in our duty to arouse Christian women, particularly, to a consciousness of this, or we shall be answerable for the consequences of our neglect; we shall be brought into account for sins of omission as well as sins of commission. Woman can and consequently ought to engage in this work. In behalf of her own sex she should do this. The degradation and utter ruin of women in connection with army life is appalling, and certainly is a motive sufficient to lead women who love home and purity, and who regard the sanctity of the marriage relation, to a vigorous and persistent protest against the system which makes such crime and shame a possible thing among civilized people.

A recent incident is a case in point. It is related by Corporal

Diffenderfer, of West Chester, Pa., who has recently returned with a company of soldiers from the Philippines. He said: " There was a somewhat remarkable scene when we left for home, on account of the wives which many of the soldiers had taken to themselves while on the island. The women over there are purchased for from five dollars each upward, and nearly every soldier has one. When we came away, of course it was impossible for the men to bring them along. But when we arrived at the port from which we sailed it was found that one of the governors of a province had sent about one hundred of the wives to the port, and every one of them wanted to come with us. There was no end of trouble, until the matter was adjusted by the officers, who persuaded the women to remain at home."

What a spectacle! What a reproach to a Christian nation which has been praying God to bless it in its effort to subjugate the poor, ignorant Filipinos by force of arms, that it might civilize and Christianize them! And then the ruinous effect of such deeds upon the soldiers themselves, and through them upon others, when they come back to their loved ones so demoralized! This ought to stir every woman to valiant deeds in opposition to war. May the Lord waken us up to our responsibility!

Women's opportunities for work along this line are so many and so varied that it would be hard to enumerate them all, but I will mention some that impress me as very important.

First, the mother's duty in regard to teaching her children in moral and spiritual things. Dr. Vincent says: " Home teaching is above every other, and should have first place. It has the first opportunity with the child. Its priority gives it superiority. It has the firm confidence of the child. It has the fervent love of the child. It has unchallenged authority. It has unconscious influence. It has the opportunity to illustrate. It has the opportunity to reiterate." No danger of beginning too early. This should be in the truest sense an infant school. And while we try to bring the great truths of religion within the comprehension of the children, we should also give them reasons why we believe certain things to be right or wrong, which others about us do not see as we do. Particularly in these days of militarism, when the pomp and circumstance of war seem to have such place with the people, should we endeavor to impress the children with the teachings of our Saviour in regard to peace. This is a very important thing, that they may be fortified and prepared to meet the temptations that will beset them as they enter school life, and come in touch with influences outside the home. If children could be taught to settle their difficulties by arbitration, they would be learning a very important lesson, and one that would be a blessing to them all their lives.

The large majority of Bible and secular school teachers are women, and they have much to do with moulding character. If they were only advocates of peace, what an influence for good they would exert in turning the current of the child's thought into the right channel. If our children are to remain in fellowship with us, and be loyal and faithful Friends, and be true to our principles and testimonies, they must have clear, intelligent views of the truth, and be able to give to the world a reason for the faith that is in them.

The hope of the future is in the children of to-day. If mothers and teachers were conscious of their blessed opportunities and great responsibilities, and were doing their best to train up the children in the way they should go, what mighty influence for good would be set in motion through the men and women of the next generation.

Our children should be familiar with all that has been and is being done for international arbitration. They should be impressed with a loftier, nobler idea of heroism than war at its very best has ever been able to inspire. They should be taught concerning the cost of war, the awful destruction of human life,—a thing which God alone can give and which he alone has the right to take,—and how enormously prolific it is of vice and crime, cruelty, drunkenness and licentiousness. Military drill in schools, many of our children's toys and story-books, and pictures in our homes and on the walls of our schoolhouses, engender and foster a military spirit.

Physical culture is important. The body should be trained as well as the intellect. Our children must have playthings and books suited to their capacity. All this could be provided for without objectionable features, if mothers and teachers would bring their influence to bear towards eliminating that which is harmful, and putting into its place that which is harmless and which would tend to educate along right lines.

What a power for good or evil the mother holds within her grasp! "I saw the Holy Spirit shining in my mother's face," said a college professor, " and her piety and faithfulness drew us, a large family, safe into the service of the Master, though our father was not a Christian until we were all grown up." Love is the highest and most potent of human qualities, and the mother has this mighty agent at her service. A habit of referring everything to the arbitration of our Heavenly Father is the very best form of government in a home; and in this way peacemakers are trained.

The mother should claim the same right to life, liberty and the pursuit of happiness for her son that is accorded her daughter. This cannot be while war exists. The peace-loving mother should go with her children into their school life. Our text-books on history, the most of them, glorify war, teaching that in the strength and efficiency of the army and navy of the nations in large measure rest their glory and power. Men of war are set before them as heroes. Until these books can be changed—a thing concerning which something has been already done—this teaching must be counteracted by that of the home. There the mother has her chance.

If women who are teachers would use their influence to secure the writing of essays and papers on peace and arbitration by students in our schools,—the public schools and those of higher grade,—the reading of these and their discussion in lyceums and literary societies particularly would result in the formation of peace sentiment, and lasting impressions would be made on the minds of those who took the time to prepare the papers and those who listened to them.

Our children and youth should know what generals and those regarded as military heroes have said against war. A gathering up and presentation of the utterances of those who know most about it, who speak from actual experience, would be a forceful lesson in education along the path of peace and international arbitration.

Women to-day ought to be in close touch with all reform movements. The way is clear for this. Those of us who are doing what we can ought to be adding to these tides of influence by inducing others to join us in our efforts,—not simply to accept our theories, but to work with us.

This is a day of organizations, particularly among women, for moral, religious, social and literary purposes. The Women's Christian Temperance Union, which is, in my opinion, the most efficient of them all, is the only one with which I am familiar which has a department of Peace and Arbitration. This, under the leadership of our friend, Hannah J. Bailey, in the National and World's W. C. T. U., is a power for righteousness. But I do not know of a literary circle among women where this has a place on the program, except among Friends or where introduced by Friends. I would suggest that in our home neighborhoods we take occasion to get a hearing on this subject, particularly before societies organized for study and investigation.

Then we have our peace literature, which is religious and convincing, and which ought to have a wide circulation. A large class of intelligent, thoughtful readers would be reached through the insertion into the papers and magazines of the day, both secular and religious, of articles on peace and arbitration. The press, particularly the religious press, is a mighty lever, and ought to be used in lifting people up into the clear atmosphere of God's truth, where they can see light in his light concerning this matter. Here is a wide field for the activities of women.

We must work outward along all lines if we would reach the masses with this truth. Above and beyond every other power in the hands of women in our Society should be our work in the ministry of the gospel. We have the privilege of proclaiming to the world, under the baptism of the Spirit, and in the name of him who came from the Father into this world " to guide our feet into the way of peace," that " unto us a child is born, unto us a son is given; and the government shall be upon his shoulder; and his name shall be called Wonderful, Counsellor, the Mighty God, the Everlasting

Father, the Prince of Peace. Of the increase of his government and peace there shall be no end." While this refers, no doubt, to the effect of Christ's work upon the heart of the individual, bringing the will of man into harmony with the will of God, it must refer also to the matter of peace among men and nations.

Therefore, we should not only be loyal subjects of His spiritual kingdom, but as his ambassadors we should bear to the world his message of love and goodwill, and, clad in the armor of God, skilled in the use of the sword of the Spirit, we should ceaselessly wage our peaceful warfare against everything which interferes with the spread of his kingdom and the establishment of righteousness and peace on the earth.

THE CHAIRMAN: We have closed the papers two minutes under schedule time, and so there will be time for the discussion of them; the discussion will be opened by S. Edgar Nicholson, of Baltimore.

S. EDGAR NICHOLSON: It is probable that among the Friends gathered in this Conference there is only one opinion as regards the undesirability, the inexpediency and the wrongfulness of war. Believing as we do, therefore, our obligations are two-fold in character. First, we must of necessity spread the doctrines of peace intelligently and forcefully among the largest possible number of Christian people, till they, with us, are possessed of a conscience that says that war is both wrong and inexpedient. Second, we must put forth constant effort to solve present-day problems in a practical way, that will make the avoidance of war not only possible, but real.

Undoubtedly Friends have been widely and grossly misunderstood on the question, perhaps at times through unwise presentation of our beliefs, and untimely denunciations of existing conditions, and sometimes because of a disinclination of others to recognize the basis of our position. By some we have seemed to be opposed to the government, with no heart of sympathy for national interests or for the national welfare, and yet measured from the standpoint of genuine and intense interest in all that makes for good government, good citizenship and the exemplification of the highest types of Christian manhood, it is to be doubted if a more patriotic people exists in our land.

To my mind, the problem of peace is the problem of co-operation with government in the effort to solve governmental problems. The peace idea projected on any other basis must fail. It is not sufficient to denounce war and say it is wrong. That may satisfy individual conscience, but it affords little consolation to the officials of government, perplexed by grave national or international disturbances, to be simply told that war is wrong in the abstract, with no spirit of co-operation manifested, and only words of censure given. I would not be understood as criticising the advocates of peace, but only am constrained to emphasize that which seems to me of supreme importance—the fact that the problem of peace is the problem of co-operation with government in the solution of its difficult problems.

When the difficulties with Spain were beginning to culminate, and the storm cloud was gathering, and men, moved seemingly by humanitarian love for Cuba, were clamoring for inhumanitarian treatment of Spain, had the advocates of peace been strongly enough allied to have given potent assistance to the President in holding in check the war spirit until peaceable measures could have worked the deliverance of Cuba, as the President evidently believed could be done, that struggle would probably have been avoided.

When Spanish rule had been overthrown in the Philippines, later events that have brought deplorable bloodshed could probably have been avoided, if peace advocates could have led the administration to immediate and friendly treaty with the natives. If it be said that the spirit of greed made that impossible, it is only to say that peace, as opposed to war, has not yet become practical and potent. For, if peace principles cannot be assimilated in our mechanism of government to the subduing of other influences which are selfish and designing, we are hardly in position to complain of the results.

But back of all this is a subject that is more vital yet to the question of the abolition of war. When the advocates of peace can be so thoroughly united and organized that they can take proper hold of governmental problems, when the issues are forming that ordinarily culminate in war, and are able to give such direction that peaceable solutions are assured, then will war be at an end, among civilized peoples at least. Whatever other results may grow out of this Conference, I believe that lasting good would be accomplished by laying the groundwork of a system for the proper study of all questions that may lead to national or international differences. Not only that, but the day of our fondest hopes would be hastened were we able to project the peace movement on such a basis that at all times there would be the closest and most cordial relationship existing between peace advocates and the administration.

I am the more impelled to this belief by the conviction that governments are not likely to abandon war because of the simple declaration that war is wrong. Deplorable as it is, and however it may indicate a condition of moral degeneracy, I doubt if the world reaches a condition of absolute peace without the manifested agencies of causes that are secular, absolutely selfish it may be, and wholly outside of purely religious considerations. The belief that peace is the rule of Christ, established for human conduct, must ever be the incentive for the right initiation of peace movements, and in fact must ever stimulate aggressive efforts in the promotion of peace, but the fact remains that we must be able to touch other forces, that of themselves will greatly aid, and perhaps be the final determining influences, in the solution of our national and international differences.

The pioneers of the agitation on the question of human slavery were impelled by the overwhelming idea that human slavery is wrong, and were possessed of a conscience on the subject that voiced itself in a thousand ways, but it was only when the more secular and selfish ideas of political expediency were injected into the question that the doom of slavery was sealed. True, had the Quaker idea on the subject been early adopted as the rule of practice, and had we been in position to impress the importance of human freedom upon the thought of the nation, the Civil War might have been avoided; but the day of settlement having been postponed, it seemed that other forces inevitably would become even paramount in the final issue.

To-day the advocates of temperance reform denounce the saloon system as being wrong and immoral, and undoubtedly the issue should be determined from that basis, but already economic questions have injected themselves forcibly into the matter, and they, with other similar agencies, will, we believe, hasten the doom of this agency of evil.

Similarly is the promulgation of the peace cause. The tendency of the civilized nations to consider arbitration as the best means of settling international differences, is probably the most hopeful indication we have of the ultimate triumph of this movement. Whatever we may do to bring about the agreement before hand to settle all differences by a court of arbitration, will make us a factor in the ushering in of the era of world-wide peace.

Another influential element working for peace is the widespread recognition of mutual commercial interests by the civilized nations. When this recognition becomes more universal, nations will be less inclined to go to war, and will be more ready to find peaceable means of settlement, and the day will be hastened when some future International Conference will unite in an agreement which, when adopted, will be recognized as binding, and wars will be remembered only in history.

Meanwhile, let this agitation go on. Sentiment created, crystallized and organized is a mighty force in public affairs. Let us be sure of our own ground, be ready to keep in touch with every other legitimate force at work for the establishment of the principles we advocate, seek to co-operate more and more in a systematic way with our government in the consideration of perplexing questions and, better than all, get in position to give direction to great governmental problems, and some glad day there will be the realization of our hopes, the sword will be beaten into plowshares, the reign of the Prince of Peace will become universal, and the prophecy will become a fact that "The knowledge of the glory of the Lord will cover the earth as the waters do the sea."

THE CHAIRMAN: The subject is now open for general discussion in five-minute speeches.

DAVID NEWPORT: At a meeting held in this city just before the Civil War there was a little woman, known to many of us, who was called to speak. Her text was this: " The weapons of our warfare are not carnal, but mighty through God to the pulling down of strongholds." She spoke, I suppose, about fifteen minutes, and when she had concluded she met with a wonderful reception from the audience.

The cause of it was the great superiority of her remarks over those of the speakers who had preceded her. It was the dark period before war. There seemed not a ray of hope. Frederick Douglas was in great agitation. Wendell Phillips thought the chains of the slaves riveted more firmly than ever. She plead that the remedy was to be found in the spiritual, in the power of the Spirit of God, and that with this there could be no failure. She thus kindled great hope in the minds of those present.

Socrates, as reported by Plato, speaking of the causes of war, says that they grow out of the carnal mind, of the animal nature, and that the remedy is to be found in the spiritual. The animal man delights in quarreling and fighting. He delights in hearing of war championship and heroism. The very thought of it pleases him. But with the spiritual man it is otherwise.

The thought I wish to express is that the cure for war is spiritual. It is the Spirit of God that worketh in men to will and to do of His good pleasure, in the home circle, in the circle outside of the home, and in the commerce and business of the world. This is the truth which we must inculcate, that the spiritual weapons are mighty through God to the pulling down of strongholds. I am not discouraged. The paper read by our brother was a very encouraging one.

MARIANA W. CHAPMAN: I find myself at heart in unity with many of the speakers; not only the last one, who declares that spiritual weapons are the best; but also with the friend who opened the discussion, who declares that a little secular work must be done, and that things must become expedient in government before they can be successful. I think you will agree with me that one of the most important things to get behind Congress is a peace constituency, and I do not know a larger constituency of peace-loving people in this country than the womanhood of America. I believe, therefore, that you will have your true peace force behind this government when you admit women to a voice in the government, when their opinions are not only influence, but are counted at the ballot-box as well.

WILLIAM L. PEARSON: George Fox used to have his "openings." You have all read of them. If any Modern got near the heart of the Almighty, it was he. I am reminded this morning that some of those "openings" were toward the house of Cromwell, and that some of his most effective work and personal conferences with men were with Oliver Cromwell.

We have a President of the United States who embodies in his character something of the Cromwellian, modified, of course, by the spirit of our own times. But have we a true insight into the Divine sources of peace, and have we the courage of our convictions, to put our power into use with the administration at the present time? We need our practical side of life. All our theories and brilliant discussions may be of small value unless we do in some way make ourselves felt by approaching those who can turn the affairs of men, politically speaking. I believe that we should make a great mistake in this Conference if we did not in some way recognize the truly benevolent purpose of the present Administration toward the islands of the seas that have come into our possession. But, on the other hand, we must by all means try to realize the leaven of war spirit that is leavening the whole lump of society, permeating it unobserved, perhaps, by the heads of government, and perhaps too little observed by ourselves. Let us beware of what is coming from it, of what is even now being effected by it. Let us do our part, as we are assembled here, and see that the usefulness of this Conference shall be the very greatest in counteracting this growing power of evil.

MARY CHAWNER WOODY: It seems to me that our peace principles have been too much theory; they have not been properly set forth in practical form; we have not had the far-sighted thinking to bring them down to practical application in times of necessity. There is no doubt, as was hinted, that the President, at the time of the Cuban crisis, was waiting and waiting and waiting for some person's "openings" to lead him into some peaceable way. It is in such ways as that that the workers for peace have failed; too much theory, not enough preparation for practical action. Our women have failed to make sentiment and thus to make ready for emergencies. When such papers as were filled with the war spirit came into our homes and the men folk of the family came in with their heads full of the war sensations and excitement, our heads were not cool enough to quiet them down. It does seem to me that, after all, whether women have the ballot or not, there is a powerful force that they may apply in the home. They must be prepared to meet such emergencies. Why cannot the President of Bryn Mawr, as she has told us, carry the girls with her on the subject of peace? We send to that institution the best girls we have. Where does the trouble rest? Was the Jesuit priest right when he said that the first eight years would determine the character of the child? It certainly is, it would seem to me, or the President of Bryn Mawr College could lead the girls on this subject. Women, let us go back to our work, to the mothers' meetings, to the women in the factory towns, to the women all over the country, to teach them to teach the children, that we may thus create the sentiment that will hold the nation steady until the men who formulate great principles shall be able to carry them through in times when great diplomacy is needed.

DAVIS FURNAS: I have been much interested in hearing from the various speakers and the various essays that have been read the idea of the fatherhood of God and the brotherhood of man. I believe in that. The All-Father who created all men and requires of all to give an account of the deeds done in the body is the controlling influence, if they will but receive it, over all mankind. Now, what I want to say is this: We have heard this morning about the proper training of children. We tell our children in the Sabbath Schools that there are people far off who are so low that we must go and teach them, and that we must give money to bring about that object. We ought to be careful not to do this in such a way as to inculcate the idea that they are a different order of beings from ourselves; that they are down almost to the level of the brute creation. We should seek to leave the impression that they are the children of, and under the influence of, the same Eternal Power that we claim as our Father and Guide; and that it is our duty to recognize them as brothers. Otherwise the children may get a very false impression of the brotherhood of man.

DR. MORROW: I have the honor of being the Secretary of the Pennsylvania Bible Society, and I have been very much struck with the use made of Holy Scripture and the spirit of prayer in this Convention. When the Peace Convention was held in Rome, there was no prayer. Nothing, I believe, gives to us such strength as our conscious dependence upon the Spirit of God.

I heard a peculiar story about an African recently of the supposed influence of the Bible upon a dog. He said to a missionary that he was in great distress about this dog. The dog had been a great fighter. "But," said he, "he ate up my New Testament, and all the fight has been taken out of him." There is a moral in this story which we may fairly enough take into our hearts, that the spirit of the Book is the spirit of peace.

When it was said just now that the ladies were to bring up their children in the way they should go, I thought of what was said in a mothers' meeting in Chicago not long ago, that that was excellent advice for the mothers, but perhaps they had better go the same way themselves two or three times. Isn't that what is needed, not merely the telling the children about peace, but doing all that we can to show a determination against the war spirit and the soldier life? There is no man in society to-day more popular than the soldier, and the mothers are not going in the way they ought to go; they are training up their children in the army spirit, or the navy spirit.

It was said not very long ago by a Jewish rabbi in this city, that the Lord Jesus had His limitations, because He used physical force in carrying out His reform; that He made a whip and drove the traders out of the temple. But it is certain that Jesus never struck a man. The translation which we have is bad and misleading. The correct version indicates that the whip was made to drive out the sheep and the oxen. Jesus never struck a man. He comes under none of the limitations of His own time. He is larger, fuller, universal. He has the right of truth to be called the Prince of Peace. I plead that we may enter into the thought of our dependence upon God. He rules. He overrules all conspiracies, all rebellions, revolutions and wars, for the purpose of pushing back the darkness and bringing in the reign of light and peace.

Dr. Morrow then offered a short prayer for the blessing of God to rest upon the deliberations of the Conference.

RUFUS M. JONES: We must never forget that there are two things we are trying to do; in the first place, we are trying to educate society by educating individuals; we are trying to establish new ideals of life, and we are doing it, first, by education. If the time is to come when the woman is to have the ballot, then we want a good woman to vote, who will vote right. Our first effort must be—whether we are thinking of the voting woman or the voting man, the man in society or the woman in society—to get a truly trained and educated man or woman who has the true ideal of life. Part of the purpose of this great Conference here is to push on this work of educating men and women and society.

But there is another end which must not be lost sight of; we have got to do something practical. You cannot get work done in this world, anywhere or at any time, except by resident forces. Two of our speakers have touched on this line; they have been showing that if we are to accomplish very much we have to hitch on somewhere, to bring force to bear. We must accomplish something with those who determine the destiny of nations. That idea has been very well brought out by S. Edgar Nicholson, and by William L. Pearson and others.

Now, would it not be a pretty good way to do that to have ten or fifteen good, strong, true, wise, valiant Quakers in the Congress of the United States? What is the trouble with that idea, and why are we not doing something in that direction?

In England there are about 17,000 Friends. Ten of them are in the House of Commons. Nobody who knows anything about the last hundred years can doubt that the man who has done most to make the principles of peace mean something to the world was John Bright. He was a fighter; he didn't believe in non-resistance, in one sense, though he did in another. He believed in being aggressive, to make his principles understood; he stood for them and lived for them and wrote for them, and he went out of office because he believed in them, and he stayed out until he was called back as a victor.

The other man who has made our great truth most known and best understood and most of a force in American society, was the poet, John Greenleaf Whittier, who was a practical politician, as everybody knows who has read his life. Probably no Friend since the time of William Penn has been more of a practical politician, determining who should be nominated and who should be elected, than Whittier; and probably to no man was the election of Senator Sumner, of Massachusetts, more directly due than to the influence and power and practical work of this Quaker poet. He carried his idea not only into his poetry, in almost every line of which it breathes; but also into the caucus, and into the town house.

I want to say, without taking up further time, that whatever we think about getting women into the right places as a remote possibility, it is a matter of immediate concern that we get the right men into the right places; and there is no reason why, in the next fifteen years, we should not have six Senators and fifteen Representatives at Washington; and I hope we shall go to work, not to wire-pull and to pack conferences, or anything of that sort, but by the proper methods to get the right men where they can work out our great ideals of life, and make the principles of peace and righteousness prevail because they become, so to speak, resident forces.

ELIZABETH LLOYD: The thought that I have is somewhat in line with that dropped by the last speaker. It was suggested in the paper last evening that we, although peace people, believe in force. Now, it seems to me that what we need to do is to substitute, gradually, but as rapidly as possible, moral force for physical force in all human relations. The time has hardly come when any of us, perhaps, would be willing to do without policemen entirely, or without jails; but in our best prisons to-day the purpose is to reform men rather than to punish them.

We all know how great is the moral force of some people. A group of men may be swearing and telling obscene stories, and one pure woman coming into their midst will cause all this to stop, not by any physical power, but by the righteousness that is within her. Now, in home, in school, in the community, everywhere, let our influence go toward the substitution of moral force for physical forces. Leave physical force for the adapting of the material universe to the use of man; use moral force in our relations one with another, and the highest kind of moral force is that which is the result of development. It is true of organisms, as of individuals, " that the first of our duties to God and ourselves is to grow."

CATHERINE M. SHIPLEY: Just one sentiment I have for the Conference:

> " One who never turned his back,
> But marched breast forward;
> Who never dreamt the right
> E'er worsted—wrong would triumph;
> Who held, we fall to rise,
> And sleep to wake."

JOSEPH ELKINTON: I would like to suggest that a message be sent to President Roosevelt, expressive of the interest and sympathy of this Conference with him in his present responsibilities, with encouragement to him to promote as far as may be in his power the attainment of peace through the influence of our national government.

THE CHAIRMAN: In accordance with the rules adopted, that recommendation will be given to the Business Committee for consideration.

EDWIN MCGREW: I came as a learner to this Convention; but I cannot allow this opportunity to pass without expressing my hearty appreciation of the messages of this morning. The questions discussed in the two papers bearing on the subject of education of children become old to us, and thus lose much of their urgency. Someone has said, " Thoughts become deeds, and may become crime " ; and it is such outcomes as these that we are to guard against, as has been suggested in the papers and in the various remarks that have been made.

With reference to the practical application of our peace principles, I feel most deeply in sympathy with the spirit of what has been uttered. Our peace work must be of such aggressive and powerful nature that it will be felt on all possible lines. We must search about to find opportunities for the expression of our sentiment. However impractical the suggestion may seem, I certainly am ready to help as far as possible in the West toward the election of any member to the House of Representatives. I am glad of this suggestion, and hope it may be worked out in the most direct way.

JOHN CHAWNER: A short time ago I remarked to a member of the Society of Friends in high standing in England, that it was my conviction that but for the pressure of public sentiment and the newspapers upon President McKinley, he would have solved the Cuban question without war. I was astonished when he remarked, "I prayed that America might go to war with Spain, and when the report of the destruction of the Maine came I rejoiced." That man is one who is anxious to see the condition of the world improved; who is especially interested in the condition of criminals everywhere. The reason he felt as he did, so he said, was because he believed it was impossible ever to get a better condition of affairs under Spanish rule, and that the Spanish rule could never be broken in Cuba without war. In other words, he was of the opinion that it is necessary to do evil sometimes that good may be accomplished. Certainly I do not agree with the opinion he expressed; but it shows us that there is a necessity still of presenting the sentimental side of this question, to say nothing against what has already been expressed on the practical side.

In conversation with another person, a Non-Conformist minister in England, I was surprised to hear the sentiment expressed in substance that the war with the Boers was a necessity; that they had oppressed the native races around them; that they had been preparing for this contest for years, and that it was unavoidable. I was surprised to find that there are many Friends who lean strongly toward that sentiment and who, if they do not openly express it, apologize for the war. So there is necessity even among the Friends of teaching the principles of peace anew.

In regard to the fact that workingmen will ultimately have great influence in the solution of the peace question, I wish to allude, in a sentence or two, to some observations that I recently heard made by two gentlemen. One of them was sometime ago in the Transvaal as a mining engineer, I think; and the other a miner recently returned from the Transvaal. The war with the Boers, it is claimed, was undertaken for the good of the English inhabitants in their territory. What is their condition now? Before the war miners received $5.00 a day. What do they receive now? A dollar and a half a day. What goes with the balance? It is supposed to go, though the miners have no means of knowing that it does absolutely go, to the government to support it in the war. Now, if the war was undertaken in the interests of the English subjects, they are beginning to feel—at least the English laborers in Africa are beginning to feel—that they have to bear the burden of it; and in the future we may suppose that they will not be anxious to see another war.

JOHN B. GARRETT: Just a few words, to allude to some remarks that have been made during the past hour. In the first place, with regard to the Friend in England who had prayed that America might engage in war with Spain, I thought it might have been a pertinent question whether he had wrestled in prayer to God on behalf of Spain that she might ameliorate her treatment of the inhabitants of Cuba. When people talk of praying that war may be engaged in, they would better, I think, look back at their own hearts and see whether their share in the amelioration of the suffering of mankind by means within their power in their own community has been performed.

I listened with great interest, as evidently the whole company did, to the suggestion of Dr. Rufus M. Jones with regard to the representation of Friends in the legislation of the land. I want the editors of the Society journals to take the matter to heart, for they, above all others, can make the idea go. But there are practical difficulties, as every one of us who is interested in this subject knows, connected with our engaging in the work of the national Congress, or even of our State Legislatures, and I want to call attention to some of these. There are functions of the national Legislature that no one of us could consistently perform. While I agree most heartily that it is desirable that there should be an influence of this sort in the national Congress, I trust that the man who comes forward as a candidate for that office will be very sure of his ground, and be determined in advance that he will refrain from those portions of the duties which attach to that office or those offices which he cannot do conscientiously before his Master.

Attention has been called to the prominence of Friends in Great Britain in political life. We all are aware, no doubt, that the proportion of Friends who have served in the Parliament of Great Britain, as compared with other religious denominations, has been and is very large, and that the proportionate influence of Friends in Great Britain over the national legislation is far greater than is the case in our own. There is one feature of their political system that contributes to it very largely; and that is, that any one who is competent to sit in the British Parliament may represent any constituency in the whole kingdom. He does not necessarily reside in the district which he represents; a considerable proportion of the members of Parliament do not reside in the districts which they represent. Moreover, the constituencies in Great Britain vary a great deal; some of them are very small, some of them practically within the giving of a single individual. There are men who wish to be represented in the Parliament by their own personal friends; and it is thus comparatively easy for one who represents a great moral idea to find that he has a constituency somewhere in the country. He can find a constituency which is ready to send him to Parliament that that very idea may find its fullest expression before the British people. No such thing is possible in the United States. In the State of Pennsylvania, with its thirty Representatives, if a man moves from one side of the street to the other, out of the district which he has represented into another, he can no longer represent what he had represented before. The absurdity of it is apparent to us all. But let us go on and work as we may, and let us take to heart the example of the poet Whittier, who did work with a clean hand and heart, and contributed marvelously to the creation of public sentiment, not only immediately around him, but throughout the country at large.

I am glad that what was said by the president of Bryn Mawr College drew from our friend Mary Woody a reference to the teaching of our educational institutions generally on the subject of peace. There is one thought I want to present to us for our comfort and hope; and that is, that the heads of the educational institutions of Friends in America, from Maine to California, are in sympathy with this Conference and its work; and we need no better assurance than we have had in this very session to-day, and in the other exercises from first to last, that the leading educational men and women of the Society of Friends in America are, as has been recognized by the Committee on Program, of all others those who have made this subject a study and are fitted and ready to educate our young people aright in regard to it. Let us be assured by reason of this fact, that there is hope of the right education in peace principles not only of our own young people, but also of the large percentage of the students of Bryn Mawr College and of our other institutions who have not had the advantage of a Quaker training in their youth.

THE CHAIRMAN: I want to say that if the students of Bryn Mawr College are somewhat warlike, I think they are the least warlike of any body of 417 young women that can be found. I only meant to bring out that the young people of the country are not rightly and thoroughly educated as they should be on the peace question.

After announcements, the Chairman declared the Conference adjourned till 3.30 p.m.

Fifth Session.

Sixth-day Afternoon, Twelfth Month 13th.

The Conference re-assembled at 3.30 p.m. The session was presided over by William W. Birdsall, president of Swarthmore College.

After a few moments of silent waiting upon God, the Chairman said:

The Chairman: I find upon the program an item, " Remarks by the Chairman." My loyalty to the Committee on Program will not permit me to pass by that item unnoticed. And yet my loyalty to those who have presented and who will present definitely-prepared discourses will not allow me to forget that the ground of any remarks I may make is likely to have been more forcibly covered in some paper which has been read, or which will be read. My consolation is that if these be vital truths, as we believe them to be, they cannot be too often rehearsed in our ears.

The progress of peace, like that of every other great movement in the world, partakes of the nature of evolution. Its real advance is to be measured not by comparing to-day with yesterday, but by comparing century with century, and age with age. When we make such comparison, it is impossible for us not to be joyful, not to be hopeful and courageous for the future.

In the present, it seems to me that there are three great causes making for a hopeful forward look. It may be that many of you will disagree with me as to one of these causes. However that may be, I firmly believe that the nature of modern warfare and the preparations for it constitute one of the causes which make it practically impossible for great nations to go to war one with another hereafter. Other lessons have doubtless been taught by the war in South Africa; but certainly this lesson has also been taught, that the company of men which goes up against a city to take it, if that city be fortified and defended upon modern lines, has an almost impossible task. The expenditure of men and of means in the undertaking of war now by any one of the great nations of the world against any other one of them will be such as to appall any ministry and necessarily give pause to any government. War, therefore, between the leading nations of the world, I confidently expect, is now a thing really of the past.

The second of the three great causes which I have in mind has already been presented to you; it is the present unity of the world, which has come about through other forces than those of the spirit, forces which are largely material, or economic, but which are vital and of the greatest possible potency in moulding the character of the time and the trend of men's minds. We depend for the furnishing of our breakfast tables and of our clothing upon the producers and the merchants of every corner of the world; we are connected in thought and in feeling, as no generation of men ever has been before, with all the peoples of the world. The people with whom we talk in the morning through the medium of the telegraph and the newspaper; the people with whom we make friends in the short weeks of a summer holiday; the people with whose institutions and whose persons we have become familiar through their writings, or through their travelings, or through ours, are not the people with whom we shall wish readily to go to war. The present and the growing unity of the world is a great force in the promotion of the world's peace.

I have put last that which is truly first, namely, the progress, the spread, of the kingdom of Christ in the world and in the hearts of men; for surely the spread of charitable thought, the growth of sympathy of man with man, and of people with people, is of his kingdom; and surely men now do love peace to a degree and in a manner which has never before been true.

And here I come to what seems to me the vital consideration of a real peace conference, namely, the growth, the spread, of the peaceable spirit. I attended not so long since a conference on arbitration, and a prominent feature of the proceedings was a discussion of the number of arbitrations that had occurred between the nations of the world in the decades of the past century. It seemed that those present regarded with disfavor some decades in which the number of arbitrations had been less than in the previous decades. They seemed to think that the progress of peace in the world was to be measured by the number of quarrels which men had had to settle by "leaving them out" to other people, and not by the absence of quarrels themselves. The growth of peace, my friends, is to come about not so much by amicably settling our quarrels as by not quarrelling. We ought to be called, as George Fox called the Protector, as I stated last evening, to that voice of God in the heart which will take us away not only from wars and from fightings, but from the occasions of wars and of fightings.

Before calling for the first paper of the afternoon, I am pleased to be able to announce a more complete carrying out of the idea of this Conference than was at first thought practicable. It gives me pleasure, as I have no doubt it will give you pleasure, to know that, at the request of the committee, Ida Whipple Benham, of the Rogerine Friends, Mystic, Conn., whose poetic work is well and favorably know through some of our leading journals, has prepared a poem, which will be read to us by Rufus M. Jones.

GENTLE AND MIGHTY.

BY IDA WHIPPLE BENHAM.

The Child that in the manger lay,
    A babe, a lamb, yet strong to bless,
Dwells in the contrite heart alway,
    And proves the power of gentleness.

"Joy to the world, the Lord has come!"
    "Glory to God, to men goodwill!"
Now hush the bugle and the drum,
    And bid the haughty strife be still.

What lips were loudest in the fray
    Of wrathful words, what hands would smite
With fist or sword, be still to-day,
    And learn the law of peace and right.

Such wisdom as from self proceeds,
    The sapient lore of worldly lust,
Forget, with all those ruthless deeds
    That, from the dust, return to dust.

Oh, not with boastful threat and blow
    Doth man achieve his true estate,
But loving, trusting, toiling, so
    God's gentleness doth make him great.

Ye leaders of the multitude,
    With their up-reaching hands in yours,
Lead to the one eternal Good,
    The Love that ransomed, heals, endures.

Yea, all ye stewards of the Lord,
    Make haste to do His perfect will;
Obey the voice: "Put up the sword!"
Obey the voice: "Thou shalt not kill!"

And ye who stretch your limbs at ease,
    Forgetful of a brother's claim,—
Down, from your couches to your knees!
    Thence rise to work in Jesus' name.

White is the harvest, large the yield;
    Lift up your eyes and see the glow
Of fair wheat shining in God's field.
    The call is sounding, rise and go.

THE CHAIRMAN: We shall now have the pleasure of listening to a paper on the "Present Encouragements for the Friends of Peace," by Professor Ellen C. Wright, of Wilmington College, Ohio.

PRESENT ENCOURAGEMENTS FOR THE FRIENDS OF PEACE.

BY PROFESSOR ELLEN C. WRIGHT, WILMINGTON, OHIO.

Edward Everett has left us a most eloquent description of the natural dawn, as witnessed by himself in an early morning trip from Providence to Boston. With the pencil of an artist he paints for us the darkness and silence of the midsummer's night, the spectral lustre of the stars, the position and appearance of the planets and constellations as the journey begins. Presently there is a timid approaching of twilight, a softening of the intense blue of the sky, a departing of the smaller stars, and a shifting of heavenly scenery by unseen hands of angels. Then follow, in order, a kindling of the east, a purple streaking of the sky, an inflowing tide of morning light, till at last, " the everlasting gates of the morning are thrown wide open, and the lord of day begins his state."

The figure is well worn, but it remains so striking a type of the beginning, growth, and glorious ending of all great reforms, and especially of that which has come and is coming to encourage the friends of universal peace, that one may be pardoned, if it is impossible to contemplate one without a reminder of the other.

The darkness and horror of past ages in their setting of blood, the advent of the Prince of Peace, the gradual and, for a time, slow spread of his teachings, the speedy growth of the same, in the past half century of rapid transit, and the surprising and almost overwhelming evidences that all nations are now yielding to the incoming light of truth, and are soon to accept the better way, form a panorama as much more glorious than the advent of day as the substance is greater than the shadow.

It is the business of this paper to bring together into one view some of the signs that make for encouragement. It is but a pleasant task to turn our thoughts to the hopeful outlook; for from every side loom up evidences that we are in the dawn of the day that is to usher in the reign of universal and perpetual peace.

To encourage is to put heart into the weary toiler and arm him with new strength for continued struggle. Nothing puts heart into the worker for any cause as does evidence of growth toward final success. But the signs of encouragement in the present can be understood and appreciated only by at least an occasional glance at the past for purposes of contrast.

In the infancy of the world men were like children, who intuitively strike at whatever injures them; who " use the fist until they are of age to use the brain." The fighting instinct, like that of hunting and fishing was developed, too, in a crude condition of mankind, by the struggle to preserve life. But these elements are now eliminated. The world has reached its majority, and its experience has changed and improved its attitude. The cruelty once condoned by a state of semi-development is no longer in keeping with the humane and fraternal feeling of an advanced civilization.

The very absurdity produced by attempting to fit old military customs of a decayed period upon the new order of things in this young, new century, constitutes, in itself, a source of encouragement; for nations, like individuals, can tolerate anything better than ridicule. How incongruous it appears for a people whose compassion has been cultivated till it builds hospitals for dumb brutes, and puts its greatest offenders to death by as painless a method as possible, to be asked to listen with pleasure to a paragraph like this from a citizen of a Christian nation:

"A few thousand massacred last Good Friday filled Englishmen with joy during the Holy Easter season, and whetted our appetite for what has followed on a larger scale at Khartoum. The reports indicate that our perfected machinery of slaughter have been effective in mowing down some 10,000 or 12,000 men who were fighting for their country, and in wounding a still larger number, who, at this very moment, are lingering out their last moments in indescribable agony in holes and hiding places into which they have crept to die. Such, sir, are the glorious doings for which bishops are thanking God, poets are writing impassioned sonnets, and over which almost all our able leader writers in the press are waxing hysterical with delight."

Can anything be more certainly working out its own overthrow than the attempt of a system to reconcile for a moment this mingling of the spirit of thanksgiving and rejoicing with the contemplation of deeds that shock and torture every nerve and fiber of modern humanity?

The system, then, in the light of the twentieth century, is self-destructive. How pitiful is the attempt to humanize anything so brual as war? But nations have a code of honor, and that code says you must no longer use bullets that flatten easily in the human body. How long will it be till the honor of nations will demand that no bullets at all shall be used?

Nations are coming to wince under charges in which once they gloried. They fear to be called brutal; none are willing to acknowledge the citizenship of Czolgosz. America knows he is none of hers. Jews are indignant, Russians offended and Poles put on the defensive whenever the question is sprung. Any ambitious motives for modern war are veiled under cover of protection for the natives of South Africa or the West Indies, or pity for the victims of Spanish cruelty.

For the first two or three centuries of the Chrisian era the followers of Christ, when asked to take up carnal weapons, said, "We are Christians and cannot fight"; but from the time when Constantine, seeing that Christianity was becoming popular and would strengthen his empire, drove his soldiers into the river and had them baptized by battalions, the idea of necessity prevailed that such nominal Christians might fight, and there grew up the notion of holy wars; and we have the anomaly of the Crusades and other wars professedly for holy purposes, until the idea became almost universal that the Christian's duty was scarcely done till he had lifted up the sword in defense of something or other.

But the advent of that gentle-spirited Swarthmore preacher who said, " I am in love with all men and cannot fight against any," began to call the followers of Christ back to the purity of their first principles, and to George Fox and his followers has been entrusted for two hundred and fifty years the sacred mission of interpreting correctly to a fighting world the real teachings of the Prince of Peace.

How well this has been done only he who gave them the mission may know; but in these later years have come an array of events that fill them with renewed hope and encouragement.

The trend of human thought in the past has been so in harmony with the idea that war is essential, that it is amazing so much has been accomplished in a little more than half a century. Instead of a few feeble folk standing for a principle under fire of ridicule and persecution, now every nation has its advocates of peace. Men and women in all ranks of life have espoused the cause.

The Polish publicist who has written so learnedly as to influence so powerful a patron as Nicholas II. has for one of his strongest arguments against war that it is now out of date. He shows that it is the absence of militarism as known in the old world that gives the United States her commercial supremacy. This is turning the eyes of other nations to our better system. The statesmen of the day are busy with the problem of devising methods that shall supersede those of war.

This change in men's minds and feelings on the subject of peace and war is a permanent one; for it is founded upon right and justice, and is the outgrowth of circumstances attendant upon advancing Christian civilization. Peace is becoming the demand of the age, and when popular opinion protests against war, its doom is sealed.

Once even the clergy exalted war as a great agent of progress. Davies, " a devout divine," urged his hearers " to cherish a war spirit as derived from God, as a sacred heaven-born fire." Others have declared that war is essential to the life of a nation; that it strengthens it morally, mentally and physically.

But David Starr Jordan shows that such utterances can proceed only from the grossly ignorant. He points out what, in the light of the age, needs no demonstration, that the warring nation is the decaying nation; because she reverses the natural law of development through heredity. She sacrifices her able-bodied to the dragon of war. She exterminates instead of conserves her best. So the warlike nation of to-day must be the decadent nation of to-morrow.

Such teaching as this from educated and intelligent men forms one of the strongest sources of encouragement.

Educators are teaching the young, not only in the schools, but from the platform and the press, that there is a grander conception of patrotism than has prevailed in the past; that it is better to live for one's country than to die for it; that it is nobler to set the example of good citizenship in time of peace than to win laurels on the field of blood.

The histories prepared for school schildren, and even for their elders, are improvements over the old, for they do not dwell so much upon revolting, detailed descriptions of battles. The model history of the future will not only exalt the peaceful exploits of industry which promote true wealth and human happiness, but will teach that arbitration is able to settle all difficulties between nations as well as between communities and individuals.

As the consequence of this modern teaching, a new generation is coming up, who advocate peace. The young men of Europe are weary of militarism and long to throw off the yoke it imposes upon them.

That world-wide movement among the young which is international, interdenominational and interracial, the United Society of Christian Endeavor, is laboring to popularize the cause of international arbitration. It presented to Congress a peace memorial signed by thousands of names, in which are such sentiments as these: "We wish to express our abhorrence of war, and our solemn conviction that it is the duty of every civilized nation to do all in its power toward making war impossible. We wish to record our desire for a speedy establishment of an international tribunal of arbitration."

Woman has learned that she has an important part in the extermination of war. When the western woman goes for the first time to the continent of Europe, she is shocked at sight of multitudes of women toiling at the manual labor of husbands, brothers, and sons who are giving to their country a grudging service demanded by an enslaving military system, and henceforth she feels that all this must be changed. Women everywhere are coming to see that war is one of their greatest enemies, robbing them by wholesale of the dearest treasures of life. So we come to have such great organizations as the "Woman's Universal Peace Alliance." and a department of Peace in both the National and the World's Woman's Christian Temperance Union, that powerful organization which penetrates the remotest corners of the earth. The International Council of Women, which includes all women's clubs of America, signed a petition asking for a permanent court. What has woman ever undertaken in united body that she has not in time accomplished?

The press, through the agency of peace advocates, is flooding the world with innumerable pages of literature. The few, feeble tracts and pamphlets of earlier days have been succeeded by addresses, sermons, prize essays, magazine articles, peace periodicals and books in abundance. Prose, poetry, satire, debate and the powerful cartoon have all been summoned to contribute to the teaching that all war is brutal, and may be done away with by the peaceable method of arbitration. If you fear that all this is but dry reading and neglected by the multitude, here is the modern method of making any subject acceptable to them.

Fiction, that form of literature which the masses read, is promising to become a mighty ally in reform work. Harriet Beecher Stowe is credited with a gigantic blow in the destruction of the institution of slavery, and modern novelists are undertaking to show the hideousness of war, and to put into attractive form sentiments averse to the common theory that war is ever to be encouraged or even tolerated.

Commerce in these later times has so bound the different nations together that the mere rumor of war in one is able to disturb the markets of the others. Shuttling trains, electric wires, steamships and ocean cables combine to make the whole world next-door neighbors. Men who deal with one another in honorable commercial relations develop friendships and fellow-feeling that shut out all desire to employ against each other rapid-fire guns or maximite. It is maintained by some who have given the subject deep thought that the ethical principle underlying commerce will of itself finally suppress war.

It is a most hopeful sign that the laboring classes, upon whom the heavy burden of war falls, are becoming more and more opposed to it. Workingmen everywhere are developing among themselves a sentiment favoring peace and universal alliance.

The study of social and political economy, which has become a part of the curriculum of almost all schools, is impressing upon all thoughtful persons how enormously costly in men and means is any system of war. France is bewailing her numerical condition as indicated by the proportionate rate of increase and decrease of her population. All nations point with pride to a fat census roll, but they are learning that war is the greatest depopulator. The financial cost of war has long been held up as a motive of prevention, but the cost of building, arming and maintaining modern ships of war, of manipulating modern equipments, and firing and exploding modern murder machines, is so enormous that it makes the past seem like child's play. And all this does not take into account that other awful drain upon the moral and spiritual forces of the world.

The past few decades have witnessed a series of peace conferences and congresses increasing in frequency and prestige, as public interest has arisen. At first these assemblies received little attention, even in the cities where they were held. Now magistrates and city officials, in robes of office, come out to meet and welcome and honor the lovers and advocates of peace. A president holds a reception for assembling delegates and invites them to his palace.

The advance steps taken by the nations for the establishment of a permanent tribunal, though depreciated in some quarters, are a source of the strongest encouragement. Never was a birthday more gloriously celebrated than that of Nicholas II., on the 18th of May, in 1899, which saw the opening of what General Harrison was pleased to call " one of the greatest assemblies of nations which the world has yet seen." The Hague Conference is said to have done more for the world than a multitude of battles. Its treaty has been called the Magna Charta of international law; The Hague the capital of the world.

This "High Court of Nations" and of Christendom will find something to do. The greater nations have called it into being, and when they have learned to use, by using, its beneficent aid, the smaller ones will be compelled to submit their differences to the same tribunal.

Encouragement grows out of the very evils that are afflicting our country. The frequent strikes resulting from the different standpoints of capital and labor, of employer and employee, are training bodies of men far and wide in the use of peaceful arbitration, which means to stop and think about it; and thus transfers disputes from brute force to the realm of thought and reason. How easy and natural will be the passing to questions of larger content, and engaging a greater number of men.

The South African War is a terrible blot on the fair name of Great Britain, but it is teaching her best citizens a lesson that will long be remembered. Sir Joseph Pease, member of the British Parliament, has recently said that in the more than thirty years of his parliamentary life he has never known, in the House of Commons, so much opposition to war as now.

Our own nation has learned many lessons from the mistakes of her policy in recent wars. Those mistakes have challenged the study and thought of the best and wisest citizens, and summoned the aid of the ablest statesmen in their discussion.

A great and sudden test of character has recently come to our nation in the manner of its chief magistrate's death, and the rank and file of citizens have borne it with a spirit that shows we are growing more Christlike, and consequently more unwarlike.

The discouraged worker will tell us that our hopes are Utopian; that storm clouds are gathering everywhere; that all nations are in an inflammable state and need but the igniting match to flash them into universal war. But the wars and rumors of wars that are left are only the shrieks of the spirits as they take their departure from the body politic of nations. All difficulties and seemingly backward movements are only evidences that our reform is following the natural trend of all reforms. The apparent retrograde movements are but surface currents; the great majestic tide is toward the desired end. These are but a few of the manifold signs of encouragement.

The Temple of Janus is soon to be closed forever. The world cannot creep back into the narrow shell whence it came. When once a reform so gigantic gets a start, its very momentum carries it onward. The mightiest contribution that has ever been made to civilization is the idea of universal peace.

Is this a namby-pamby optimism that believes all things are going to come out right whether we work or not? No; our mission is inherited from our forefathers. Their spirit cries out to us, " Go on! go on! You have a thousand things to encourage you where we had one. Let not our toil have been in vain. Make use of every strategic point; guard every avenue of defeat; keep the flag of peace floating."

Eternal vigilance is still the price of success, and a meeting like this is but to arm ourselves anew with weapons for our peaceful warfare for peace.

We dare not stop. We are like builders with a heavy beam poised above our heads, ready to be placed, with steady, united hands, into its sockets.

The greatest of all sources of encouragement is that the silent and invisible forces are for us. The stars in their courses are fighting against our enemy as they did against Sisera. The Lord God Omnipotent reigneth.

THE CHAIRMAN: The next paper will be upon the subject of " Internationalism," by Hannah J. Bailey, Superintendent of the Peace Department of the World's and National Woman's Christian Temperance Union.

INTERNATIONALISM.

BY HANNAH J. BAILEY, SUPERINTENDENT OF THE PEACE DEPARTMENT OF THE WORLD'S AND NATIONAL W. C. T. U.

The world is gradually moving towards internationalism. Business naturally takes a leading place in the movement. One part of the world does not produce what another part does, consequently trade must be established between the different sections, and thus indirectly are they brought into harmony, for it is to the advantage of all to be at peace. There are thousands of business men who are selfishly opposed to warfare, inasmuch as it greatly interferes with their foreign trade. Some think that for the sake of self-protection duties should be charged upon all imports; others believe in free trade, and still others in reciprocity. The question arises: Which of these methods is best adapted to the interests of internationalism? And this question is answered according to one's own preference and advantage financially.

Because of business requirements, an International Postal Union has been established, all nations which have joined it agreeing to send their first-class mail to all others in the union for five cents per half ounce. A universal postage stamp is now needed. It is embarrassing for those who wish to have postal communications with people in foreign lands to have no practical means of enclosing return postage. This is especially so in the case of authors who want to submit manuscript to the inspection of editors of foreign publications. When we realize that the postage stamp itself is a thing comparatively recent, we can hope that one that is international may materialize in the near future.

This suggests the thought that there may be also an international system of money, and no doubt it will be the decimal system which originated among the savages, who did their counting upon their fingers. This is the system now in use, as we all know, in the United States and Canada.

This brings us to the thought of finances considered internationally, and what a great factor is this. The Rothschilds and the house of the Barings have long been known, and exerted a financial influence in all the civilized world. When, a few years ago, the balance hung between a gold and a silver standard in the United States, trade was not only much paralyzed in this country, but the whole world waited breathlessly for the result, knowing how much was at stake; and none but those who understand the financial market can comprehend the terrible stagnation that is brought about by warfare. The very rumor of a war in this country will cause no small stir in Wall Street, New York, and in all the great money centers of the world.

Modern inventions have done much towards making the world one family. The steamships and the locomotives have gone to the uttermost parts of the earth. The steam cars not only traverse the desert, but have invaded the sacred soil of Palestine and have made their way across Siberia; and now great international railroad systems are being talked of. The telephone, the telegraph and the electric light are now found not only on all of the continents, but likewise in the islands of the sea.

Dress has become largely international, as a glance at the pictures of the lady members of the homes of royalty of the world will show. At a world's fair the different nationalities of the most notable visitors can hardly be distinguished by their dress alone. France sets the fashion and the world follows. Such a state of affairs has advantage from an economic standpoint, but it is destroying, in a measure, race individuality. The missionaries of Japan tried to induce the native women to keep to the native dress because it was so much more artistic in style than that which was being donned by them as obtained from the French fashions.

We often wish that internationalism would bring into use one language. There never has been a universal language since Tower of Babel times. Latin was for years the language of the courts. The English language is fast spreading over the world. The simplicity of its structure makes it well adapted to any people. But will the Anglo-Saxon race be the one great final race upon the earth? Some do not believe this, and they declare that England will have to fall as have other nations, for God has not forgotten the terrible opium trade she has imposed upon China, and the more terrible wars for which she is responsible. We deplore that, though the United States has been guilty of less, yet, as a nation, her hands have not been free from the blood of others. The American band was playing " There'll be a hot time in the old town to-night " while hundreds of human beings were sinking to their eternal destiny, and the cause of their death was the fact that they belonged to Cervera's fleet. There would be nothing but the bitterest disdain for a man who would, while singing a street song, deliberately push a man into the sea; but what is the difference? Ah, friends, is such a system of settling international difficulties civilization? Is it Christian?

International fairs—the Columbian Exposition, for example—do and have done much towards bringing the nations into closer harmony.

But most of all can this desirable result be brought about by utilizing the International Court of Arbitration. The Peace Congress at The Hague has been one of the great blessings that have come to the world. The international peace conferences that have been held annually by peace workers for years have, doubtless, exerted a great influence in bringing this about.

It is an encouraging sign of the time that some of the colleges have professorships of international law, and one can advance the cause of civilization by furnishing funds to institute such a chair where there is none. Law is the opposite of war, as order is of chaos. Some seem to have the idea that those who would dispel militarism from the earth would allow wrongs to go unrighted. Nothing could be farther from the truth. All wrongs should be righted as far as humanity can right them, but the advocates of peace teach that they should be adjusted in a sensible manner—by arbitration, and not in the haphazard manner of warfare, where chance plays so important a part and the suffering and sin are simply indescribable.

We get some idea of the darkness of present internationalism from the late Chinese trouble, where the powers of good and evil were contending for the mastery. From a human standpoint, China was opposed to the entire civilized world, and she then learned the meaning of internationalism. The Chinese Minister at Washington explained it well. He said that if obliged to leave the United States, he did not know where to go. He did not care to return to China, and there was no foreign country open to him, for China was at war with all the world. How happy, indeed, is "that nation whose God is the Lord," the Prince of Peace.

Hegel, the great philosopher, has shown very plainly that no man lives for himself alone; that there is an artificial life, as it were, for which the child must be disciplined; hence arises the need of culture and education, these to adapt the child to the institutions which await it—the home, the church and the state. We might go further and say that no nation exists for itself alone, but each exists for all others, and the sooner the world learns that the highest good of each nation is the highest good of all nations, the better it will be for all. When one nation suffers because of warfare, all nations suffer indirectly. The trail of the serpent is upon all; hence, from the standpoint of political economy, if for no other reason, militarism should be universally denounced.

It would greatly promote a true internationalism if all the influence for militarism and the so-called glory of war should be obliterated from the school books of the nations. If school histories should give accounts of the achievements of governments, nations and of prominent individuals, of scientists, politicians, educators and philanthropists in times of peace, or independent of warfare, omitting the mention of war, except as an event, the cruel practice of settling international difficulties by force of arms would soon be relegated to the past and men would "learn war no more." If the honor and glory now bestowed upon warriors who have done the most harm to the losing side were given to worthy poets and other authors, to inventors, discoverers, leaders in righteous causes, in moral reforms and in genuine religious teaching and the promulgation of the gospel of the Prince of Peace, there soon would be "no need of arsenals and forts." The song of the angels on the first Christmas morning would be the victory song of the world, and all nations would join in the march of Peace.

Christ prayed that his disciples might all be one. Some believe that this means there must be but one denomination, and that the entire Christian world will come to be one religious organization. It is probably immaterial what our individual opinions may be upon non-essential points, but it is quite important that we be agreed upon the great underlying facts and elements of Christianity.

We hear a great deal in these days about universal brotherhood. It is true that God is creator of us all and that "one touch of nature makes the whole world kin," yet does not the Bible everywhere distinguish between the children of God and the children of the evil one, between the children of light and the children of darkness? Not until the heathen and the unregenerate in Christian lands are brought to Christ will the world be one in Christ Jesus. Let us pray earnestly for that time.

The kingdom of peace will surely some time be established on earth. What the prophet has foretold must surely come to pass:

"And he shall judge among the nations and shall rebuke many people; and they shall beat their swords into plowshares and their spears into pruning hooks; nation shall not lift up sword against nation, neither shall they learn war any more."

When the World's Fair was being held in Chicago there was one tent occupied by South Sea Islanders exhibiting their native wares. A large placard was posted near the entrance of the tent upon which were printed words reading like this: " Visitors are requested not to ask these people about the now-abandoned practice of cannibalism among their ancestors, as they do not like to hear it spoken of." There will be a time in the future when the Anglo-Saxon race will be ashamed to have the present practice of warfare alluded to. It is humiliating now, that the twentieth century opens with "wars and rumors of war." May God grant that when another century dawns upon the world its inhabitants will have forgotten the barbarism of warfare and will only know it as a matter of history that had to be recorded to be complete, although it must be so to the shame of our children's grandchildren.

An important factor in promoting true internationalism is the recent practice of holding international conventions in the interests of religion and of philanthropy in different parts of the world. The Christian Endeavorers, the Young Men's Christian Association, the Woman's Christian Temperance Union, the Peace Societies of the world and the women's international organizations are on the list of those who have thus promoted international co-operation and the cause of peace.

The president of "The Women's Universal Alliance for Peace," the Princess Wiszniewska, said at a banquet of peace in Paris, that more than two millions of women had joined the movement of "war against war." The president of the International Council of Women, May Wright Sewall, of Indiana, is an earnest advocate of peace, and the topic is always given a very prominent place on the program for all public meetings of this organization of organizations of both a national and international character.

The World's Woman's Christian Temperance Union, with a membership of more than three hundred thousand, has a Department of Peace and Arbitration, which has been organized in eleven different countries and in twenty-nine States in our nation. Its literature and influence have been extended into every civilized nation in the world. It has found many warm advocates of this beautiful cause among missionaries, and it has been chiefly through their helpful efforts that the initial steps have been taken in introducing and organizing this department work. The work has been done chiefly by the methods of lectures, sermons, Bible readings, utilizing the public press, organizing peace bands and introducing peace teaching in Loyal Temperance Legions and Bible Schools. Also peace principles have been promulgated by much personal work done by national, State, county and local superintendents and their helpers. Telling resolutions have been introduced by them into many conferences and conventions of various religious and philanthropic organizations. Petitions, memorials and protests in the interests of peace have been circulated, and letters bearing requests have been sent to public officials. Influence has been exerted against military teaching in public schools and Bible schools; also against prize-fighting, lynching, capital punishment and every other phase of man's cruelty to man. So much of the work done under the auspices of the W. C. T. U. is educational that the results of its best efforts on the line of peace as well as some others cannot be known until some years have passed, and perhaps not until many of the workers have gone into the life beyond.

There are many who would die for their country, but what is most needed to-day is men and women of courage who are willing to live for their country, to live " for the cause that needs assistance," and " for the wrong that needs resistance." That is a heroism consistent with a twentieth century civilization. The most costly, noblest heroism is the living sacrifice, the sustained resolve, the courage of conviction, the daily consecration of powers to God and to humanity.

" The world is our country and all mankind our countrymen " is the sentiment of true internationalism.

" Only the Golden Rule of Christ can bring in the Golden Age of man."

THE CHAIRMAN: A paper upon " Peace Principles in Political Life and Institutions " has been prepared by Augustine Jones, Principal of Friends' School, Providence, Rhode Island. Augustine Jones found himself unable to be present; the paper will, therefore, be read by Timothy B. Hussey, of Maine.

PEACE PRINCIPLES IN POLITICAL LIFE AND INSTITUTIONS.

BY AUGUSTINE JONES, LL.B., PRINCIPAL FRIENDS' SCHOOL, PROVIDENCE, R. I.

The most essential outcome, so far, of political institutions, is the establishment of peace and domestic tranquillity within the civilized nations themselves. Municipalities and citizens, in modern times, submit their causes to organized courts and to arbitration for settlement, and have outgrown trial by battle and the brutal methods of antiquity, within the domain of the nations where there exists real government.

The recent treaties and international efforts to apply the same ethics in international contests, which are so satisfactory in giving peace within the nations themselves, are the strongest possible evidence of modern progress towards the peace of the world, and the most inspiring promise for the future of the race. English history illustrates the pacific effect within States of the modern political structure, the union of many small communities under one government. The many great federations in modern times of once belligerent but now peaceful communities, dwelling together in unity, all suggest by irresistible logical sequence the holy alliance of the governments of the world, in support of one universal court of international arbitration. This paramount subject demands the sympathy, wisdom and energy of every Christian on the globe.

The writer was admitted this past summer to the court rooms of the Permanent International Court of Arbitration at The Hague. The nineteen most important nations have already, with certain restrictions, appointed judges to that court, and joined in treaty obligations to abide by its conclusions. This structure is the creation of nineteen States, or political institutions, resting themselves on numerous other subordinate political institutions down to the individual citizen. If you know what war is, you cannot enter this sacred court room, dedicated to peace on earth and goodwill to men, without a throbbing heart, for this is indeed holy ground. The tremendous shocks of war, which would in years to come have convulsed nations, toppled over thrones, fixed the fate of empires, changed the map of the world, extinguished life and light in thousands of happy homes, may hereafter on this spot be prevented by the potency of law and time-honored precedents, administered with reason and justice.

We have thus far outlined what the complete work already accomplished through politics is, and what gigantic work politics has yet to do before the millennial peace possesses our planet.

But there is, however, a more vital and practical portion of our subject to be considered; that is, political life, or politics in action, leavened with peace principles. Politics is the science or practice of government for the preservation of the peace and prosperity of the State. Peace is, then, one of the most important objects to be sought in government.

If the principles of peace are to be active in politics, they must take hold of public opinion, " the governing principle in human affairs," as Alexander Hamilton said, with a strenuous purpose born of conviction that they are the greatest need of human society at this moment, that they are the very essence of Christianity, which is love to God and to men. The principles of peace must be agitated, until the public mind is awakened to its highest duty; then politics will be potent to advance the cause. Christian ministers ought to be the anointed heralds of this gospel; they ought *ex officio* to proclaim these principles upon every house top, and every Christian soul ought to join in the chorus, to agitate and agitate without ceasing.

I very much doubt if this question would have been presented here, if there had not been two different kinds of politics in the world. One seeks the public good at personal loss and even suffering; this is heroic patriotism; the other barters the public interest for selfish, mean ends. Men of this last class can have very little interest in the peaceable fruits of righteousness. If they seek your vote, it is in general for a purpose which you cannot approve, and you find it a critical work to make any entangling alliances with them. These are the two extreme classes in politics, with totally different ethics. We must, however, take into account that few men are wholly bad or good, and that there is a large number of men in politics who are rather neutral, moved from time to time, like the ballast box, with the changing wind and tide.

Can any man who belongs to the upright class of politicians who act from lofty ethical motives have influence and be useful with and among politicians of all classes and bear through it all a stainless character and an uncorrupted soul? One very acute observer of public men once asked: " Who touches politics and is thenceforth clean?" We answer without hesitation, John Bright, Charles Sumner, and a host beside them.

Probably no man was ever more thoroughly imbued with peace principles, ever endured more in his own person for them, ever bore aloft the white flag of peace more irresistibly and gloriously than Bright, indifferent to the jeers and scoffs which fell firelike on his spirit, sensitive as a woman's, but majestic and unconquerable like Cromwell's, England's greatest orator.

How was it that this man, almost alone, saw great public evils as no other public man seemed to do, with the eye of a prophet; saw, and with a voice which had no equal for power and beauty, spoke words of truth and soberness, often unheeded, nevertheless words brim full of wisdom, loud warnings of impending danger? Strange to say, he never gave false alarms. The causes which he advocated were sustained by subsequent history, with hardly an exception. No other public man's record was ever more absolutely vindicated by time and events.

He himself attributed it to his lifelong training in the Society of Friends. He had been taught to mind the Light within, Christ within and conscience, to avoid all expedients in public and private life which did not accord with the inner witness. He says:

I do not know why I differed from other people so much, but sometimes I have thought it happened from the education I had received in the religious sect with which I am connected. We have no creed which monarchs and statesmen and high priests have written out for us. Our creed so far as we comprehend it, comes pure and direct from the New Testament. We have no thirty-seven articles to declare that it is lawful for Christian men, at the command of the civil magistrate, to wear weapons and to serve in wars—which means, of course, and was intended to mean, that it is lawful for a Christian man to engage, in any part of the world, in any cause, at the command of a monarch, or of a prime minister, or of a parliament, or of a commander-in-chief, in the slaughter of his fellowmen, whom he might never have seen before, and from whom he had not received the smallest injury, and against whom he had no reason to feel the smallest touch of anger or resentment. Now my having been brought up as I was would lead me naturally to think that going 3,000 miles off,— for it is nearly as far as that by sea,—to carry on the war with Russia in the Crimea, was a matter that required very distinct evidence to show that it was lawful, or that it was in any way politic or desirable.

John Bright for two years (1854-1856) constantly opposed the was with Russia, almost alone. He suffered great abuse from the press and from other sources. He had been very popular, and received everywhere welcome plaudits, swelling the notes of praise for years, but his firm attitude against the wars with Russia and China cost him his seat as representative in Parliament for Manchester, and serious illness came to him from political anxiety. Birmingham immediately elected him as her representative, in which office he remained during his life. He has given the following vivid description of his conflict:

Well, I cannot forget all that took place on that occasion. There is much of it I wish I could forget. I wish I could forget the slanders that were uttered against me; slanders from many writers of the press, and, I am sorry to say, some of the most bitter were from those people who are supposed to write for the religious newspapers. I should be glad if I could forget that I was at one time hissed and hooted by mobs, and forget, further, a story that I was burnt in effigy by those I was most anxious to serve; and, finally, that in consequence of the course I took on a great public question, I lost my seat in Parliament for one of the first constituencies in the kingdom. But I may recollect that, after all, I never lost the sense, and I have not lost it yet, that I did what was my duty to my country, under the trying and difficult circumstances in which I was placed.

He favored always " peace, retrenchment and reform." His most notable speeches, some of them, were made against increase in armament, against more extended defences. He was intensely opposed to meddling in the differences between foreign nations. He struggled to avoid entangling alliances with other countries. This had been the policy of Sir Robert Walpole, Charles James Fox, Sir Robert Peel and others, though not successful always. But Sir Robert Peel, noble, self-sacrificing, patriotic, was the chief prototype in the political character and course of John Bright, in international affairs. A double portion of the spirit of Elijah did rest on Elisha. Peel was taken away suddenly, but he left a worthy exponent to uphold and vindicate his political doctrines.

John Bright was opposed in 1882 to the war in Egypt, as he was to all wars everywhere, including the Afghan and Zulu, and he very soon resigned his seat in the Cabinet, an office worth to him ten thousand dollars annually, beside the dignity and honor which attended it. This he did without hesitation, although it might estrange him from his life-long political and social friends. He has given, fortunately, his own most interesting account of this painful severance. He said in the House of Commons, July 17th, 1882:

The House knows, at all events, those who have had an opportunity of observing any of the facts of my political life for forty years, know, that at least I have endeavored from time to time to teach my countrymen an opinion and doctrine which I hold, which is, that the moral law is not intended only for individual life, but is intended also for the life and practice of States. I think in the present case there has been a manifest violation of international law—and of moral law—and therefore it is impossible for me to give any support to it. I cannot repudiate what I have preached and taught during the period of a rather long political life. I cannot turn my back upon my belief and deny all that I have taught to many thousands of others during the forty years I have been permitted in public meetings and in this House to address my countrymen. One word only more. I asked my calm judgment and my conscience what was the path of right to take. They pointed it out to me with an unerring finger, and I am humbly endeavoring to follow it.

The most conspicuous feature of John Bright as an apostle of peace principles in political action, was his firm foundation upon the bed rock of Christian New Testament ethics; there was no confusion in his mind. His course was directed by the true polar star of morals. He said again in 1858:

May I beg you, then, to believe, as I do most devoutly believe, that the moral law was not written for men alone in their individual churches, but that it was written as well for nations, and for nations great as this of which we are citizens. I believe, too, that if nations reject and deride that moral law, there is a penalty which inevitably follows; it may not come at once—it may not come in our lifetime—but, depend upon it, the great Italian is not only a poet, but he is a prophet when he says:
 "The sword of Heaven is not in haste to smite
  Nor yet doth linger."

How his soul would be stirred if he were now living, over the sickening details of the South African war. The Zulu war was but as a fly by an eagle to the violence of this one, and yet how earnest was his protest against that. If he had been in Parliament these recent months, the present British Cabinet, dishonored and discredited by unholy conquest, would have felt the weight of his tremendous moral prestige, his cogent and irresistible eloquence, and yet above all his consummate ability to convince and change votes. It may reasonably be doubted whether the present war could have had existence if Bright and Gladstone had been alive and in the councils of the nation.

The last words of his which I shall quote ring out like inspired prophecy of the recent sad events in British annals. He said, you remember: "We have the unchangeable principles of the moral law to guide us, and only so far as we live by that guidance can we be permanently a great nation, or our people a happy people."

My friends, those were words of soberness and wisdom. The English people have not, in this unjust and cruel war, been under the "guidance" of the moral law, and they are not now a happy people. Multitudes of their noblest youth have perished; their homes are desolate, mothers refuse to be comforted. Her public debt increases fearfully. England has lost her exalted, proud leadership and supremacy in the galaxy of nations. Her enemies, biding their time, in the hour of her bitter distress, in a long-drawn-out war with less favored communities, scoff at her, and if they dared, would evidently extend her afflictions and weaken her. There is only one safe course for men and nations alike, and that is to do right.

I have chosen John Bright, with his forty years of experience in the British Parliament and in public life, a thorough outspoken apostle of peace principles, fearless, able and consistent in his support of the cause in every vicissitude of his political fortunes, because he is considered historically the greatest and most conspicuous advocate in political life who has voiced those principles. His life work in upholding the cause of peace before the whole world at its commercial center, himself long a prominent member of the government of the most powerful nation in the world, his noble moral character, each and all contributed to extend his ceaseless influence world wide. He has settled forever, both in Parliament and in public meetings all over the kingdom, that peace principles can be effectively presented and agitated with great success. He has shown that, under the influence of a venal and warlike press, a senseless delirium for war may be created, which subsides after cruel slaughter and havoc, and this is followed by sober reason, repentance and sorrow; that there have been no wars for centuries which in the end have been by wise and pure men regarded as necessary or useful to mankind. John Bright and his coadjutors did more to advance the peace cause than had been done for centuries in all lands before their time.

From the group of men that surrounded John Bright the gospel of peace was carried to the heart of Alexander of Russia, and the light that was then set up still burns brightly from the throne of all the Russias. Hence we have the Conference at The Hague. No one can study faithfully the influence of these persons in this cause, and reasonably doubt that by agitation the public mind may be aroused to the enormity of evil, and that public sentiment is omnipotent in political life and institutions.

Fifty years of congresses of nations held in different countries, composed of eminent, representative publicists and statesmen, and conferences like that now held annually at Lake Mohonk, have created public opinion and powerfully inspired political institutions with peace principles, the fruit of which appears in treaties, in a court of international arbitration, and even in a touch of altruism in the very laws of war.

We might properly include the influence of all the distinguished men, writers, orators, agitators and earnest Christian souls, unknown to the world but registered on high, who have struggled in season and out of season to enlighten their fellow men, to create public opinion, and who have, without knowing it, been guiding political life and institutions.

The recent international reciprocity movement, which seems to promise very much in the future for the peace of the world, is the masterful work of political organizations seeking profit chiefly through peace principles. The white-winged ships of commerce, and the great and small ocean steamships, freighted with the products of every zone, are gradually gathering the nations into communion and intercourse, which must end at last, if continued, in the federation of nations, in arbitration and peace, developed and directed by the political life and political institutions of the world.

We must not be in haste for heavenly perfection, but take knowledge of the Divine patience which has brooded over erring humanity many centuries. How little does the race yet comprehend that Light which came to this world two thousand years ago, and has never ceased to enter constantly thick spiritual and intellectual darkness. Yet progress is certain; now slowly, now rapidly, the light of civilization extends. There is a vast difference between the savage, barbaric life that once was and the enlightenment in the most favored nations of to-day.

Truth seems to us sometimes to retire before the armies of the aliens, but it is really ever uppermost, and following we may always look for great and permanent advance. We verily thought a few years since that we had come out at last into the eternal sunshine of peace, but we were hurled back suddenly by the two most enlightened nations into dark clouds and cruel war, without necessity or reason.

But the bitter lesson which is following these deliriums of war and blood will teach us, if we can learn it no other way, the wickedness, foolishness and extravagance of both conquests.

The burdens of war in all ages fall upon the poor and weak most heavily; they are slaughtered, they are taxed, they suffer most. They are God's outraged poor everywhere, broken-hearted mothers, sisters and lovers, whom no sympathy can reach, only pity, for it is the iron fate of war. The Christian ministers might close the gates of war forever, but instead they, with lusty enthusiasm, blow the bugle blast and let loose the dogs of war, consecrate the simple, childlike victim devoted to war and his weapons, and exhort him to do anything but remember his New Testament and its words, "Thou shalt love thy neighbor as thyself."

The remedy is enlightened Christian public opinon, in political life and institutions.

THE CHAIRMAN: The discussion of the topics raised in the papers of the afternoon, which will continue for not more than half an hour, will be opened by Dr. Edward H. Magill, of Swarthmore College.

EDWARD H. MAGILL: If the discussion of these papers means finding any fault with what has been presented, I surely have nothing whatever to say. These three papers, being naturally connected, have presented a very bright and hopeful outlook for the cause of peace.

I have only a few words to say on the one point of "Internationalism," presented in one of the papers this afternoon, just to emphasize what has been said. Six years ago a system of international correspondence between professors and students in different nations was started by Professor Millet, who lives in Southern France. He thought that it would be a good thing for the sake of the study of the languages that students should interchange letters and correct each other's letters, and also that it would be a very valuable means of making the citizens of the different nations acquainted with each other and thus tend to remove misunderstandings and causes of war. To-day there are between 12,000 and 15,000 letters going all the time between the nations of France, England, Germany, Italy, the United States, Spain and Canada. What a significant thing it is that the central bureau in Italy, in Milan, should be under the charge of the Peace Association. E. T. Moneta is president of that peace society, and he conducts the bureau there. Dr. Hartman, in Leipzig, is very much interested in the cause of peace, and he is conducting the bureau there. Professor Millet, in France, who invented the system and has done so much to put it forward, and is a prolific writer, sends me whole reams of paper on the subject of peace. He writes much for the journals of France. His wife is president of a peace society in France. W. T. Stead, the editor of the *Review of Reviews*, who is so highly regarded by most of us, but who has lost recently much of his standing in England, largely because of his bold stand against the Boer War, is interested in the movement. His office is the central bureau for England. The central bureau in this country is not far away (at Swarthmore, Pa.).

We have first, then, in this work, the teaching of the languages; but we know that the correspondence will make pupils acquainted with each other and that thus will come about an exchange of views and a wider acquaintance among the young people of the rising generation.

We have got to wait until this generation passes away before we can expect the great things that we have been speaking of this afternoon. When I was a boy I could wait till to-morrow or the next day, or perhaps the day after, for anything I wanted very badly, but not beyond that. Now, if I can get something accomplished in four or five generations, or before the twentieth century is over, I shall feel comfortably well satisfied. We shall have to be satisfied to get perhaps late in the twentieth century these things that you have heard predicted this afternoon. In a few days we shall finish one year of it, and we shall have ninety-nine more years left to do work in.

I will close by saying that the secret of the whole business of making all such changes is to begin with the young, to begin in the home, and then to continue in the school, in business, everywhere, to carry out these principles of peace, of brotherly love, of the golden rule. A Golden Rule Brotherhood was established a year ago last August in New York. Its purposes were fully set forth at the Pan-American Exposition at Buffalo this year. It has a small actual membership. But the Golden Rule Sisterhood, as May Wright Sewall, its president, reported in Buffalo, has a membership of several millions. The way to get to be a member of either of these is to make up your mind that you are going to act on the Golden Rule. Everybody knows that the Golden Rule is a very old story. But it is an entirely new thing to put it in practice. Those, therefore, who make up their minds that they will obey it every day, as far as possible, will be truly members of the Golden Rule Brotherhood or the Golden Rule Sisterhood, and will thus help to bring about the great results at which we are aiming.

THE CHAIRMAN: The papers presented this afternoon are now open for general discussion.

STEPHEN R. SMITH: This expression has weighed with me much to-day: "Whatsoever thy hand findeth to do, do it with thy might." I have listened with great interest and rejoicing to the many splendid papers that have been presented and the discussions that have followed them. I have been enthused with them. I have enjoyed seeing the city of Philadelphia, its great buildings and its City Hall. But at the entrance to the hall there is an equestrian statue of a warrior of the flesh; then there is at the top the grand monument to William Penn, who was pre-eminently the preacher of righteousness and of peace. His "holy experiment" in government was a great deed. His treaty with the Indians was the only one that was ever cemented without an oath, and said to be the only one ever kept between nations. But there I beheld, staring me in the face at the orifices of the building, six grim engines of destruction. Friends, we need to change public opinion on these matters. If we have been enthused here, we need to take that enthusiasm home with us and engage in home missionary work. We need the spirit of Christ in our souls, our whole being filled with the Holy Ghost, so that we may do our work effectively, as George Fox did his. Let us not forget, as we go home, that we do not wish to have it said that this Congress was simply a mutual admiration society. Let us put our shoulder to the wheel and work while it is day.

THE CHAIRMAN: I would like to suggest to my friend Stephen R. Smith that possibly those disused and decrepit cannon in the plaza of our City Hall may be symbols of the wornoutness and uselessness, the "gonebyness," if you will allow me to use the word, of the system of war; for certainly no one could fire them off, and they are perfectly harmless.

DAVID FERRIS: I have listened with intense interest to the various papers read, and the views expressed on this vital question of war, now so earnestly engaging our attention. We, who call ourselves Friends, are almost unanimous in pronouncing all war inconsistent with the teaching of Jesus and with the spirit of Christianity. I have nothing to add by way of argument. I want to endorse the views expressed. Though variously worded and given from different points of view, they all converge to the same general conclusion. I unite with that conclusion.

I wish lovingly to exhort Friends to more faithfulness in living this vital testimony of "peace and goodwill"; that it may permeate our life and pass from us as the healing from Jesus; that we may live, as George Fox said, "in the virtue of that life which takes away the occasion of war."

I have felt that during the past three years, while the war fever, like a moral pestilence, has swept over our land, we Friends have not exerted the influence that we should have done on public sentiment regarding war. Why? Because too many of us have compromised, have excused, have palliated the wrong. While many have worked earnestly to stay the curse, there have been many others who have used such excuses as these: "God can bring good out of this seeming evil," "We must be loyal to our government." Our political affiliations have been a source of weakness. Choosing the least of two evils is not an uncommon plea. Some of us have even gone so far as to justify the present Philippine war. These Friends may be honest and sincere, but I think the war excitement has warped their judgment so that they cannot see clearly.

Will not such excuses, if carried to their logical conclusions, justify any iniquity or cruelty that the mind can conceive? So our "trumpet has given an uncertain sound," and we have not exerted the influence against the present wars, which a faithful upholding of this precious testimony would have given us.

Even in our most unselfish and honest endeavors to promote justice and truth we must expect opposition; "for so persecuted they the prophets before" us; or as our Quaker poet says:

"Every age on him who strays
From its broad and beaten ways
Pours its seven-fold vial."

We need a higher courage than is shown on the battlefield, for we must sometimes bear the condemnation of those dear and near to us.

> "Hard to bear the stranger's scoff;
> Hard the old friends' falling off;
> Hard to learn forgiving.
> But the Lord his own rewards,
> And his love with their's accords
> Warm and fresh and living."

Do not justice and true patriotism and our Christian profession of peace plead with us to unite in using our influence with our country and government to give freedom to these injured and oppressed people who have been so long and so earnestly struggling for it? Can we not all unite in this good work?

> "Have we been faithful as we knew,
> To God and to our brother true;
> To Heaven and earth?"

Are these meetings we have been holding an augury of our future united action to bring peace to our country? If so, we may take courage and have faith that a brighter day is dawning; for when all Friends can be united in a righteous cause they will carry conviction with them.

In all the papers read and the addresses made the Christian standard of overcoming evil with good has been upheld. It has been a great satisfaction to attend this Convention. I feel it is the opening of a better day for Friends. It is a reunion full of hope. Let us work cordially together for the help and uplift of humanity, and the work will draw us nearer together in Christian love. Then, if we can unite in trying to influence our government to give the Filipinos their liberty, that we may hope will be eventually successful, then we will have done our part to

> "Break the chain, the yoke remove,
> And strike to earth oppression's rod.
> With those mild arms of truth and love,
> Made mighty through the living God."

ANNA BRAITHWAITE THOMAS: I have been deeply interested in this question of internationalism. The means that have been brought forward in the last few years for bringing the nations of the world into harmony with each other are altogether in line with the root-truth of the Society of Friends. You may remember how George Fox said, "Friends, be universal in your spirits." A belief that the Spirit of the Lord deals with every human soul should make us interested in every individual whom God has created. It makes no difference whether they are black or white, Americans, English, Boer, Filipino, Chinese, or what not. It is this principle

of the love of God to every individual soul that has made me a
peace woman, and lead me to try to put peace principles into action.
I have been thrown in the course of my life with people of different
countries. As a girl, I went with my parents on a religious visit
through Europe. I was brought in that way into close touch with
the people in France, Germany, Switzerland and Italy. I became
intensely interested in many of them; I saw their religious life; I
was present in meetings where the power of the Holy Spirit came
upon us, and I was baptized into sympathy with many of the people.
Could I afterwards view with any satisfaction the thought of
war with those people whom I knew and loved individually? I
have since been brought into close touch with Christian people in
Norway and Denmark and other places. I have relatives and
friends in the East, in Japan, in China, in South Africa, even.
When we get into this Christian touch with other peoples, we begin
to understand that war cannot be God's will. When such beautiful
ideas as those of peace are held up before us, we say sometimes,
"That is idealism." Well, what is idealism? Idealism is the
truth, I believe; and whenever we see anything beautiful or true or
good, we may take it for granted that that is God's will. The beautiful
ideal of peace, universal peace, I am not prepared to wait
even one century for the fulfillment of it. Why should we wait?
If the Christian Church, if even the whole body of Friends, would
rise in power, in the power of God, we could bring in the day of
peace much sooner than the end of this century.

The Conference then, after announcements and a moment of
silence, adjourned till 8 p.m.

Sixth Session.

SIXTH-DAY EVENING, TWELFTH MONTH 13TH.

The Conference re-assembled in Witherspoon Hall, for its sixth session, at 8 p.m., under the presidency of Joshua L. Baily. A few moments were given to silent waiting upon God.

THE CHAIRMAN: Those of us who have had the privilege of attending the sessions of the Conference yesterday and to-day cannot have failed to notice the gradual development of the doctrine and practice of peace as set forth in the different papers which have been read.

First, " The New Testament Ground of Peace," as presented in the admirable paper of Professor Russell, and then " The Elements of Peace Doctrine in the Old Testament," as unfolded in the scholarly paper of Doctor Barton, all showing the gradual progress leading up to and reaching its full development in the teaching of our Lord.

The Decalogue brought down from the mountain in the hands of Moses, and our Lord's Sermon on the Mount, were shown to be harmonious parts of one beneficent scheme in which was manifested the Brotherhood of Man as well as the Fatherhood of God. We were shown that the early Christian Church was uniform in its testimony to the peaceable nature of Christ's kingdom, " I am a Christian and therefore I cannot fight " being the all-sufficient reason assigned for the maintenance of their peace principles.

Passing down the centuries we were shown how primitive Christianity declined as Church and State became united, men forsaking the teaching of the Prince of Peace and seeking the spread of Christianity by force of arms. It was claimed that not until the middle of the Seventeenth Century were the peaceable principles of primitive Christianity revived by the preaching of Fox and Penn and Barclay. We were made sorrowfully aware of the sad extent to which the members of the Christian Church, not excepting our own portion of it, had so often failed to bear a consistent testimony against all wars and fightings.

" The Inherent Immorality of War " and " The Christian Idea of Force " were the subjects of two valuable papers, the clear teaching of both being profitably emphasized by several speakers.

We were reminded of the duty of parents and teachers to inculcate the principles of peace in the home as well as in the Bible School, and " The Opportunities and Responsibility of Woman for Promoting Peace Principles " were presented in an earnest appeal.

The peace principles which should govern us in political life were also forcibly presented, and the consistent position in opposition to all war so steadfastly maintained by the illustrious Quaker statesman of England, the late John Bright, was commended as an example worthy of emulation.

And now, having gone this far, it is proposed that we this evening review the field from quite a different standpoint. It seems almost like taking a backward step to open anew the question as to " the extent to which peace principles are practicable," and yet this is the query propounded as I read it in the printed program for this evening. It having been shown to us that the Gospel of Peace is graven in the very bed rock of our Christianity, that for the maintenance of their testimony against war the early Christians, as well as the early Quakers, suffered imprisonment and divers tortures, and even the loss of life itself; and in view of the many examples already quoted of the triumphs of peace principles under the most adverse circumstances, is it still an open question " To what extent are peace principles practical? " Fortunately, the committee has confided the discussion of this question to one so well qualified to handle it that I am quite content to leave the field to him.

THE CHAIRMAN: " To What Extent are Peace Principles Practicable? " is the topic which will be spoken to by President Sharpless, of Haverford College.

TO WHAT EXTENT ARE PEACE PRINCIPLES PRACTICABLE?

BY PRESIDENT ISAAC SHARPLESS, HAVERFORD COLLEGE.

Is it ever right to do wrong? Will the achievement of great and beneficent results justify the commission of an act which, but for these results, would be immoral? Has a man the right to put his conscience in the path of progress and impose the consequences of his beliefs upon other people? May we hold a theory as right in itself if in practice it is impossible?

These and a great many similar questions immediately arise to the man who is asked to solve the problems of life in the world as at the present constituted. They do not arise simply in that abnormal condition of things which we call war, but are ever present with us in our ordinary civilization in times of peace. We employ detectives who lie and drink and dishonor trust and friendship because we say they are necessary for the suppression of crime. The whole criminal administration is in use of methods in which a perfectly moral man could hardly join. Business life is not always conditioned upon perfect trust and honesty, and there are those who would say it would be impossible to succeed on this basis. The code of politics justifies the commission of a number of at least doubtful acts, which, for good ends, are winked at by excellent people. The first man that you will meet on the street will tell you that while a state of society which practices the precepts of the Sermon on the Mount would be ideally beautiful, yet they are entirely impossible of fulfillment under the present circumstances and may be laid aside for better times. It comes to us as a moral tonic, but at the same time a matter of surprise, when we hear a successful business man announce that he would not accept a directorship in any company or own a share of its stock if any questionable methods for securing legislative favors were necessary to be adopted.

There is no doubt about the answer of the early Friends to these questions. They were not opportunists. The least matter of conscience was worth more than the whole world. Better lose life and goods, and sacrifice all future apparent good of society, than violate one iota of the moral law. They could lose; they could suffer; they could die; but they could not do wrong.

But government, business, society and politics at the present time have codes of morals of their own which are perfectly understood and justified by many excellent men, but which are greatly different from the code of the New Testament. There is no subject on which this divergence is more conspicuous than the subject of war. The questions are again and again asked of " peace men " : " How are you going to apply your principles to existing conditions? What would you have done if you had been in charge of affairs at Revolutionary times, or during the Civil War? Your theories seem to be in accord with the highest Christian sentiments, but they are not applicable. It becomes necessary to fight, and theories of right and wrong have to give way in the face of present necessities." There are a great many who consider themselves good " peace men " who will go to great lengths to avoid a war, and who fully recognize the evils of war; yet they say that under desperate circumstances the evils of peace would be still greater. They say that any abstract principles lose their validity, and that of the two courses possible we must take the one that, in our judgment, seems to produce the fewest evil results.

To this class of people several replies may be made. One is that they cannot possibly judge what the results will be. The wisest of us are short-sighted, and we can probably in every case reverse the motto of Paley and say that whatever is right is expedient. If a Christian martyr had argued that he could do more for his cause by living than by dying in some obscure village of the Roman Empire, he would have had a plausible case. He might have supposed that many Christian converts would have been the result of his later efforts if he would only temporize a little and utter some meaningless phrase signifying his devotion to the genius of the Emperor. But we are now quite sure that his death meant more to Christianity than his life could ever have been. Luther might easily have argued that his influence at Rome in favor of reform within the

Church would have been far more potent than his probable isolation and apparently suicidal attacks upon it. But from the point of view of expediency he would have made a great mistake. The cases in history of men who bravely took the losing side because it was right will occur to every one of you, and in looking back you will recognize that nearly all the great impulses toward better things which the world has received have come from this sort of people. The blood of the martyrs has been the seed not only of the Church reforms, but also of all reforms in politics and society. The fear of consequences has been the plea of the coward and the time-server, and the little gains that the best of them have made, even when their intentions have been good, do not stand out in history.

I cannot now argue the question as to the abstract righteousness of war. For our present purpose we will assume that the answer is in the negative. But it will not do simply to stop here. It may serve the individual conscience of him who takes this view and induce him to say that for himself this settles the whole question. And so it should. But he has duties to others as well as to himself, and if he desires to avert from society the evil effects of warfare he must indicate some method of living which will seem reasonable to others. It is very right that there should be among us those who plant themselves firmly on the high ground of principle and say, "Come what will, war is wrong and no exigencies can make it right." But there are very few people, even Christian people, who believe this. They may, at some future time; but I think there is some obligation upon ultra-peace men to show how far they will extend their principle, and under what conditions peace regulations of society can be enforced.

We have on one extreme the teachings of Tolstoy and his disciples, who claim that all resistance is wrong, and consequently that all government is wrong, for government at its best is only a method to resist invaders of personal rights. Hence the whole machinery of police and jails and courts of justice, and laws and executives should be abolished, criminals should be met only by forbearance and passive resistance, and the great example of universal love should be shown to the world, let the consequences be what they will.

We do not feel sure that there is not more in this theory than most people are willing to admit. We have found in our ordinary experiences that a man who is met in a generous spirit will practically always so respond, and that most of the difficulties which come to us are the result of deviations from absolute justice and kindliness on our own part. It is probable that there are men so ruthless and unfeeling as to strike at the rights and even the lives of patient, generous and bravely suffering victims, but such people are, I believe, much more rare than we usually assume. In what company will not the life and honor of a helpless child be perfectly safe? How very few there are who would insult or injure old age or sickness! So we say that every approach toward the position of

Tolstoy, even if that position be in itself an extreme, is a gain for the world, which is altogether too sceptical of the strong defences of purity and righteousness. But it is not necessary to carry the matter to this extreme. Usually among the so-called " peace men " a distinction is made between police and military measures. The one is permitted, the other is reprobated, and I suppose the line with most of us would be drawn, not at the denial of all resistance, but at the use of methods which would be in themselves criminal.

It is probably a mistake to call Friends non-resistants and non-combatants. They have not been so in the past. In the seventeenth century they resisted with unflinching courage and mighty success the efforts to quench their privileges and narrow their duties. No braver fight ever occurred. They have never had but one opportunity to attempt to conduct the State according to their principles, and that was in early Pennsylvania, and we must pause a little time to find out how, in this practical test, they applied their doctrine of the wrongfulness of military measures.

In 1688 the colony was asked to form a militia. The governor appointed by Penn was an old Cromwellian soldier, who urged it upon the council, which was largely Friendly. After a conference the Quaker members gave as their decision: " We would not tie others' hands, but we cannot act. We would not take it upon us to hinder any, and we do not think the governor need call us together in the matter. We say nothing against it and regard it as a matter of conscience to us." Not infrequently similar demands came from the crown. The universal custom of the Quaker Assembly was to throw the responsibility upon the non-Quaker lieutenant-governor. In the matter of appropriating money for military expenses their practice was varied. In 1709 they appropriated £500 in response to the promise of the governor that it should not be " dipt in blood." Two years later they made a similar appropriation without the reservation, and Isaac Norris, a Friend minister of high standing, defended it on the ground that it was simply a supply for the government, and the fact that the government chose to spend it in war was not a responsibility of theirs.

When, as a result of ill-treatment of the Indians and French intrigue, the troubles began on the frontier, between 1740 and 1750, there were many demands made upon the Quaker Assembly for money for military purposes. These, after some haggling as to terms, were generally voted, though the purpose for which they were to be applied never stated warlike expenditure. In one case it was for bread, beef, pork, flour, wheat and other grain. Franklin said that the " other grain " was construed to mean gun powder, to which construction the Assembly appears to have made no objection.

A line of forts stretching from Easton to the Maryland boundary was built with money so expended, and several laws were passed organizing a militia. In the latter case it was always provided that no one was to be forced to perform military services. The meetings were expected to keep their own members out of it. It was a favorite phrase in a law, "Whereas this province was settled, and the majority of the Assembly have ever since been of the people called Quakers, who, though they do not, as the world is now constituted, condemn the use of arms in others, yet are principled against bearing arms themselves," etc., etc. This seems to have been the Quaker policy through the whole of the provincial days. They were convinced of the unlawfulness of war for themselves, but did not attempt to impose their principles upon others. After the first ten years Penn and his successors never appointed a Quaker governor. If they had it is difficult to see how the province would have been governed. It may be a question of casuistry whether a man should make it easy for some one else to do that of which he himself does not approve provided the second man's conscience is not troubled. But whether right or wrong, that seems to have been the consistent policy of the Pennsylvania Friends in provincial days, and there is some justification for those who say that pure Quaker principles are not adapted to government, in the policy of the Quakers themselves when in power.

They thought, in 1756, they must resign their places in the Legislature. The executive branch of the government had declared war against the Indians, and it was the opinion of the wisest Friends, both in England and America, that the exigencies of the case were such as to demand the entire withdrawal of Friends from the responsibilities of government. This was in itself a confession of failure. They could have remained in power apparently indefinitely, so far as the electors were concerned. In the fall of 1755, after Braddock's defeat, and when the Indians were ravaging the frontier, twenty-eight of the thirty-six members elected to the Assembly were Friends. Their constituency evidently had faith in their methods of solving the difficulty, and were willing to try these methods further.

So far as I can see this condition of affairs could have lasted until the Revolution, for their political machine was in excellent order and they were practically sure of re-election. I think that they intended to resume their places in the government after the troubles, which they believed would be temporary, should have been overpast. But there was continual rumor of war on one side or the other for twenty years, and then the great cataclysm occurred which ended their influential connection with the government. Whether, in the light of subsequent events, they did right in voluntarily withdrawing is a question. At any rate it would have been a more perfect experiment in the practicability of peace principles if they had remained in power as long as they were the honorable recipients of popular votes, and so had shown whether or not their theories were available in stormy times. The truth of the matter seems to be that the virtues must go together. Justice to the Indians and French and adjacent colonists was an indispensable condition of peace. I am not at all convinced that a Quaker government in America, in 1776, could not have also solved the great question of English oppression without a war, if it had had the opportunity during the preceding years, and the eradication of slavery in the State at the time it was abolished by the meetings might reasonably be supposed to have obviated the necessity of our Civil War. If, therefore, peace is to be practicable among nations, a large amount of other virtues must also exist. And until this is possible we will have to admit that there are limits to the application of our doctrine. I believe that both John Bright and General Grant are credited with the statement that all wars of the present century migh have been avoided if reasonable and cool views had prevailed in advance. But in a great majority of cases one side or the other has a desire to fight for the sake of fighting.

We might, therefore, come to these conclusions: First, that it is our duty to fight for the right and against evil, and fight hard, by methods which are not themselves wrong. Second, that a man or a society that believes war to be wrong must keep out of it, let the consequences be what they will. Third, that one cannot impose his views upon others, who, with equal honesty, have come to a different conclusion; that he must respect the motives which take many men into war, and give them the honor which their terrible self-sacrifice deserves; for to the man of fine feelings and honest convictions nothing could be more repellent than enduring the horrors of battle and the awful demoralization of camp life in place of the comforts and duties of home and civil society. Fourth, that as all the virtues work together, any one who advances the cause of righteousness in any direction is a friend of peace, and especially he who shows a man or a nation how to practice forbearance in the face of injury, and to deal kindly and generously with an opponent is doing his best to remove the causes of war. But, as these causes will continue to operate, it is our duty, by the establishment of arbitration and other methods, to avert wars, even when otherwise they would be inevitable.

Upon these points certain remarks may be made. It is impossible to avoid giving aid and comfort to wars and warlike tendencies unless one goes to a desert isle and lives by himself. Even if we do not join the army we pay taxes for its support. I do not know that any peace man omitted to write checks after the opening of the Spanish War because stamps were necessary to make them legal, and these stamps were expressly a war tax. Any one who has read the records of Friends during the Revolutionary times knows how difficult it was for them to hold their position of neutrality between parties and of consistent opposition to everything that pertained to war. Some drew the line at personal service, some at payment of war taxes, some at handling the paper money issued in support of the war, some at selling supplies to the army, and some at subscribing to tests of allegiance to the government while at war. The spirit and results of the war are so inextricably mingled with our general civilization that he who lives in it must support them inevitably. But while it is difficult to draw the line this much is clear, that certain acts are unquestionably over the line, and he who takes the ground that war is a violation of the Christian moral law must not confuse his mind by arguing that it is right for him because the cause is just, or the consequence apparently good, or the necessity dire. For himself the line of duty must be marked out regardless of where it will lead. Any compromise yields mental confusion and gives away his cause.

But when we come to judge our fellows we have no right to place our standards upon them; whether through education or conviction their consciences are different from ours. Many doubtless take part in martial display or actual warfare from love of glory, or love of adventure, or love of money, but there is a solid residuum which regards war as an inevitable and at times a justifiable evil, and takes it up with reluctance and at a great sacrifice. We cannot fully judge of motives, but we know that this class contains a very considerable number of our fellow citizens, and I should be unwilling to oppose any measures, like honest pensions or honors, which a grateful nation would adopt to give expression to its appreciation of exalted self-sacrifice. I do not think that we should necessarily keep clear of flag-raisings and other public ceremonies of this sort, for the Stars and Stripes represent a great many things in America besides military display. The flag stands for liberty, civil and religious; for equality; for a democracy which is unquestionably stronger than in any other nation of the world, all Quaker principles of incalculable preciousness. It stands for commerce and trade, and in the main, too, it stands for peace, for our government has done more than any other to advance this cause by promoting arbitration and by self-restraint. We will have to admit also that splendidly beneficent results have sometimes followed a war, and that military heroism is not an empty name.

Seeing, then, that the success of sound principles in practice is to depend on the education of the community and the removal of causes which tend toward strife, we have before us a very practical field of work. I do not mean that we should cease to point out that the spirit of war and the spirit of the New Testament are contrary to each other, and so gain converts to strictly peace views; but we must remember that it is hard even for us who have looked at the question for years from a peaceful standpoint to understand just what is right in all cases. We can give our right hand of encouragement to the men who are establishing the principles of arbitration between nations and individuals, and we can oppose legislative actions which encourage martial feelings among boys in schools and colleges. But we may have to admit that pure righteousness cannot be applied; that a strictly peace man could not be President of the United States though he might be a policeman on our streets; that we cannot explain to all opponents just how our principles would work in the present tangled condition of affairs; indeed, we may hold that they will not work at all in certain emergencies, and like John Bright after the bombardment of Alexandria, and the Quaker legislators in Pennsylvania in 1756, we will simply have to withdraw them and live quietly until better days come.

On the other hand we must have a firm faith that they are right, and, therefore, because right is always strong, that they are much more capable of application than the world believes or we can see, and in this faith we can keep our own consciences clear, and labor hopefully for the slowly growing peace sentiment to ripen its beneficent fruitage. With our two centuries of vantage we ought to develop the inspiration and the leaders of practical advances, and not be satisfied simply with the instruction of our own membership.

THE CHAIRMAN: With your indulgence I will now make use of a part of the time which by the program is allotted me, but which I did not occupy in my opening remarks, to relate two circumstances which came under my own observation illustrative of the practicability of peace measures. Some of you may remember the great strike on the Pennsylvania Railroad which occurred some twenty or more years ago. At Pittsburg, where the disturbance appears to have commenced, a very serious riot ensued. Hundreds of cars belonging to the railroad company were burned, and buildings and other property valued at millions of dollars were destroyed. The local soldiery were ordered out, and several regiments were sent to the scene of the riot from other parts of the State, and it was only after much bloodshed and loss of life that the rioters were overcome and peace restored.

The strike extended to Philadelphia. Here great trains of cars stood motionless upon the railroad tracks, the fires were drawn from under the locomotive boilers, and the angry strikers were gathering in groups along the lines of the road. The danger seemed imminent. The Mayor of the city—William M. Stokeley—quietly and privately called together at his office a select number of business men for consultation as to what should be done. "Call out the military," "Telegraph the Governor for additional troops," was the advice of the majority. "Not that," said the Mayor; "my experience is that the presence of soldiers under such circumstances only excites the riotous spirit and provokes resistance. Give me several hundred additional policemen and assure me of the money that will be required for their pay and you may hold me responsible for the peace of the city," or words to that effect.

There was no time to be lost. The recommendation of the Mayor was adopted, the gentlemen present agreeing to be responsible for the expense incurred. The Mayor had in part anticipated the action of the citizens and had already summoned a large addition to the regular police force, and with some further increase he was able to place men all along the line of the road where violence seemed to be most threatening, orders being given to quietly and gently disperse the strikers wherever they appeared to be congregating and to counsel them to return to their homes. What was the result? Without the firing of a gun, or the shedding of blood, or the destruction of property, the riot was prevented and the peace of the city preserved, and all this, mark you, without the presence of a soldier.

Another instance let me relate, an exemplification of practical disarmament which I met with in a recent visit at Nassau, on one of the Bahama Islands. There are four very strong fortifications commanding the harbor of Nassau. One of them, Fort Charlotte, is on a rocky height almost as unassailable as the Heights of Abraham at Quebec. But all these forts are dismantled. There are many cannon there, but they are all spiked, and only bats now inhabit what were once the quarters of the soldiers. There has been no other condition there for nearly a third of a century. There is a fine-looking police force, made up of negroes, but not a soldier under arms on the island; and the inhabitants suffer no hardship from the lack of military protection. An old woman put the whole matter in a nutshell when she queried of me, " Do you ever hear of fighting men going where there is nobody to fight?"

One other circumstance, not of personal observation, but historical, seems to me quite worthy of mention in this connection. Many of you will remember that in the war of 1812 between Great Britain and the United States there were many very disastrous engagements on the lakes which separate the United States from Canada. Indeed, the naval fleets of both nations were almost entirely destroyed. I think that it was John Quincy Adams who, after the conclusion of peace, was first to suggest that the great lakes should be declared neutral waters on which no war vessel of either nation should thereafter be permitted. It was not long after that, under the Presidency of James Monroe, John Quincy Adams being Secretary of State, this provision was carried into effect by solemn treaty between the United States and Great Britain, and now for more than three-fourths of a century along the coast lines of this great chain of lakes and upon the waters thereof—an area of even greater extent than the Mediterranean Sea—the white-winged Dove of Peace has held her unbroken sway. Is not this a notable example of the practical application of peace principles?—an example which other nations may find it wise and beneficent to follow, that thus there may ultimately be brought about the reign of peace throughout the earth.

THE CHAIRMAN: We shall now have an address on "William Penn's Peace Work," by the President of the Indian Aid Association, and a member of the Board of Indian Commissioners appointed by the President of the United States, Philip C. Garrett, of Philadelphia.

WILLIAM PENN'S WORK FOR PEACE.
BY PHILIP C. GARRETT, PHILADELPHIA.

Three prominent figures were chiefly influential, during the sixteenth century, in perpetuating the life of the Society of Friends. The passionate fervor of a number of very zealous converts doubtless added great momentum to the movement; but these three men —the one as the originator and organizer, the second as the expounder of a new and somewhat startling propaganda, and the third as its practical exponent, conserved and established this revival of pure primitive Christianity. These remarkable men were George Fox, Robert Barclay and William Penn.

The rôle of William Penn was largely in the line of civil and religious liberty and peace, but at all events to illustrate in his own Province, and also in his citations from the lives of devoted Christians in all ages, the truths they all advocated.

In so far as the Quaker movement was a peace movement there was one striking fact about the three. Two of them were the sons of distinguished warriors. Penn had been himself a soldier, and even George Fox was bona fide offered a commission in Cromwell's army.

Undoubtedly they were all men of peace; but I would call attention to the fact that their antecedents would have made them men of war, and at the outset it was seemingly not yet revealed to them that the inevitable result of accepting the Gospel of Christ was the abandonment of war. It was not that they did not fully accept his revolt from the Mosaic law of revenge, "an eye for an eye and a tooth for a tooth"; only that their thought had not been forcibly directed to the extent of the revolution, into which their independence of the later religious traditions, and reversion to the original type, were leading them.

The early Friends made no specialty of peace; they had no patent for it; they made no aggression upon war. From the nature of their belief they were necessarily opposed to war, simply because they sought to be Christlike Christians; and it was impossible to imagine their Divine leader in the heat of battle, slaughtering his fellow men and the lilies of the field incarnadined by his holy hand. It was not conceivable. And so while they did not attack war as an institution to be perfected by science and machinery, all physical combat was to them unallowable.

So secondary a place did Robert Barclay assign to war in his Apology, that he introduced it last of all subjects, under the singular head of "Salutations and Recreations." He begins his arraignment thus: "The last thing to be considered is revenge and war, an evil as opposite and contrary to the spirit and doctrine of

Christ as light to darkness." This is plainness of speech. In another place he avers that "it is as easy to obscure the sun at midday as to deny that the primitive Christians renounced all revenge and war."

We therefore see that the early Church was really as stalwart on this subject as the Society of Friends, and that Christians have simply fallen away from the primitive faith in this as in many other respects. Our call is to call them back in these last days to the ancient foundation upon which Christ builded his Church. But we cannot forget that military officers were referred to by our Saviour without reprobation as belonging to an established institution which he himself did not attack specially. The centurion was a just man, and one that feared God with all his house.

George Fox, like his Master, made no direct attack upon war, but warned his followers when offered great places and commands in the army, to "keep out of the powers of the earth, that run into wars and fightings," and "denied them all." To those who offered him a captaincy he said that he "lived in the virtue of that life and power that took away the occasion of all wars"; and he wrote to Cromwell that he "denied the wearing or drawing of a carnal sword or any other outward weapon against him or any other man," and that he was "set of God" to bring people from the causes of war and fighting "to the peaceable Gospel."

Robert Barclay treated war much in the same vague way. War as a separate and concrete monster was reserved for the modern reformer. The theorists of the seventeenth century cultivated the peace of God and all its blessed fruits. Fox and Barclay were theorists. Penn was practical, and, like the reformers of the twentieth century, would abolish wars. There is a difference in the two attitudes. Even Penn, though grappling with the subject in a more personal and concrete way, held somewhat aloof from our modern ultraism.

The comments of George Fox on the suggestion that he himself serve in Cromwell's army sound rather like the words of one who has other work to do and another mission to perform, than those of one to whom this method of settling scores was abhorrent per se. So his well-known saying to his courtier friend, when consulted as to wearing a sword, "Wear it as long as thou canst," was not the utterance of a man who was abhorring the institution of war, but of an apostle of the inner light, of a prophet who pointed every Christian to the teacher within the soul, of the Baptist who called men to the baptism of the Spirit as the only true baptism. Indeed, these inspired men had not yet come to facing the specific evils of war and slavery, but were still combating the spirit that led to all such evils. The true Christian divinity, until now, needed an apologist. Men were imprisoned and beaten for believing in it, notwithstanding Christ's own assurance that "he that speaketh a word against the Holy Ghost it shall not be forgiven him, neither in this world nor in the world to come."

In the first century of Quakerism, then, war was not regarded as a distinct science, or an institution to be condemned or condoned, but simply as the natural expression of man's evil nature.

William Penn, however, through the unique opportunity aforded him by the debt of the Stuart king to his father, the admiral, God having put it into his mind to " beat this spear into a pruning hook," and seize this chance to establish a model government, was brought into more direct and effective contact with government and war than his coadjutors, Fox and Barclay; and it thus happens that the most perfect opportunity in history—the most perfect possible —fell into the hands of a Quaker:—the opportunity to demonstrate, as a ruler, the entire practicability of conducting government without war.

Not only so, but the situation into which the providence of God introduced him threw him into circumstances the most difficult for the preservation of peace, and therefore the most conclusive, when the experiment proved successful; for he was brought face to face—not with civilized and Christian nations, but with painted savages, who had never yet heard the Gospel of Christ. It was in the midst of these that he showed government could be conducted without one drop of blood being shed.

Amid difficult negotiations, questions of intrusion on their territory, and of purchase and sale of it, with people of antipodal customs, Penn contrived to live on terms of perfect justice, in amity and mutual esteem with the native redskins. His neighbors, the other English colonies, were in nightly fear of torch and tomahawk. And yet, for two generations, a province capable of containing ten million souls was governed with conspicuous success without soldiery. The experiment well called " holy " lasted well nigh a century—a full generation after the death of its author,—endured until the peace-loving Friends were ousted from the government of Pennsylvania, and, but for that, might have continued to this day.

But although, soon after the middle of the seventeenth century, the Scotch-Irish and more combative element of the population obtained the mastery of Pennsylvania, the colossal statue of its Quaker founder, surmounting the dome of the metropolis, attests the pride of her people in her founder, and her belief in his unrivaled statesmanship. In this twentieth century the plant that his right hand planted is blossoming out into a world-bloom. The success of the demonstration cannot be gainsaid. No completer proof is practicable than that made by William Penn of the entire feasibility of maintaining a nation without arms, and this perfect experiment stands out unchallenged and shines as a beacon light from the seventeenth century to the twentieth that needs not to be relit. A nation can be, for a nation has been, conducted without arms for three-quarters of a century. On one occasion Lord Baltimore tried to make war upon the colony, and sent an army from the south, but his lordship discovered that it required two to make a quarrel. He found no one to fight, and so marched back again, and the boundary was subsequently settled in peace by Mason and Dixon, for this invasion was on account of a boundary dispute, which is a frequent cause of war.

Fiske attempts to belittle the experiment of Pennsylvania, ascribing the seventy years' peace, not to Penn's efforts to maintain it by justice and conciliation, but to what he calls " Indian politics." It is clear to me that Fiske is mistaken, and that in other hands than Penn's the colony would have been an Aceldama, like those further East. Fiske did not know how complete was the goodwill between Onas and the Indians, nor was he apparently aware that other Friends beside Penn traveled north and south through the wilderness, among the most dangerous aborigines, unmolested and welcomed. They were welcomed because without guile or selfishness they were full of love, and love begets love. The shrewd and penetrating sons of nature would not harm them, and in their presence the tomahawk slumbered.

The New England colonists could not live at peace with the red men, because they themselves were quick to provocation and prompt to arm.

After Penn's return to England his deep interest in the great cause that had so much engrossed his thoughts was undiminished, and in his retirement from society and the world he still devoted his pen to the cause of his divine Master. Ten years after the colony was launched on its voyage of demonstration he gave forth this second memorable contribution toward the permanent peace of the civilized world. The lurid clouds that veiled the sunset of his life had begun to gather around his head. His enemies had temporarily wrested from him his province; they had smirched his irreproachable character with false charges of treason on account of his friendship with King James, and he was in involuntary retirement. It was at the time that he wrote his beautiful " Fruits of Solitude." It was then that he extended his thoughts of peace beyond the limits of Sylvania to the federation of man, and wrote his Essay for the Present and Future Peace of Europe.

The scheme was a great one, greater in its practical than in its theoretical or Quakerly characterization; and it was greater as coming from the same factory as the conclusive experiment in Pennsylvania which was now well under way. The mind that gave forth this essay was the same which inaugurated and ultimately perfected this divine demonstration. It was therefore authoritative on the subject of international peace. Penn's voice was a voice to be heard on this subject; and it would have been heard if the world's ears had been open. But " men love darkness rather than light because their deeds are evil," and with the carnal ear they love the confused noise of battle rather than the " still, small voice."

It was not in the irony of fate, but in the ordering of an all-seeing Providence that William Penn was the offspring of a distinguished admiral in the British navy, who was invested with knighthood for his services in war. This courageous advocate of peace was himself a warrior in his youth, but changed. " Out of the strong came forth sweetness." The evolution was not a sudden one. The familiar portrait in armor, which his grandson, Granville Penn, says is the only portrait ever painted of him, truthfully represents him as a soldier. " His spirit," wrote Granville Penn, in his memoir of Admiral Sir William Penn, " was high and enterprizing; and the forwardness he displayed on the occasion of a mutiny of the soldiers in the castle of Carrickfergus, induced the Duke of Ormond to think of giving him the active command of the company of foot attached to his father's government of the fort of Kinsale." His father's objection perhaps saved him from a military career.

He had already been deeply impressed by the preaching of Thomas Loe, who, like himself, had been an Oxford man, and within the next year after the affair at Carrickfergus he was irresistibly drawn to attend another " conventicle" where the same Friend again preached. For thus participating in a " tumultuous assembly," so called, he was cast into prison. And thus began a faithful service in the Lamb's army, which lasted to the end of his days.

Three years later his father, the admiral, died, and his filial son thus gently refers to his profession of arms: " How far he was a master of his art, both as a general and a seaman, I leave to the observation of his friends, his own constant success, and what hereafter may come to public view of his remarks."

Love and admiration for his father may account for this tepid reference to the military art, but to a certain extent it pervaded his view of the subject. This was on the courtier side of his character. In his opposition to war he was hardly an extremist; or perhaps I should say more accurately, was not violent. He had the inclination of the practical statesman to see all sides of a question. He approved to a certain extent of the use of force, of police, for example.

And when we now come to deal with his scheme for the peace of Europe, we shall find that it contains features which Friends of the present day would regard as inadmissible. The essay is too long for the limits of this occasion, and much of it is occupied by an argument in favor of the plan. It is only needful to refer to two sections, which contain the kernel of it. The author intimates that it was suggested by the design of Henry IV. of France, or of his Minister, Sully, to bring about by force, or forceful diplomacy, a somewhat similar union of the European States to which each should contribute its appropriate quota of a common armament. The main feature of the essay was an imperial Diet, or Parliament, which was to sit once in one, two or three years, before which sovereign assembly should be brought all differences depending between one sovereign and another that cannot be made up by private embassies before the session begins.

The Diet was to represent the nations of Europe, and he proceeds to particularize by naming the number of representatives from each nation. There were only six from England, while Germany was assigned twelve, France ten, Spain ten, and Italy eight, all more than England, which shows the changes time has wrought in the relative importance of these powers. He goes on to say: "And if the Turks and Muscovites are taken in, as seems but fit and just, they will make ten apiece more." "Sweedland" and Poland were each to have four, although the half-barbarous Muscovites have swallowed or partitioned the latter out of existence since.

The remarkable feature of the scheme is found in the following lines, which sound somewhat warlike: "If any of the sovereignties that constitute these imperial states shall refuse to submit their claim or pretentions to them, or to abide and perform the judgment thereof, and seek their remedy by arms, or delay their compliance beyond the time prefixed by their resolutions, all the other sovereignties, united as one strength, shall compel the submission and performance of the sentence, with damages to the suffering party, and charges to the sovereignties that obliged their submission."

He somewhat naively adds: "To be sure Europe would quickly obtain the so much desired and needed peace to her harassed inhabitants; and consequently peace would be secured and confirmed in Europe." Although the last paragraph smacks of "practical politics," possibly somewhat too much, we must allow for the age in which the writer lived, and admit that he is far in advance of that age. If Penn had been more powerful, perhaps if it had not been for Ravaillac's dagger, Europe might have been as far advanced in the direction of peace in 1700 as it has been brought at the House in the Wood in 1900.

It is remarkable that this scheme, which is worthy of The Hague Conference, and is one of the most statesmanlike and feasible propositions ever emanating from a potential source, has not attracted more notice than it has, especially that it did not receive more attention with Henry IV.'s endorsement than it appears to have received, from the publicists of that period. I believe that even William Ladd, the so-called Apostle of Peace, did not mention it in his prize essay (published about 1840) on a "Congress of Nations." Clarkson refers to it briefly; so does Janney; but Hepworth Dixon seems to be the only biographer who has discovered that the plan "attracted much attention at the time." I have not found any reference to it in the English histories. It may be rather presumptuous to claim for William Penn a potential position at the time this essay was published. It was written when he was much under a cloud, indeed when he was actually a prisoner under surveillance in his own lodgings, on account of Fuller's charge of treasonable conspiracy to seat on the throne one of the pretenders.

Penn was finally heard and acquitted by the King himself; but he was scarcely in a position to give him much influence at the time.

I can only briefly revert to the third unique lesson taught by William Penn on the subject of peace and war. It is regarded as vital, even to a nation peaceably disposed, that it should maintain an army for defence, in case of an attack from without. But I have already referred to the originality of the reception of Lord Baltimore's invasion. There was no beating of drums and summoning of minute men by William Penn's forces, no defending of bridges with muskets, no ambushes, no panic.

The slumbering country disarmed the invaders, who were met by grazing herds beside the still waters, against which their arms were valueless; and thus Penn proved the fallacy of the above common assumption, and the futility of armies for defence.

Has he not demonstrated three great facts?—First, that a country can be ruled without war; second, that Europe may safely reduce her armaments by uniting in a Diet and pooling her forces, and, third, that armies are not necessary for defence.

Alas! that the sun of this glorious man should have set in gloomy clouds; but few have left behind them grander memories of duty done, of seed sown, and promise of golden fruitage, with earnest of perfection.

In our estimate of the contributions of William Penn to the long movement against the hydra-headed monster, war, we may safely rank them high on the roll of historic accomplishments. Probably no other man has evolved from his laboratory more practical and conclusive proofs, either of the advantage of abandoning war or of its feasibility. But his glory is of a kind that seeks no blazoned heraldry nor lofty monument; better the simple white stone at Jordan's.

The Chairman: "The Present Position of the International Peace Movement" will now be presented to us in an address by Dr. Benjamin F. Trueblood, of Boston. Dr. Trueblood is well known to you all as the Secretary of the American Peace Society.

THE PRESENT POSITION OF THE INTERNATIONAL PEACE MOVEMENT.

BY BENJAMIN F. TRUEBLOOD, BOSTON.

Remarkable changes have taken place in the world in respect to war since George Fox first " saw " and was " taken up in the love of God," became an " heir of the gospel of peace," was " brought off from outward wars," and began the great gospel peace testimony of which the whole Christian world has learned.

In order to be able to utter the old message of the gospel of peace with freshness and power in our time as he declared it in his, we must know where we are, what are the conditions around us, what conquests of peace have already been made, and where and how the spirit of war still lies entrenched and unsubdued. Seventeenth century methods will not do now. We are facing the demands of a new time, and we should give all diligence to understand its behests.

George Fox did no specialized peace work. The time was not ripe for it. It was against war as such, the sum total of its spirit and deeds, that he let go his broadsides of gospel truth and experience. Peace sentiment had to be made, for as yet there was none. That was largely the task of his day. With the system of war, as a political institution, he did not attempt to deal.

At the middle of the seventeenth century war was substantially perpetual. It raged continuously. No practical means of arresting it was then possible of realization. Men did not wish it arrested. The only thing that had been accomplished toward its diminution was the disappearance in considerable measure of private war, whose brutalities had filled the Middle Ages. Not even this would have gone had there not been plenty of fighting in other forms. The so-called humanizing of war, the lopping off, that is, of some of its incidental cruelties and sufferings, had only just begun, through the influence of Grotius. Nothing had been done toward lessening the practice of duelling. International war was not more prevalent than civil war, which raged everywhere and kept every country of Europe distracted and laid waste with fire and sword. George Fox himself, after his majority, lived through three civil wars, one of which lasted nine years.

But now, after two hundred and fifty years, how different the circumstances! Christianity, education, commercial development, progress in science, in economic knowledge, in political institutions, in modes of communication and travel, have wrought marvelous changes. Private war is no longer heard of. Few people now know what it was. The duel, as a serious life-and-death encounter, has disappeared in large measure from civilized countries. Civil war has practically passed away in what we call Christendom, with the exception of parts of Latin America, where it remains as a savage sort of spectacular social distraction. Races and peoples occupying the same territories have ceased fighting and been compacted in various ways into settled nationalities, within which social order reigns and the institutions of law dispose of what few quarrels still remain. Large sections of human society and great areas of territory have thus been brought into what is practically perpetual peace. Only international wars and those for territorial or commercial expansion still remain. Even these are much less frequent than formerly.

If peacemakers are to do their work intelligently in our time and not waste their strength beating the air, they must acquaint themselves with the facts of this large elimination of war already accomplished and not paint the world any longer in seventeenth century colors. Recognition of the remarkable gain which has been made gives strong practical ground for insisting that international and colonial wars also may just as easily be abolished, and that it is no credit to either the intelligence or the moral character of the civilized powers that such wars have not already been made impossible.

Since the seventeenth century the development of peace sentiment and its organization have been no less remarkable than the decline of war. The two have been, in fact, different sides of the same movement; for it is impossible that war should have declined unless there had been a sentiment against it, expressing itself effectively in one way or another.

In the seventeenth century, and even in the eighteenth, there was no organized, co-operative peace work, unless we call that of the Friends co-operative. There were not enough workers at any given time to co-operate. Henry IV., Crucé, Grotius, George Fox, Rheinfels, William Penn, and in the next century, St. Pierre, Locke, Leibnitz, Montesquieu, Condorcet, Turgot, Rousseau, Adam Smith, Lessing, Herder, Bentham, Kant, did their work each in his own way and practically alone. These were great men, and, with their philosophic plans of perpetual peace, they made a great record, but no popular movement gathered about them. To-day, such has been the transformation of sentiment that there are now no less than four hundred and fifty peace associations, each with a membership of scores, hundreds or thousands, doing their work without intermission in many countries. They count among their adherents numbers of the most capable men living. But these societies do not represent a thousandth part of the sentiment which is now for peace, some of it working effectually in other organizations, and some of it lying around loose and going to waste.

There are now regular international peace congresses, undreamed of even a century ago, national and local arbitration conferences, a great peace union of many hundreds of members of the national parliaments, a permanent international peace bureau, an international law association of distinguished jurists and publicists working for arbitration and other means of promoting more amicable relations between nations. There are also distinguished specialists like John de Bloch devoting their time and their fortune to the destruction of war and its implements, and eminent authors, read all round the world, bringing war rapidly under the ban of literature.

Thus peace sentiment has not only developed very greatly, but has also reached a state of powerful and permanent organization. Of this fact every friend of peace ought to inform himself, to acquaint himself with the history of the movement, and in some way to connect himself permanently with it. To attempt to do peace work single handed and alone in our day, without co-operating with the body of organized laborers, is as serious a mistake as if one should attempt single handed to build his own house, gather his food and clothe himself. It is a bit of saintly ignorance or egotism of which too many sincere friends of the cause are guilty. Individual work, which everybody ought to find, and even the work of particular societies, can be most effectually done when it is done in fellowship with the work of others.

Since the days of Grotius and George Fox international association, then little known except in matters of war, has developed marvelously in all sorts of peaceful ways. Travel, trade, swift communication by ship and wire, the intermingling of peoples and races, treaties and conventions for various common interests like the Postal Union, into which every organized government in the world has entered, have made the world already one neighborhood, have awakened a wide sense of brotherhood, and contributed immensely to the promotion of general peace. The present status of international relations in these matters is a much better gauge of the gain which peace has made than the sum of all the peace associations organized or peace and arbitration conferences held, important as these are as agencies. These associations and conferences are simply the prophetic scouts of the great societary movement which is coming steadily and irresistibly on.

No less remarkable has been the progress since the seventeenth century in the application of pacific methods in the settlement of disputes between nations. The need of such methods began to take deep hold of men's minds from the beginning of that century. Henry IV., in the very dawn of the century, advocated, as is well known, a federation of Christian Europe. Grotius, in 1625, pleaded with the Christian rulers to employ arbitration instead of such incessant and ruinous fighting. Crucé, in 1623, deeply affected by the continual shedding of blood for the most trifling causes, and by the consequent ruin of commerce, advanced a project for an international tribunal, the first known to have been made. Hesse-Rheinfels, in 1666, proposed a "society of sovereigns" for preventing war. Pufendorf, six years later, in his "Law of Nature and of Nations," advanced a similar scheme. William Penn, in 1693, worked out his famous plan for a diet or parliament of nations. Early in the eighteenth century Saint Pierre, following up the work of his predecessors, elaborated in great detail a design for perpetual peace. In 1758 Vattel, the distinguished Swiss jurist, again brought forward a project of arbitration. Toward the close of the century Bentham, in England, pleaded for a European fraternity in the form of a common tribunal; and Kant, in Germany, advanced the bold idea of an international state through the process of federation.

These plans of perpetual peace or projects for the prevention of war were the highwater mark of political and humanitarian thinking when the nineteenth century opened. During that century, just closed, we see the principle of arbitration, over which these great minds had been working, gradually blossom out in practice, like a magnificent century plant. Plans for a congress and court of nations continued to be put forward by men of the highest rank —John Stuart Mill, William Ladd, David Dudley Field, Bluntschli, Leone Levi, Professor Corsi, Lemonnier, Hornby, and others; by the Peace Congress, the Interparliamentary Union, the International Law Association, by bar associations and by distinguished government ministers. But, while this work was going on, the governments themselves fell under the influence of the rising tide of opinion and took to arbitrating their controversies.

During the century just closed nearly one hundred temporary tribunals and arbitral commissions were established for the adjustment of disputes, some of them disposing of several cases. In the second decade of the century three cases were thus adjusted. In the third decade five. By the end of the century so common had become the practice of arbitrating disputes between nations that the number of cases had run up to just under two hundred. More than sixty of these were in the decade just closed, or an average of over six per year for the whole ten years; and the nations participating in them number thirty-seven. This is a record of extraordinary historical significance, and yet so little is it appreciated or even known that it has found its way into not a single well-known book of history, the most of it into none at all.

While these arbitrations were taking place, the movement for a permanent international tribunal, which began to take definite shape in the first half of the century, developed to such an extent that it became the chief feature of the entire peace movement in the decade from which we have just passed. It was supported by all the peace organizations, by the Interparliamentary Union, the International Law Association, by bar associations, by the great organizations of women, by social clubs and religious unions, by influential sections of the press, by legislators and diplomats, by parliaments, and at last by presidents, kings and emperors. It grew in its last stages into a veritable crusade of great extent and power.

Out of these three long centuries of peace thinking and planning, of organized peace effort and the practice of arbitration by governments came the Hague Conference and the setting up of the Permanent International Court of Arbitration. This august institution, in which nineteen powers, practically the whole civilized world, are already represented, formally declared open on the 9th of April last, was not the work of the Czar of Russia, nor of any knightly crusader, nor of any bar association or particular organization. Nicholas II. was the providential instrument of calling the Conference. He did his great deed at the right time and in the right way. But when the Conference met, with three whole centuries of momentum behind it, it proceeded to do the work which those centuries had prepared for it, as if the Czar of Russia had never been born.

The Hague Court, now only just eight months old, has not yet done any business (the Supreme Court of the United States did no actual work for two years and a half), but it is itself the grandest piece of business in a political way that has ever been done. It is not a failure from the fact that it has not yet had opportunity to do anything. It never can be a failure, however it may have to be supplemented or even superseded by something more perfect. The Pan-American treaty of 1890, never ratified, was not a failure. The Anglo-American treaty of 1897, rejected by the Senate, was not a failure. The Italo-Argentine treaty of the same year, never formally adopted, it seems, was not a failure. Nothing done in the historic development of a great principle is ever a failure. The peace movement which has such a splendid history of three centuries behind it—to go no farther back—and of which the Permanent Arbitration Court is the consummate present expression, has yet wider sweeps of triumph before it. Of the appearance of these when the time has ripened, through the workings of the Divine Providence and the faithful efforts of the friends of the cause, no one who believes in the omnipotence of God, of truth and of love, will have the least doubt.

It seems, at first view, an incomprehensible anomaly that, while war has so much decreased and the cause of peace has made such large gains, the standing armaments of the nations have reached such a point of development in size and expensiveness as at the present time. But these very armaments, ludicrous as the thought may seem, are in their way an evidence of the growth and spread of peace. They would have been impossible two centuries ago, when every part of society was kept exhausted by continual fighting. Their economic possibility lies in the vast increase of wealth which the general disappearance of civil war has given opportunity to produce. They are feeding upon and devouring the fruits of peace and without it could not continue to exist.

But these armaments are also an evidence that the old brutal spirit of greed, hatred and violence still survives from the past. They have primarily no relation to the internal affairs of the nations. Their motive is the surviving greed, ambition and hatred, which, since their citizens ceased to fight among themselves, the nations have turned more fully against one another and let loose in such totally un-Christian and atrocious ways upon weak and ill-civilized peoples.

These bloated and frightfully costly armaments are at the same time a conspicuous evidence of the surviving moral stupidity and primitive brainlessness of these great internally peaceful groups of men, in not practicing toward one another the common sense which they have learned to use within themselves, and in destroying in this colossal way the wealth which they are so anxious and careful to create in their internal life and by foreign trade.

The considerations which I have adduced are sufficient to indicate clearly the present position of the peace movement, and of the great evil which it is seeking to abolish. They also point out the specific ways in which our task at the present time may be most effectually performed. These may be summarized in a few sentences:

1. We may fairly insist that the large elimination of war which has already taken place gives just ground for believing that all war will ultimately be done away; that we are not acting as enthusiasts and dreamers when we thus declare, but are reasoning upon the most solid historical grounds; and that it is those who maintain that war will never be entirely abolished who are irrational and sentimental.

2. Since, speaking in general terms, only international wars and those for territorial and commercial expansion remain, we should direct our chief efforts against these, instead of against war in the abstract, and should endeavor to make it plain that at this age of the world's advancement they are wholly needless, economically unprofitable and in every way unworthy of nations professing a high degree of civilization, love of right and liberty, and claiming to be guided by Christian principles.

3. We should make every possible effort to secure the establishment of the reign of law instead of brute force in the realm of international affairs as it has been so largely established within the nations, and should maintain against all comers that there is no more reason in our time for international anarchy than for anarchy and civil war within the civilized States.

4. We must let our testimony ring out straight and uncompromising against the growing military and naval establishments of our time, as entirely out of date, as economically ruinous and morally debasing to the populations of the countries, and as having now no ground for existence except that of greed, jealousy and hatred worthy only of barbarians.

5. We must throw our influence at all possible points toward a larger friendly association and co-operation of the nations—in trade, in travel and residence, in treaties and conventions for promoting common interests, in scientific and hygienic investigations, and the like.

6. In view of the remarkable success of arbitration the past century, we ought to declare in unhesitating terms that the settlement by this means of two hundred controversies of nearly every conceivable kind, in every one of which the difficulty has been finally and permanently disposed of, leaves no ground for believing that there is any sort of international dispute which may not be arbitrated without the least loss of honor or prestige.

7. We are fully warranted in claiming that the civilized nations, by the setting up of the Hague Court, have cut from beneath them the last ground for believing in the necessity of war, and that they cannot hereafter appeal to brute force without self-condemnation and self-stultification.

8. We must recognize, enter heartily into and co-operate in all possible ways with the organized peace propaganda, as the most effective way of fitting ourselves for our own personal work and making our voices heard in behalf of this greatest of all social movements.

While doing our work along these specific practical lines, marked out for us by the general condition of the times in which we live, we shall have opportunity to work in at every turn all the old ethical and Christian arguments against war, which will never lose their force and appropriateness until the sound of the last cannon has died away and the last fit of international passion has spent itself.

THE CHAIRMAN: The papers which we have heard this evening will now be open for discussion. The discussion will be opened by William C. Dennis, who has just been chosen by Albert K. Smiley as the new Secretary of the Lake Mohonk International Arbitration Conference.

WILLIAM C. DENNIS: Dr. Trueblood has referred to the fact that private war is a thing of the past. It seemed to me that it would be interesting to consider for a short time the method by which private war disappeared, as this may possibly throw some light on the way in which public war will finally disappear.

There were at least four stages in the history of the disappearance of private war. When our Saxon ancestors wandered over the forests of Germany, private war was entirely unregulated; it was their method of doing justice between man and man. There were no rules; when one man injured another, the family of the injured man went and took vengeance on the wrongdoer in any way they saw fit. They could surprise a man at any time of day or night and kill him. That seemed a little bit hard; so afterwards private war was regulated. A rule was established that if one man had murdered another the relatives of the injured man could not go in the night-time and attack the one who had done the injury; they must go in the daytime. Thus private vengeance began to be regulated. There is an old English statute that if one man accidentally fell out of a tree and killed another man by falling on him the relatives of the latter must fall out of the same tree on him and kill him.

Finally, the *State* got to be a little stronger, and courts were set up as an alternative for private war—not as a substitute, but as an alternative. An injured man might proceed to take vengeance according to the rules, unless the offender offered to buy himself off. In that event the case went to the court. That was the third stage, where the court and the private war were alternatives.

Then, of course, came the last stage, when private war was finally abolished by the court taking its place. That was the history of the disappearance of private war.

Public war has so far followed a similar course. In the first place it was unregulated; there were no rules. Prisoners were killed in the early days, perhaps even eaten. Then they came to be finally sold as slaves. Still, there were no rules. Then came Grotius and the Laws of War; war passed into the stage of regulation. Now we have just reached the third stage—the stage where we have an alternative to war, the Court of International Arbitration. In the time of Henry II., or just previous to his time, the courts were itinerant; they were not regular, stated courts at permanent places. Henry set up in addition a permanent Court of Appeal. We have just done the same thing in the matter of arbitration between nations. Heretofore we have simply had tribunals of arbitration made up for the occasion; now we have a central, permanent court, not yet compulsory.

There is still one great step to be taken, to make the resort to the court compulsory, as it is now in private affairs. I was talking the other day along this line with a member of the Society of Friends, a man who does not believe very much in the immediate future of international arbitration. He pointed out the fact that private war was quite limited; that the two individuals who engaged in it belonged at least to the same tribe, that there was some connection between them. He went on and pointed out that private war did not cease until a strong central power was established. "Now," he said, "if my analogy proves anything, it proves that before we can get rid of war between nations there will have to be a strong international political State to stand behind a tribunal of arbitration," and he thought it would be a long time before we came to this stage, and until that time the future of arbitration was very doubtful indeed.

It does not seem to me that he has met all that the analogy requires. In the first place, we have already a sort of international State. That is what we have been hearing about to-day. In the times of the Saxons, England was a heptarchy; now the world is something of that sort. The Dual Alliance and the Triple Alliance have come very near reducing the warlike unities of the world to three; and however bad they are, it is better to have them reduced to three than to have thousands, as there were in the past. The concert of Europe, imperfect as it is, unsatisfactory as it has been, has at least accustomed the nations to acting together. We have thus the germ of a political, international State. We have been hearing to-day that we have in process of formation an international State in a different sense, namely, socially, religiously, industrially, commercially. We have in that way an international State such as our Saxon ancestors never dreamed of. National bounds were then conclusive; society did not go outside the State; it did not usually go outside the community. Nominally the church went outside of the State, but not very much. Now, as has been repeatedly pointed out to-day, society is international. Labor unions are international; your laborers in Germany do not want to rejoice over the misfortunes of laborers in France. However much we may regret that close lines are being drawn between capital and labor, it at least has its advantage; it is abolishing the national lines. Thus we do have an international State, socially, politically, religiously and industrially in the sense they did not have in the days of our Saxon ancestors.

History does not have to move exactly in circles; it may sometimes move in spirals. The unification that we have had in the past has been by force. England was made into one country by force; we got up to the present state of unification largely by might. We shall not get the unification of the future by force, but by consent. I do not think it is physically possible to get it by force. There will never again be such a favorable opportunity as in the time of Napoleon to establish a world-empire by force. Democracy is making it so that one man cannot get the start of the world as Napoleon did; all the rest are acquiring the intelligence to combine and stop it. Probably no great nation will ever be defeated worse than France was defeated by Germany in 1870, and yet Germany never thought of annexing France. The war would have been going on yet if Germany had attempted to do anything like that. If the unification of the future is to come by consent, it is natural that it should not come first to the executive. A world-State made by force would naturally come to the executive first; but a world-State made by consent would naturally move along the lines of least resistance and come through the organization of the judiciary.

For all these reasons it seems to me that the analogy of the abolition of public war along the same general lines as that of private war does not require that we have any international State in a political sense before we see the success of an international tribunal like that at The Hague.

This way of the judiciary first is the Quaker way, the method of William Penn. Two hundred years ago William Penn made the first proposition, so far as I know, for a strictly judicial court. Other people planned national councils, but they were more or less political or religious schemes. He proposed a court, pure and simple; and we as Friends ought to take up the work that he initiated; we ought to stand behind and promote the one practical step which can be made now, which is the supporting of the Hague tribunal. Our immediate duty is to see that it is made absolutely impossible for this country to go to war without submitting to that tribunal any dispute which it may hereafter have with any nation.

The Chairman: We have now time for four five-minute speeches.

Joel Borton: The object of this gathering is to confer in reference to the outlook for peace, and it is no doubt an opportune time for this. I have wished since we have heard these excellent papers and discussions that we had the ears of the world. We who are assembled here are all peace people; but we have been sleeping, and it is time that we were aroused and aroused somebody else. Had we been aroused six years ago, as we are at the present time and have been in the past three years, there would have been, in my judgment, no war. The outlook for peace at the present time, however, is to me quite encouraging. As was said this morning, nations do not care now to meet one another in war; the destruction of life, the loss of property, are too great. Again our close connection with other nations by commerce, by religion and education is an indication that we cannot afford to go to war. The manner in which nations are tied together to-day by the cable makes us no longer individual nations; the people of the world are one people. War, for these reasons, must cease.

The Hague Conference, the International Court of Arbitration, already referred to, is to me one of the greatest steps in the right direction. But all is not yet done. What we need to do is to arouse ourselves to action and to stir up the sleeping sentiment about us. I know of no better motto for us than those words of the late ex-President Harrison, uttered in New York, that " Christ in the heart and His love in the nation " is the only cure for all the ills that confront us to-day.

Howard M. Jenkins: I wish to take only about a minute to say that in my judgment the presentation made by most of our historical writers, by most of those who have had the attention of the American people and of other people, in regard to the Indians of Pennsylvania, has been made with the intention of detracting from the fame of William Penn. This is very largely due to the genius of that prince among American historians, Francis Parkman. Parkman has been followed by pretty much everybody else. He took his ideas from two sources: first, the New England idea, which was that the Indian was a heathen and ought to be exterminated; and, second, from the presentation by the writers of the State of New York, particularly Albert Gallatin, who had the idea that the Indians of Pennsylvania were always and entirely subject to the Five Nations of New York, and were in general such a poor lot that Penn's living in peace with them was no particular credit to him.

That is the theory which runs through all our history of Penn's work with the Indians, and against which the writers of Pennsylvania have either not contended at all, or have contended in vain.

It is an illusion; it is not true; I think it is totally unfounded in fact. The Indians of the Delaware Valley were much like the other Indians of the United States. Penn and the early Friends, the early colonists of Pennsylvania, lived in peace with them because they adopted a true and honest and generous peace method.

WILLIAM L. PRICE: It seems to me that those old sages made their pious claim rightly when they treated war as only the negation of the things they should stand for. They were constructive people; their religion and their economics were full of construction; they stood for something positive, something in advance of the other people. Now it seems to me that for the Society of Friends to meet in Conference of this kind and merely send out the same old message against war, does not put it on constructive grounds at all, or in advance of its always understood position. It means almost nothing simply to proclaim again what the Society has always stood for. It would mean much if this Conference or any similar conference should take up the lines of constructive, economic thought that have been intimated here—questions of broader trade association, and more perfect relations between the nations. It would be a constructive work and one on which the Friends could start the world if they would take up the peace message of our President who was shot, his last and greatest message, in which he said, that too long we had stood alone, and the time had come when we must reach out our hands to all the world. I think that shot should go around the world from this kind of convention far more than a mere peace proposition. Then there is another point, and that is, that "The kingdom of heaven is at hand" means something, and has always meant something. The trouble is that we have always expected the kingdom of heaven to come from without; whereas Jesus meant that it was at hand in the sense that it was in the hands of the people to whom He spoke, that it was in their power to bring it in then, not after awhile, not after growth, but immediately. That was always true, and it is still true.

The Conference then adjourned, after a moment of reverent silence, to meet in the Twelfth Street Friends' Meeting House at ten o'clock on Seventh-day morning.

Seventh Session.

Seventh-day Morning, Twelfth Month 14th.

The Conference gathered at 10 o'clock, on Seventh-day morning, in the Twelfth Street Meeting House, with Arthur Perry, of Boston, Mass., presiding.

The session opened with a period of devotion, during which vocal prayer was offered by Anna Braithwaite Thomas, of Baltimore, and remarks were made by Isaac Wilson, of Canada, in which he expressed his gratification that the Conference had met and that the Friends were thus trying in a more practical way than previously to carry out their high profession, and his desire that all might abide in the spirit of living prayer, that the power of the life of peace might be individually realized.

The Chairman: I esteem it a privilege to preside at a session of this Conference, and thus to some extent be identified with its work and its purpose, for its work is the re-statement and upholding of the time-honored testimony of Friends in behalf of peace, and its purpose to consider ways and means of doing away with the horrors of war by abolishing war itself.

Time and again the Meetings for Sufferings or Executive Meetings of our several bodies have addressed memorials on this subject to those in political power, which have been as beacon lights on the pathway to peace.

The present Conference affords opportunity for the re-examination of the foundation of our peace principles, and the issuance to the world of an appeal for the support of international arbitration. We are accused of having high ideals and impractical theories. But history has in many instances demonstrated the wisdom as well as the possibility of referring international disputes to special courts of arbitration, and to-day the great nations of the earth have united in establishing the Hague *Permanent* Court of International Arbitration. The practical and sensible course for the advocates of peace is to bring every possible influence to bear to secure the reference to this court of international claims which have failed to be settled throught the ordinary diplomatic channels.

It is also important that we uphold the hands of those in authority in the administration of the affairs of our country who openly proclaim that they desire that peace shall prevail. It is an old adage that responsibility sobers and steadies one's judgment, and it is a well-known fact that the great rulers of to-day seek to avoid war, and resort to it only when forced by an overwhelming force of popular opinion; and even when nation does go to war with nation, each seeks to throw the responsibility upon the other.

Another practical work, then, in the direction of peace is the creation of a wholesome, right and pure public sentiment upon this question. Papers have been read before this Conference bearing directly upon this suggestion, namely, the necessity of educating the rising generation to right ideas of force and patriotism. In this connection I am tempted to add an incident or two in illustration and support of the ground taken in Dr. Thomas's very excellent paper on the "Christian Idea of Force." In the late civil war many Friends were drafted, among them a young man, who, while confined in camp pending the disposition of his case, refused to join in military duty, and for continued disobedience was ordered to be shot. When brought before the men who were to execute him, he uttered these words: "Father, forgive them, for they know not what they do." The soldiers refused to shoot, and the mounted officer, in his anger, attempted to drive his horse over the man, but without success, and he was ordered back to quarters. Who, in this incident, was the real hero? Who displayed true courage? Who had real force?

Again, a father and son, drafted into British military service many years ago and refusing military duty, were condemned to be shot. The woman who was to lose husband and son sat between them, holding the hand of each when the fatal shots were fired; where was the courage then—in the soldiers behind the guns, or in that wife and mother and those heroes who gave up life rather than violate conscience? We do not mean to misrepresent or belittle the courage or patriotism of soldiers, but these are the great truths that we want to teach our children. We do believe in force, and we do believe in courage, but the greatest force is the power of the Spirit, and the highest courage is that of self-sacrifice.

Agitation and education, co-operation with all who sincerely desire that peace shall prevail, will advance our cause. I trust that the committee will act favorably upon the suggestion that this Conference send resolutions of sympathy to President Roosevelt, assuring him of our confidence in the sincerity of his purpose to preserve peace, and of our desire to uphold him therein. We cannot endorse all the methods by which some would maintain peace, but we can commend the purpose in view. President Sharpless showed us last night how almost impossible it is even for Friends to be absolutely consistent in their testimony against war. Let us be charitable to those who cannot go the full length with us, and work with them as far as they will go. I do not look to see war abolished simply because it is wrong and unchristian, but because the time is coming when, even from a worldly point of view, it will be inexpedient, and the very selfishness and avarice which were once the cause of wars will then compel peace.

THE CHAIRMAN: The first paper on the program this morning is by Henry W. Wilbur, of New York city; subject, " The Duty of the Christian Church at the Present Time in the Movement to Abolish War." As he has not yet arrived we will take up the next paper, by President James B. Unthank, Wilmington College, Ohio, upon the subject, " Mistakes and Failures of Friends in their Peace Work."

MISTAKES AND FAILURES OF FRIENDS IN THEIR PEACE WORK.

BY PRESIDENT JAMES B. UNTHANK, WILMINGTON COLLEGE, OHIO.

To make the mistakes and failures of one's own denomination the subject of inquiry and discussion seems such an ungracious act that I hesitate to undertake it. Most of us who are here to-day owe so much to the Society in which we were born and reared, and look upon it with so much love and veneration, that the idea of such investigation suggests ingratitude and disloyalty.

It would be a much pleasanter task to recount the story of our successes and achievements. And yet if Friends still have a mission in the world, if they are called in the providence of God to serve the cause of righteousness and truth in the future, there may be more profit in resolutely and dispassionately considering our mistakes and failures than in congratulating ourselves on what we have already accomplished for the world. It is, therefore, in no spirit of carping or criticism that I undertake the task assigned me; and if any statements made or sentiments expressed in this paper seem severe or disagreeable they are not made with any feeling of unkindness or irreverence, but with a sincere desire to tell the truth and promote the cause we have met to consider.

I shall not discuss the subject from the historic standpoint, as that would be more curious than practical; but I desire to treat it more from the philosophic standpoint with the purpose to show if possible the causes of our failure.

In the first place, then, there is one principal mistake that Friends have made with respect to their attitude concerning this peace movement, and all the others have grown out of it and are subordinate to it. There have been two main causes of this mistake, as I understand them, and it shall be my purpose to show how these causes have operated to produce their results.

The principal mistake has been in a failure to inaugurate and carry on energetic, well-organized and persistent efforts to disseminate peace principles. Our efforts have been too desultory and uncertain to produce lasting effects.

The mission of Friends has always been, at least until recent years, largely directed to professing Christians rather than to those outside the churches. Our distinctive work has been educational and reformatory rather than evangelistic. George Fox's message was primarily addressed to church members, " professors," as he was accustomed to style them; and early Friends were largely gathered from the established Church and the various dissenting bodies of that day. Ever since that time the idea that took such strong hold upon the founders that they held advanced views upon certain essential doctrines of Christianity, which were neglected by others, has prevailed and still persists to a large degree.

This being the case, it could hardly be otherwise than that our mission, as we apprehend it, should be to enlighten the conscience of those professing Christ's name, and bring them up to higher standards of faith and practice rather than to increase the number of nominal Christians. In some of the questions upon which we took high ground we have had large influence and have been mainly instrumental in effecting several important reforms in religious and social matters.

We have done much to bring about the separation of Church and State, thus securing religious toleration and freedom for all denominations. The repeal of conventicle acts, the abolition of tithing taxes, of judicial oaths, of enforced military service, have been largely due to the efforts of Friends.

Our influence in some of these movements has been out of all proportion to our numerical strength, and affords just ground for that pleasant retrospect in which we are somewhat wont to indulge. The question naturally arises, Why have we been able to accomplish so much in these directions while in the matter under consideration by this Conference we have achieved so little? I take it for granted, of course, that at least partial failure in our peace work is conceded by all. Certainly no well-informed person, no matter how strong his Quaker proclivities, will assert that we have done all that we might have done and ought to have done to promote this great reform. The reason for this difference in results lies partly, I think, in the fundamental difference between the two cases, so that the means and methods used successfully in one case were wholly inapplicable to the other. Failure to see this distinction led naturally and inevitably to a failure to adapt the means used to the end to be obtained.

The efforts of early Friends were primarily directed against religious oppression in its various forms. They were zealous and aggressive in advocating the right of religious freedom for themselves and other dissenters. This brought upon them the violent opposition of the ecclesiastical and civil authorities. They soon found themselves confronted, in Mr. Cleveland's phrase, " by a condition instead of a theory."

As Friends they could not forcibly resist the civil law, nor could they conscientiously obey its requirements. The only thing they could do was to go to jail, and the only thing the authorities could do was to send them there. Here was a situation in which the

Friends had the decided advantage of their opponents, although it may have appeared quite the reverse. But it was a situation exactly suited to Quaker tactics, to use a military phrase. Thirteen thousand Quakers in English jails for conscience' sake, with an indefinite number of others ready to follow their example, was too strong a protest against intolerance to go unheeded. The authorities were utterly nonplussed by the non-resisting Friends, who, however, showed no signs of weakening in regard to their main contention. The right demanded must be conceded or larger jails must be built. They chose to grant toleration as the easiest, most practical solution of the difficulty, and so Friends won their case. Thus our first and greatest conquests were won by meekly and patiently suffering for a conviction. Thus we had early stamped upon us by the very conditions of our origin that peculiar disposition that has since characterized us as an organization, to wit: a genius for suffering rather than for action. If Friends could promote a cause by going to prison, by standing in the pillory, by suffering the spoiling of their goods, they were always ready and sometimes apparently anxious to do so.

But these qualities, it will be observed, are passive rather than active, and can only be useful in promoting truth under certain well-defined conditions. They are in marked contrast with that aggressive activity which characterized Fox and his co-laborers in that earlier stage of our historic development that preceded the persecution. Since the first generation of Friends passed away it has been their sufferings that have been commended and held up for approval as a shining example. We have heard little of their aggressive zeal and energetic activity; this seems to have been lost sight of in our excessive admiration for their patient virtues. So thoroughly then have we become imbued with the idea of the value of meekness, patience, forbearance and suffering, so inwoven have been these virtues into our organic structure that it becomes a question whether we are longer capable of that high and noble enthusiasm, that strong and powerful impulse to activity, that ardor and zeal for positive convictions that must characterize the individual and the Church whose mission is reform. Advanced ideas, combatting, as they often must, traditions hoary with age, ignorance dense and widespread, selfishness comfortable and conservative, and in fact every form of human weakness and depravity must be promoted and disseminated by other and more active agencies.

I am not disparaging or under-valuing these noble qualities. I honor and respect them as essential to the reformer; but unless they are combined with more active virtues they are of little worth. A man must first be aggressive enough to get himself hated sufficiently to be thrown into jail before he can help a cause very much by suffering for it in that way. A mere desire to go to prison, to become a martyr, may indicate a very morbid and unhealthy mental condition. These things are only the incidents and accidents in the life of him who works for the promotion of some worthy cause. Really there is not now, nor has there been in English-speaking countries for many years much opportunity to suffer in the cause of peace. War is a temporary, sporadic condition of society, not a chronic or normal one. To oppose war in the abstract as wrong in theory would not be objected to anywhere. To refuse to perform military service in a country where armies are raised by conscription may be considered as criminal and punished as such, but it can hardly be regarded as a protest against war itself. To oppose a particular war when in progress may become treason and be punished as such; but it is not likely to have much weight, if any, against the war system. War is an evil that must be corrected by educational methods, by appeals to the higher and nobler instincts of human nature, by inculcating sound principles of morality, by creating in the public mind a truer sense of justice, by convincing public sentiment not only of its inherent immorality, but also of its utter unreasonableness as an expedient; and this educational work must be carried on in time of peace while the public mind is not inflamed by those passions and prejudices that render all appeals to reason and the finer sensibilities futile and vain.

Here has been for the past two hundred years and more a fine opportunity for the exercise of those active and aggressive qualities that characterized the first Quakers, but which seem to have died out when the first generation passed away. The great mistake which Friends have made in their peace work is that they have not worked at it. The only reason why a movement of such transcendent importance, one that is sustained by the best interpretations of Christianity, by the purest morality, by the most weighty considerations of equity and expediency has not made more progress is that it has not been preached with that enthusiasm and eloquence and logic that it deserves.

We as Friends must bear our share of this responsibility, for we have been the natural and avowed champions of this doctrine for two centuries and a half, and we have not produced that impression on society that we ought to have done—have not come up to the measure of our great opportunity.

Here was a cause worthy of the best efforts we could have put forth; worthy of our wisest counsels, of our clearest thinking; a cause that appeals to every high instinct in human nature, to every manly virtue, to every chivalrous feeling; a cause whose success means the well being of millions of human beings, whose failure or postponement means untold misery and distress to the innocent and helpless victims of war; a cause which deserves the most unselfish devotion and the most energetic support, and yet it has failed to arouse us to any high pitch of enthusiasm or action. During the period covered by our history the cause has made great strides forward, to be sure; but I regret to feel that we have not even contributed our share of the efforts and sacrifices that have produced this progress. Why do I think so? Because the evidence of such service is wanting in the history of our Society. We could not have been as active and energetic as we should have been without making our mark in history. Where are our great names, distinguished by their learning and eloquence, and glorified by their devotion to this cause? Where is that body of noble literature that ought to have grown up amongst us in our efforts to promote so noble a reform? We shall search for both in vain.

I have now given what may be termed the historic reason for our failure to fulfill that great mission as a reform organization that seemed especially marked out for us by the hand of Providence, and of which Friends have been dimly conscious through all these years. I propose now to give what may be regarded as a sort of constitutional reason, based as it is on the inherent nature of Quakerism itself.

Now it may be necessary for me, for fear of being misunderstood, to preface this part of the paper by the statement that I am a genuine Quaker. I accept and believe most of the essential doctrines of Friends as I understand them, and do not desire to be understood as speaking from the standpoint of a hostile critic.

The second cause of our failure to inaugurate and push forward an energetic and vigorous campaign against the war system is to be found in the misunderstanding or perversion or misapplication of some of our favorite doctrines. Any truth may be exaggerated or extended beyond proper limits, and thus become grave and even fatal error. And the most spiritual truths seem most liable to this abuse. Take the doctrine of peace itself which we have met to consider. I am not at all certain but that Friends have carried their opposition to carnal warfare to such extremes that they have made it apply even in the spiritual realm as well; and that practically they have become so peaceful, so inoffensive, that they are even opposed to an energetic, uncompromising warfare in favor of truth. It is supposed that we belong to the general Church Militant on earth, that though the weapons of our warfare are not carnal but spiritual they are mighty through God to the pulling down of strongholds, and that we are engaged in actual contest against the powers of darkness and sin.

The Christian life is a warfare and we are not to allow our disbelief in the use of carnal weapons to dull the edge of our opposition to error and wickedness, nor are we to slacken our ardor for truth from fear we may incur somebody's displeasure.

Friends have never been in danger perhaps of committing the error of the man in the story who wanted peace so much that he expressed himself as being determined to have it, even if he had to fight for it.

The doctrine which has above all others, perhaps, distinguished Friends is that of the immediate influence and guidance of the Holy Spirit. It has always been regarded by us as a particularly sacred truth. It is the *sine qua non* of our theology; and yet it is particularly open to misconception and misapplication.

I doubt if there has been any mistake from which we have suffered more in our peace work and our work along other lines than from the wrong notions we have entertained concerning this doctrine.

In the first place, this claim to immediate revelation has developed a tendency amongst us to exaggerate, if I may use a term so strong, the supernatural element in moral and religious matters, and has led us to depreciate and discredit the ordinary means and methods by which desirable ends may be promoted. Too exclusive dependence upon divine guidance and wisdom may lead to a neglect of the natural processes of reaching judgments and determining right causes of action.

I fear we have been so jealous of this doctrine that we have been wont, at least in the past, to look with distrust upon superior natural endowments, and especially to regard intellectual culture and training as dangerous because incompatible with deep spirituality. In matters of a purely secular nature we try in all our undertakings to adapt the means to the end to be accomplished. We study the case in order to discover its nature and difficulties. No use of our powers of observation, of investigation, of analysis, of reasoning, appears to us out of place in such a matter. We know that such a method of procedure is immeasurably better than dependence upon momentary impulses or fortuitous circumstances.

When we come to matters religious or moral we throw aside our common sense, discard ordinary methods and especially disclaim any use of our rational faculties, on the ground that they are inadequate to these higher purposes. This may be quite true, but it does not follow because the natural powers are insufficient that they are therefore useless. They are to be supplemented, not superseded, and only when we have exhausted ordinary means for accomplishing noble ends and aims have we any reason to expect the extraordinary and supernatural to be supplied. The two are in no way antagonistic, but harmonious. Abuse of this doctrine has led to many false notions concerning things sacred and profane. There is really no ground for the distinction so often made in the minds of many between the ordinary and natural forces and what may be termed spiritual forces so far as their sacredness is concerned. They both have the same origin and both are doubtless equally approved for the specific purpose for which they were intended. I think our false ideas, therefore, of immediate revelation have led us into too exclusive dependence upon what may be termed extraordinary means and to the consequent neglect of those ordinary means and appliances that may be used to influence men's minds and conduct. We have been so afraid of "creaturely activity" even in matters of moral and social reform that we have not made a proper use of those natural powers and forces that may be legitimately used under all circumstances for the promotion of right ideas. Behind the dogma of the utter worthlessness of mere human effort undirected by divine guidance we have taken refuge until it has become a stock excuse for chronic inactivity and shirking. If man is something more than a mere automaton, if he is a creature endowed with responsibility, then the very possession of powers of reasoning and persuasion is a sufficient warrant for the exercise of these faculties in behalf of righteousness and truth.

Again, the idea of personal responsibility growing out of the doctrine of divine guidance has led to the development of an extreme individualism amongst Friends, which, while it has promoted individual initiative and action, has not been favorable to concerted, harmonious and systematic effort of the Church as a whole. In its very nature it is unfavorable to that deliberative study and discussion of means and methods necessary to secure organized and systematic co-operation along a pre-determined line. Until recently such a thing as a Conference like this was almost wholly unknown amongst us. Consequently we have had no well-matured plans, no systematic organization for carrying on a vigorous and persistent propaganda for the abolition of the war system and the introduction of less brutal and more rational methods of settling differences. Our efforts have been individual and sporadic. We have lacked that cohesion, that *esprit de corps,* necessary to united, well-considered and harmonious action. We have failed, therefore, to wield that influence that comes from a compact organization. My time limit is reached. I can only add that I trust that this Conference may mark the dawn of a better day, when we shall work more unitedly and more effectually for the promotion of this great cause.

The Chairman: The next paper to be presented is on the subject, " The Duty of the Christian Church at the Present Time in the Movement to Abolish War," and will be read by Henry W. Wilbur, of New York city, who has now arrived.

THE DUTY OF THE CHRISTIAN CHURCH AT THE PRESENT TIME IN THE MOVEMENT TO ABOLISH WAR.

BY HENRY W. WILBUR, EDITOR OF THE " YOUNG FRIENDS' REVIEW," NEW YORK CITY.

To speak a word in the line of the topic of this paper, without being censorious or rancorous, will not be easy, and may be impossible. If the purpose so to discuss the question is not even approximately realized, it will not be on account of the unwillingness of the spirit, but because of the weakness of the flesh, provoked by the evidence of an unchristian and warlike temper exhibited in the name, but against the fame, of the Church.

Accurate and accepted definition will make a good foundation upon which to build the fabric of orderly statement and logical, dispassionate discussion.

A Christian, as the dictionary describes him, is " One who believes in the religion of Christ, especially one whose inward and outward life is conformed to the doctrines of Christ."

According to the same authority a church is " A formally organized body of Christian believers worshipping together."

Having found out what a Christian is, and that a church is simply men and women of the specified exalted character banded together, it is in order to ask, What is the duty of these collective Christians to-day in the movement to abolish war?

Manifestly the answer to that question will depend upon whether war ought to be abolished at all. If the battlefield is a sort of training school for teaching the Christian graces; if it develops a measure of love and a line of activity which will give the Church a stronger grip upon the hearts of men, then the Church should become a recruiting office, and the individual Christian a man-of-war.

If, on the other hand, war is contrary to the spirit and teaching of the Gospel; if it destroys rather than conserves life; if it inspires hate of one's fellows, to say nothing about his enemies, then war ought to be abolished, every Christian ought to be an abolitionist, and the Church a universal peace society, chanting the song of the angels as it promotes peace on earth and goodwill among men.

The dictionary definition of war is all too brief and technical to describe the bloody issue involved in what is called " A contest between nations or states carried on by force of arms." To determine whether war comports with Christian teaching we shall need to understand what inspires it, what sort of conduct characterizes its progress, what effect it has upon those who engage in it.

Considered in the light of common sense, war is the old feeling of personal vengeance transferred to and practiced in public affairs —the law of Moses followed by the nations as against the law of Christ. It is national savagery, the tooth and claw spirit exhibited in government; the brute made manifest in collective human nature; an exhibition of the primitive and undeveloped, recognized as unchristian in personal human nature.

Two nations have a misunderstanding; they fancy that the crooked path will be made straight and the obscure way plain, if the way is lined with death and the path strewn with devastation. When the end of the carnage comes; when the strife has burned itself out in the besom of destruction; when one side has been impoverished as to its cash, and decimated as to its manhood, and must sue for peace, the nation which has inflicted the greatest damage, and piled up the largest number of the adversary's dead, flatters itself that this horrible evidence is proof positive that its quarrel was just. The condition would be ludicrous were it not so tragic.

The picture has not been overdrawn. No artist ever wielded a brush dipped in colors adequately scarlet to tell the whole sad story of carnage over which the god of battles presides. But false education and unchristian ideals have warped the human judgment and calloused the conscience until the clear vision of the Son of Man does not illumine the understanding.

Hosea Bigelow's statement, " As for war I call it murder," will meet the witness of the sober second thought in the minds of most men. " Learning and art, and especially religion, weave ties that make war look like fratricide, as it is," says Emerson, and the sentiment meets with a hearty amen in many quarters. But wars come and go in the main because sentiment is not crystallized into conviction and organized into public conduct.

We are not considering the topic from the standpoint of the past, but of the present. The anthropomorphic literalism of the ancient Jewish theologians need not hamper us. Their dim perception conceived of the Almighty as a man of war and a god of battles; but the spirit of the new dispensation, the religion of life and love which the Master established and the spirit of truth, first pure and then peaceable, which he left as a legacy to his disciples for all time, does not admit of the life-destroying trade of war.

The human imagination, whether Pagan or Christian, at all familiar with the Sermon on the Mount, or the wayside ministry of Jesus, has never conceived him playing the rôle of warrior. His armament can never be more carnal than the sword of the Spirit; his feeling for men less than a race-including love. It is idle, therefore, to spend time proving that the Prince of Peace was not a warrior, or that war cannot exist when that perfect law of liberty which he brought to light prevails.

It should be remembered that we are not considering the third, the eleventh or the sixteenth century, but the twentieth. We are confronted with duty as magnified in the lens of the larger light and liberty of two thousand years of accumulated Christian experience. The present concern is not condemnation of the wars of the crusades, but the abolition of war to-day.

We are now face to face with a query: What can the Christian Church do and what ought it to do to assist every effort looking towards the abolition of war? Manifestly it can become a potent, practical moral force in the world, as well as stand for a distinct type of theology. It can put forth a concerned and consistent effort to make real the practical gospel. It can stand at the parting of the ways and plead for peace, while it does its best to displace the war spirit which delights to destroy life, by the brotherly spirit whose meat and drink is to preserve and protect life.

The world needs a vast deal of teaching regarding right principles. Centuries of combat have left the race possessed of monumental errors and manifold subterfuges. War has always been the practice of the nations under provocation, and the supposition is that what always has been always will be. But that is simply one of the world's misconceptions. It has been the misnomer of the conservative and the axiom of the advocates of things as they are, ever since the spirit of procrastination began to oppose the spirit of progress.

The Church is admirably equipped to assist in the removal of this misconception. Her own history has been a constant evidence that established custom, hoary-headed habit, the beaten track of conservatism, does not constitute the divinely-appointed order of social, moral, intellectual and spiritual progress. The Church should teach the possibility of a growth in grace, not a permanency for disgrace; an evolution in righteousness, not a self-satisfied content with partial accomplishmment, low ideals, and the notion that any condition less than perfection has been blessed with everlasting life. The Church should labor to remove the misconceptions and misnomers of the ages.

One of the world's misconceptions is that the spirit of peace is effeminate; that to fight is manly, and to refrain from a quarrel provoked by brutality is to play the coward's part. The Church should teach manliness, that manliness which has the manliness of the Master as a model, and there was nothing effeminate about that. Who has ever dreamed that the calm, consistent manliness which did not demur at the crown of thorns, and which marched unflinchingly to the cross and Calvary, was cowardly?

It is better to dodge the blow of the bully than to sink to the level of the bully by paying him off in kind. That is peace for the man personally, and peace with honor just the same. It is better for the nation to let provocation real or imaginary, evaporate in the crucible of diplomacy; to invoke the delay of the sober second thought, than to resent injury on sight, and resort to the nonsensical philosophy that two calamities make a blessing. That is peace for men publicly as a nation.

What better business can the Church be in than teaching the young people, and the old people for that matter, for whose instruction in righteousness she is responsible, the simple duty of ruling one's own spirit. Peace is the product of thoughtfulness, of reason, of self-control; war is the offspring of passion—the first flash of hate in the powder pan of anger. A better motto over the church door than " Remember the Maine " is the words of Habakkuk, " In wrath remember mercy."

Among the subterfuges which obscure the world's thinking none are more vigorously or viciously pushed than the notion that national grandeur, greatness and permanency rest upon military power and prestige; that the nation which will not or cannot fight shall surely die, if it is not already dead. This view of the case has been tremendously exaggerated and distorted, until the conclusion has been almost reached that the one essential of national permanency is a military footing, and that the breath of a healthy nation's nostrils is the spirit of war.

Yet we have a standing refutation of this monstrous folly before our eyes. It is only about three hundred years since the mighty Philip II. passed away from earth, and ever since that time Spanish history has been marching backward, and fighting vigorously all the while in the midst of retreat. Spain did not go to pieces and lapse into weakness because she forgot how or became afraid to fight. Her history illustrates the essential fallacy which inheres in many of the theories which men advance to account for the grandeur and stability of nations. With no lack of bravery in battle; with a loyalty to the power ordained in government which almost amounted to adoration; with reverence for religious authority, which is one of the most mighty cohesive forces in the world; with all this, Spain has decreased from being a national giant, until now she is one of the puniest pigmies among the European Powers. Evidently, the calculating machine of the materialistic ready-reckoners in national affairs has slipped a cog. There seems to be something necessary to national growth finer than force, and without which force is unavailing.

The magnificent machinery of the Church ought to be steadily employed in teaching the truth regarding the forces and factors which make for national strength, because they tend to purity and peace.

Among the stumbling-blocks to the Christian's constant and consistent testimony in behalf of peace is the dwarfed and stilted notion of patriotism constantly pressed upon him by the preachers of his Church, the politicians of his choice, and the party paper from which he gets his intellectual pabulum, and his civic and often his moral ideas. "My country, right or wrong," is this shibboleth, and he concludes that that means that his citizenship must endorse what his manhood repudiates.

An analysis of his shibboleth would take away all of its sting, and the power it has to enslave. Of course a man's country is his, good or bad, just as his body is his, black or white. He had no power to choose the place of his birth or the color of his skin. But that does not mean that the citizen shall rejoice when his country goes wrong. His business, on the other hand, is to contribute the effort and the influence which shall at least tend to make his country right. He may love it when wrong, but the test of his loyalty as a citizen in the State and a Christian in the Church is that he shall then love it in sorrow, and labor with an eye single to its secured righteousness.

May we not learn another lesson from Spain, the finished product of bald conservatism and blind, unthinking, parrot-like devotion? Buckle, the historian, says: "Loyalty and superstition, reverence for their clergy, were the leading principles which influenced the Spanish mind and governed the march of Spanish history." Leaving Buckle, may we not conclude that time has shown that mere loyalty to a machine is not the stuff of which enduring national character is made? Loyalty that is simply blind endorsement of the powers that be, though they be diabolical, has killed more civilizations than it has cured. We are living in an age of the world when moral quality and the ability to discover and apply new principles are the things that count. What the nations need to-day worse than standing armies, or steel-plated cruisers, or submarine destroyers, is conscience. The duty of the Christian Church is to inspire, educate and make tremendously alive the constructive conscience.

The progress of civilization and the history of Christianity prove conclusively that free government is the product of originality in thinking and liberty of expression. The government cannot be benefited by the progressive spirit of its individual parts unless they express themselves. No government will progress in righteousness if its citizens approve its wrongdoing. For the citizen to tell the government when he thinks it is wrong is not treason, but concerned patriotism. Anglo-Saxon civilization would have gone down hill with Spain had it not stood for progress, encouraged growth and conferred the power of initiative and the privilege of reform upon its individual citizens. The Church is a moulder of citizens. She ought to teach an independent and progressive rather than a parrot-like and thoughtlessly acquiescent patriotism. In short, she ought to make of every man and woman a force for social righteousness, and every voter an advocate of peace, even in the midst of war and the political vituperation which war engenders.

The Church has the right, and it is her duty to demand that her generally and specially retained advocates shall not misrepresent the Christian ideals. When the jingoes in and out of Congress, in the spring of 1898, were bombarding an unwilling President to begin war with Spain, some of the heaviest cannonading came from the pulpits of the country, and the exhortation in behalf of blood-letting is still the speech of not a few of those who declare that they are "ambassadors for Christ."

A few months ago, when the President of the United States was stricken by the bullet of an assassin, the most vehement regrets that lawless personal vengeance was not summarily visited upon the murderer came from supposed teachers of Christian ethics, occupying some of the popular pulpits in the land.

The champion defender of the looting practiced by the armies of the Christian allies during the late unpleasantness in China holds the parchment of an ordained minister and the brief of a Christian missionary. Examine the authoritative declarations of Dr. Gilbert Reed regarding this matter. On page 582 of "The Forum" for Seventh month, 1901, Dr. Reed, in writing about "The Ethics of Loot," said:

"For the crime thus committed by the instigation of the Manchu court, it seemed at the moment that no punishment could be too severe. 'Raze the city to the ground!' 'Burn the palace!' 'Let ruins mark the site of the greatest crime of the century, and prove a warning to coming centuries.' I am not sure in the new moments of reflection . . . but that the first thought if carried out would have been for the greatest good of the greatest number. As a mild modification of such drastic proposals there grew up the romantic system of looting."

On page 584 of the same magazine Dr. Reed thus delivers himself:

"A somewhat similar mode of looting was that of entering houses other than those occupied, and taking the best that could be found. Old residents of Pekin not only knew where the wealth was, but generally distinguished between the Chinaman who was a friend and him who was a foe. For the former they sought protection; from the latter loot. Personally, I regret that the guilty suffered so little at my own hands."

To make the efforts of loot doubly sure, in the *North China Herald* of Third month, 1901, the same Dr. Reed said:

"Now and then I branched out to loot from those who were our enemies, and I only regret I didn't have more time to loot from such despicable wretches, instead of leaving so much to others, including not a few loot critics. If, however, those from whom I have looted want their things back let them meet me face to face and I will 'take the matter into consideration.'"

The point is that the duty of the Church is to assist in the abolition of war, which engenders in men such unchristian character, and while she is doing that she should insist that her representatives do not misrepresent her.

Made up of the disciples of the Great Teacher, the Church cannot in consistency do less than teach the Christian ideals regarding personal conduct and public policy. A prominent educator in a recent magazine article said: "Our highest politics aim at conserving the arts of peace; our first poetic lessons are in an Iliad that cannot be appreciated without a bloodthirsty joy in killing." The adult communicants of the Church, and the children whom she is educating to recruit her membership, demand at her hands impressions upon their hearts and consciences of holier ideas regarding the tenderness and awfulness of human life than Greek, Roman or Norse heroes tell or teach.

The Christian test of valor and manhood is not made on the battlefield, where the very environment tends to make one sell life cheaply. On the contrary, the Christian hero is he who in unselfish devotion binds up the wounds inflicted on life's Jericho road, and helps emancipate from the servitude of sin a submerged human spirit. From the standpoint of the Founder of the Church, the Good Samaritan is a more ideal type of the Christian than the great soldier. A wide and expanding field of labor looms up before the Church at the present time to teach her own her own truth.

Perhaps the conclusion of the whole matter can be pressed into a paragraph. The sanest method at the present time to abolish war is to displace the war spirit in the hearts of men, and in the purpose of the nations. That is the sure cure for the curse of war. But it may be too slow and too primary to suit the quacks upon the one side, and the impatient enthusiasts on the other. Whatever will help to remove the war spirit will be valuable, and the educational and moral labor necessary to that end is in the direct line of the duty of the Church.

There is encouragement, of course, in the fact that the economic drain involved in war discourages a resort to it, and tends to make the nations slow to wrath when the temptation comes to engage in battle.

That it is no longer easy or desirable for nations about equally matched to refer their differences to the arbitrament of the sword, also has its value in the direction of peace. The wars of the last quarter of a century have in the main been wars of the strong against the weak, and have demonstrated the essential moral and physical cowardice on the part of the modern warriors. That, also, will have the tendency to shame the strong nations into the more peaceful attitude. Part of the duty of the Church is to discourage the temper and conduct of the bully among the nations.

But when we consider the case in its fullness, and all the tendencies now prevailing, the center of the movement to abolish war, is, as has been said, to displace the war spirit. That is a task which belongs to all the educational processes, beginning at the cradle and continuing to the end of present-world life. Producing that result is a large part of the purpose permeating the genuine Christian system, although it has only to a limited extent been taken up by the Church. Manifestly the duty of the Church is to be practically and potentially Christian.

The whole temper of the present movement to abolish war might be changed for the better if the Church would use her influence in any practical and forceful way in promoting the discussion and propaganda of the movement. It goes for the saying that the Church could discourage warlike methods and belligerent language in treating the peace problem.

Just as all men who criticise government are not traitors, so all men who have not yet become peace advocates are not heathens. May we not charitably consider them partially developed Christians? It will be well to remember that all men have in some particular come short of fulfilling all provisions of the law and the gospel, and the blindly warlike Christian is simply defective at a different point than some of us. Christian sympathy with the frailties of men lies at the base of all well-regulated efforts at practical reform.

True, the progress towards peace has been a snail's pace, but the progress goes on. It is the duty of the Church to push the car of progress, not to obstruct it either by her opposition or her indifference.

The problem of peace touches our political and public life, and demands that the Christian citizen's relation to government shall be up to the level of his Christian ideals. If the Church is true to the mark of her high calling she will lend a hand in developing that kind of citizens.

From within the circle of the Church, holier than the French cardinal ever dreamed, there should proceed no curses, not even for the warrior. Her function is to inspire and uplift, to develop an intense love for men, and the life which they possess. In this atmosphere the spirit of war would die for the want of nourishment.

But the Church will not be mechanically lifted from her lethargy. Her progress and her work in the world as a body of collective Christians will depend upon the extent to which her individual members follow the leading of the Christ-spirit as it speaks in their hearts, and invites them to a more abundant righteousness and a larger peace.

As the individual Christian follows this holy leading, the ambitions of the warrior and the destroyer will cease to allure him, and the promise which will make his soul stretch its wings, and be glad in its strength, will be the apostolic declaration, "How beautiful are the feet of them that preach the gospel of peace and bring glad tidings of good things.

THE CHAIRMAN: The next is a paper upon "The Makers of Peace," by Dean Elizabeth Powell Bond, of Swarthmore College.

THE MAKERS OF PEACE.

BY ELIZABETH POWELL BOND, DEAN OF SWARTHMORE COLLEGE, PA.

This conference must be of the nature of a prayer. Our souls are reaching out toward the infinite soul for light and guidance and help to see how we may be makers of peace. And although it may seem a futile thing for a few hundred men and women to come together for interchange and illumination of thought, still, our hearts may glow with the faith of Hartley Coleridge's lines:

> "Far is the time, remote from human sight,
> When war and discord on the earth shall cease;
> Yet every *prayer* for universal peace
> Avails the blessed time to expedite."

There is on exhibition in this city a powerful picture entitled, "The Conquerors." It is an epitome of the story of war. Out of the sombre, far-away background come the conquerors three abreast on their great war horses. Cæsar is in the forefront, with Rameses and Alexander on either side. Close behind press Attila and Napoleon and Sennacherib, and lesser conquerors beneath their barbaric and their Christian banners. Their "way to glory" is through an avenue of dead men lying tier upon tier on either side. In these unnumbered hosts of dead we may fancy "the five hundred thousand chosen men of Israel" whom Abijah and his people slew with great slaughter; the ten thousand that fell down at Napoleon's word of command; the more than ten hundred thousand slain in "great Cæsar's" conquering marches. But "the conquerors" can no more go forward. Death has reduced to the ranks these men of might; now, they stand, naked souls in the presence of the Supreme Commander!

True, these conquerors are conquered. But down through the ages, in the blood of their sons, and their sons' sons. have come the seeds of war from their fatal sowing! True, we have not Cæsar and Alexander and Napoleon; but we have the commanders of all the nations of the earth, still carrying on wars for defence, and wars for mastery, and wars for the spread of civilization!

Said a school-master of a preparatory school, not long ago, in my hearing: "The work with boys seems to me to be very much like writing upon the sand of the seashore. You think you have made a deep impression at some point, and along comes a wave, and it is gone." What is true of the schoolboy seems hardly less true of the human race in its preparatory school of this world's life.

A few months ago I stood for the first time beside Grant's Tomb on the Hudson. As I came to the impressive structure, the brief inscription, the dead soldier's own words, " Let us have peace !" seemed to me a message from out some higher, purer sphere. It gave me a strange feeling of translation into another time and place. Here was a memorial from a grateful nation to a military hero; an expression in enduring marble of gratitude for service, in part, it is true, with cannon and sword. And yet there are no emblems of war to remind us of the soldier. The sculptured figures that seem only to accent the fitting simplicity of the marble structure bear the olive and the laurel—emblems according well with the eloquent appeal of the hero, " Let us have peace!"

Is there anywhere in the world beside a monument to a military hero, that thus perpetuates his cry for peace? Let us be thankful that this high-water mark of civilization has been reached. A wave of militarism has gone over us, and has swept away apparently the standards of national righteousness that would express themselves in such a memorial. Military heroes of this generation will doubtless be commemorated with emblems of war; but there stands the eloquent record in marble, that once in our national history, the victorious soldier pleaded for peace!

War is not an evil to be legislated away any more than smallpox. War is a disease of souls, and so long as the germs of war find in the crudeness or selfishness of men the conditions for their growth, so long will armies recruit themselves for aggressive warfare upon the weak, or for defense against the invasions of the strong.

When, in 1897, the war against Spanish rule in Cuba was threatening, the New York letter in the Philadelphia *Ledger* said that men were tired of peace, that they were blasé, that they were hungering and thirsting for the excitement of war. And it is true that men flocked to the camps to make ready for battle, with much of the spirit of college boys putting themselves in training for athletic contests. In monarchical countries where the power of one man is to be maintained; where the exaltation of the King means the debasement of all other men class by class, it is easy to see that the "divine right of kings" must intrench itself behind a standing army. But within the borders of a Republic there is every chance for peace. Said Charles Sumner, in 1871, in his address on the duel between France and Germany: "All hail to the Republic, equal guardian of all, and angel of peace. Our own part is simple. It is, first, to keep out of war; and, next, to stand firm in those ideas which are the life of the Republic. Peace is our supreme vocation. To this we are called."

What does it mean that in two decades after this noble address, men of this Republic had become tired of peace, blasé, thirsting for the excitement of war! Must it be, that like waves upon the seashore, tides of human feeling from unfinished human nature must at intervals wash away the foundations that seemed built upon everlasting principles? Blasé in this thrillingly interesting world, where scientific research is bringing us clearer glimpses of creative plans and method and power; and making us to feel more and more at one with God! Thirsting for the excitement of war, when there is the glorious excitement of making two blades of wheat grow where one grew before!

Do away with war—you and I in our greater or lesser places in the world! It is a seemingly hopeless task for the individual, one here and another there, to work against the strongly intrenched armies of the world. The world believes in its armies—it does not believe in Christ. This is our terrible unbelief: "Lord, help thou our unbelief!" There is a tradition that when the Egyptians prayed to Osiris for release from a plague of crocodiles, deliverance came through the little ichneumon that diligently destroyed the eggs of the great reptiles.

We may not be able to place in our National Congress the men who would be makers of peace in the national councils. Prompt co-operation with the executive officers of the nation may not turn back the tide of war that now and again rises in human history. It may be long years before woman shares in the active responsibilities of government. We cannot yet have her service in that way against war.

But there is a service that comes within the power of every human being, from the least to the greatest, from the young to the aged, from the unlettered to the scholar—the labor to destroy the seeds of war. The small seeds of war are in human souls, forever starting into life, forever striving for possession. The impulses of selfishness are the seeds of war. Whenever we would seek our own advancement at the cost of some other soul, then these seeds of war quicken in their native element. Whenever we wantonly infringe upon our neighbor's precious rights, in trade among men, or in social relations, these small seeds of war respond with electric swiftness, and strike root, to irritate and torment and despoil the beautiful possibilities of the day or the year. Even the jangling of untuned nerves may be the stimulus of these baleful seeds into malarial growth. The makers of peace have been named the children of God. In their energized heart of love the seeds of war wither away. If we could be loving enough in our relations to men, no seeds of war could ever spring into bitter thought or hateful action between man and man, nor into cannon-led battalions between nation and nation. Then, how the desert places of life would grow " ten thousand roses on forbidding walls "! Then, how all the energy that is paralyzed by discord and heart-achings would be turned to the joyous doing of life's work. Then, would the billions of dollars expended in the last century's wars, be diverted from the work of destruction, to the work of building up.

Let us cherish hearts of hope to measure the progress of the world, not by its laggard steps and seeming retrogressions, but by the heights which it now and then touches, and go forward with the unfailing patience of Him to whom a thousand years are as a day!

The Chairman: We shall now listen to an address on " The True Spirit of Peace," by Dr. William L. Pearson, of Penn College, Iowa.

THE TRUE SPIRIT OF PEACE.

BY PROFESSOR WILLIAM L. PEARSON, PENN COLLEGE, IOWA.

Peace is not simply a state of pacification. It is not merely a condition in which conflicts of words and weapons have passed away; nor does the cessation of inward struggle naturally issue into peace. Its content expands beyond the definitions of the lexicographer. Neither do courts for compromise and arbitration usually comprehend it.

The peace of Christ and of unity means all these, and far more. But neither the world nor the church has fairly conceived it. Peace is not negative; it is particularly positive; it is not merely the absence of conflict, but the prosperity of realized divine blessing. In nearly every apostolic salutation after " grace," by which one enters into the presence and favor of God, " peace " is the great comprehensive blessing of life. In the kingdom of God, next to righteousness, which must forever be the foundation, peace with God and men is the precious, practical fruit of the Holy Spirit.

Hence it is that the placid face and gentle manner do not always indicate a peaceful spirit, just as a calm surface of the sea does not necessarily imply a quiet deep sea. From the springs of a worldly or a wilful life come up mire and dirt, even when the restraints of society and the discipline of a better civilization apparently control it. There is not in it the real peace that constitutes Christian self-mastery.

On the other hand, the mind permeated, empowered and dominated by the Spirit issues into life and peace. Peace as God's gracious gift vouchsafed by the Holy Spirit of adoption with favor into the Heavenly Father's family embraces all other blessings in the life of his regenerate and faithful children; and, according to Isaiah and Paul and Jesus, none others know genuine peace. " Peace " was among Christ's last benedictions upon his disciples before his death, and his first blessing after the resurrection was, " Peace be unto you." No other has the prerogative to confer this blessing, supreme and peculiar beyond all understanding in its power to guard heart and thoughts, so that one may say,

> " These surface troubles come and go,
> Like rufflings of the sea;
> The deeper depths are out of reach
> To all, my God, but thee."

Thus we see the genuine Christian peacemakers are they who have been constituted such by Christ himself. It was his not merely to break down every wall of partition and bring all classes and conditions and nations and races face to face in order to eliminate their differences; he is not merely the matchless peacemaker by virtue of his authority over men, but himself is our peace, and constitutes his elect at once possessors of peace, and henceforth proclaimers of God's peace and goodwill to men. Practical Christians are naturalized citizens of the kingdom of grace, peace and assured prosperity. Such are " the peacemakers that shall be called the children of God." One can never be a servant of the Prince of Peace in the full, free sense without possessing his Spirit of peace, the supreme satisfaction that always arises from the consciously accepted heavenly irenicon. In the case of Christ, the spirit suffered in Gethsemane and sank on Golgotha, when his own right arm might have protected him, or legions of angels might have been summoned to his help. Too few fully realize the fact that if he had not thus possessed himself in the spirit of peace, our peace would never have been made possible by the breaking of the bonds of death and the grave; he would never have been the Prince of Life and Peace. At a time when furious factions sprang up in a night, and bands of zealots daily ran mad, was not the world poor, indeed, to have only one Son of Man, who, being empowered by the spirit of peace within him up to the point of self-mastery, could triumph over evil and the evil one? Yet such an one! King of Peace because he was King of Righteousness, King Eternal! It was thus that he, the author of peace, is authorized both out of the depths of an unfathomable experience and with the sanctions of the almighty, loving Father to announce in his own name, to all sincere peace seekers, "*Pax vobiscum*" (Peace be unto you).

We should give encouragement to every honest effort towards peace, and where the Church neglects God's gospel of peace it may be our duty to co-operate with even the agnostic. The heroism of Professor Virchow and his two coadjutors, who used annually, in the face of ridicule, to offer in the German Parliament their resolutions looking to disarmament, should receive our hearty applause. And yet, we are Friends—but friends of Christ only if we do whatsoever he commands. In the Society of Friends Christ's word ought to be the voice of the eternal: "The way to work the works of God is, first, to believe on his Sealed and Sent, and to take one's commission from him for the work of God." Only thus shall we feed on the Bread of Heaven, know the Life Eternal, possess the true spirit of peace.

What man may ever, in his own name, assume the divine prerogative? Whose is the right to bestow peace upon his fellowmen? Can priest or potentate bestow the blessing? Who may thus exalt himself above his kind and dictate the terms of peace? Rameses II., Israel's oppressor, made conquest of Palestine and Syria, and would gladly have exalted himself to say to a conquered world, "Peace be unto you," but in a drawn battle with the Hittite emperor he met an equal and was rescued, as he believed, from the midst of his foes by the intervention of his god Amon. Yet, he who would assume the exalted prerogative over men, did not hesitate to engrave his own instead of the name of Amon on the tablets of victory, to efface his god's in order to insert his own name, and even to erect statues of himself in the temples of the gods, to take his place in the midst of the Egyptian trinity. Somewhat similarly a modern Bismarck, and then a Wilhelm II., after the old king and general had constructed an empire by conflict and conquest, would announce the *Pax vobiscum* as umpire of the European countries, declaring "The bayonets of all Europe point towards Berlin." In the same spirit many a proud prince or august ecclesiastic would have peace on earth, along with the universal sway of his own will.

How wide the contrast between all these and the spirit of Paul, the first to make conquest for Christ in Europe! Differing Christians were to "give diligence to keep the unity of the Spirit in the bonds of peace," in order to "attain unto unity of the faith and of the knowledge of the Son of God." Among differing races and ranks of men, wherever and whenever disputes arose, and especially among themselves, the Christians "should thankfully welcome the unfailing arbitration of the peace of Christ in order to the unity of the body." "Let the peace of Christ rule, arbitrate, in your hearts, unto which ye were also called in one body, and be ye thankful." The spirit of peace first seeks the divine equation in every one's own inward conflict, and submits every issue between men to the Prince of Peace, remembering that "the Lord's servant must not strive, but be gentle towards all." Hence it would have been entirely foreign to Paul to utter in his own name among the brethren any sort of *Pax vobiscum*. The spirit of peace is impossible, as is peace itself, in the would-be autocrat peacemaker. Instead of the *Pax vobiscum* of divine prerogative, and unlike every autocratic ecclesiastic, this prince of apostles would say to those of like faith with him, "*Pax nobiscum* (Let us have peace)."

It is characteristic of the spirit of peace to stand immovable upon the conceived will of God, daring to do right, willing to suffer wrong rather than do wrong. Let us open our eyes to the awful fact of sin, with all its fearful consequences. The world has been and is sin-cursed, and selfishness, iniquity, conflict and suffering must obtain for some time to come. "No variableness nor shadow cast by turning" upon the stage of diplomacy, political or ecclesiastical, can conceal such condition before the increasing light of God, and while the twentieth century Friend must withstand all war and war spirit, yea, rather stand for the coming Messianic reign of peace, as firmly as our stalwarts of the seventeenth century did, we should be the last people on earth to become misled by sweet sentimentality on the subject. Events of the last five years have compelled the advocates of peace to pause and read the signs of the times. Haply it was only to sound forth again to peoples and rulers their appeals for peace and peaceful methods, and protest upon protest has gone up to heads of governments, sometimes from labor unions and other fraternities, but slightly understanding the spirit and ideals of peace. This is all only negative. But the ardent advocates of peace must never forget that their *first* business is to possess and to proclaim both the Prince of Peace and his peace evangel, a thought too often overlooked in times both of continuous peace and of exciting conflict of arms.

And yet the Christian testimony contains more than word or deed. Every worthy testimony is a testimony with the spirit; it *is* spirit and life. Christ freely yielded up his life *to* his enemies, *for* his enemies' sake, and as freely commended his spirit *to* the Father *for* the Father's glory. It may not be forgotten that he who offered his life for us also breathed his spirit upon us, and that an all-sufficient, soul-satisfying self-sacrifice calls for an ever-living, suffering Saviour realized in us as touched with a feeling of all human infirmities. Hence in the advancing revelations and experiences of a Paul and a Peter, the baptism and fellowship of Christ's sufferings became ideal in the higher phases of Christian life and service. Christ ever has crowns for those who will bear the cross, but he must continue to bear the cross alone who will too eagerly snatch the crown. In the sinful, suffering world's conflict they were to make up that which was lacking, not of the atoning sacrifice, but in the afflictions of Christ for the body's sake. The royal son of heaven's and of Israel's king was also the son of the Hittite's wife, of a Moabitess, of a harlot, and possibly of a Jezebel. It is neither dry dogma nor poetic fancy, but a fact of first order in the divine providence, that the spotless, suffering High Priest and King "passed through the heavens" to the lowest rung of the social ladder, and home again. Somehow, in "the light of life," it is kingly and Christlike to answer thus truth's call, and only thus may truth slowly and surely build upon and in the foundations of society and thence rise in triumphant grandeur.

The London Meeting for Sufferings is pre-eminently the most unique and extraordinary ecclesiastical body of modern history. And while the conditions in England differ from those in this country, one only need fairly feel the weight of war-burden resting upon many of those meetings to fear lest the war-god may some day find the American Society of Friends asleep with the weeping Spirit of Peace perched over her head.

May modern Friends, like Christ and Paul and Peter, have the true spirit of peace! Aye, more; we *must* have it in order to be Christ's true peacemakers, in order to be the Friends our fathers were, and under the clear sky of the twentieth century we may, must be, more than

"Half our fathers' shadows cast at noon."

We should be taller and broader and stronger than they. Our question is only as to the power of the spirit of peace. Examples might be multiplied anywhere in the history of the Society of Friends.

Let two examples suffice. When every one, every ecclesistical society or political party who dared, appealed to the sword with the furious zeal of a mistaken divine authority to enforce his own creed and claim, when the first Friend, with hundreds of faithful followers, was spending one-fourth of his forty active years in dreadful dungeons, and much more under dire persecutions, Thomas Carlyle, surveying the whole latter half of the seventeenth century, spies out a single figure of masterly Christian fortitude, and writes: "There is in broad Europe one free man—George Fox, the greatest of the moderns,—he looks heavenward from his earth and dwells in an element of mercy and worship." But this is not the whole of it. The Spirit of God, who will conform all of us into the spirit of peace—for the unity of the Spirit is in the bond of peace —impelled George Fox eagerly onward to proclaim and promote life and peace among his fellows. Drinking in the elements of the divine nature, the true spirit of peace becomes partaker of an extraordinary divine-human benevolence, the brotherly love which is suffused and surcharged with the divine love and obliged to find an outlet in the lives of men. It was this spirit of peace which filled and possessed William Penn and led to the " Holy Experiment," whose real meaning is only beginning to be fully felt.

Finally, the gentle, supremely courageous, suffering, true spirit of peace is a prophet's voice in the wilderness, faithfully speaking forth the word of the Lord until his generation sees it. Only an example. It was given John Bright alone to speak the word of God in Parliament as to the Crimean War. More than thirty years afterwards, driving one Sabbath evening to the London Station for the last time, and passing the monument upon which is inscribed " Crimea," he remarked, " The ' a ' should be transposed, and let it read ' A Crime.' " To this all thoughtful Englishmen would now say, Amen!

On my first visit, many years ago, I first read appropriately posted aloft in the bell tower of Independence Hall in Penn's City of Brotherly Love, Longfellow's lines, " Peace on Earth," which shall fittingly show the prophetic view of the spirit of peace:

> " Down the dark future, through long generations,
> The echoing sounds grow fainter and then cease ;
> And like a bell with solemn sweet vibrations,
> I hear once more the voice of Christ say, ' Peace ! '
> Peace ! and no longer from its brazen portals
> The blast of War's great organ shakes the skies,
> But, beautiful as songs of the immortals,
> The holy melodies of love arise."

THE CHAIRMAN: The subjects presented in the papers will now be open for discussion, and the first speaker will be Amos Saunders, of Brooklyn.

AMOS SAUNDERS: As I say what I have in mind I hope that I shall not be understood as criticizing our fathers of the past, or those of us who are here.

It is a sad fact to me that we have only one hundred thousand members instead of one million. If we had the latter we might go before the Congress of the United States and demand, whereas now we have to be simply suppliants and perhaps receive in response the hint that we are anarchists.

There is another sad fact, and that is that we have so few men who are capable of speaking to the great crowds that gather in such assemblies as the Christian Endeavor National Conventions and other places; that we have not those who can command those immense audiences and declare for peace in such a way that the world must hear. In the large cities we have so few men that are able to move the masses and lift men up into the great Gospel of peace that our Master declared.

It seems to me that we need constructive work, beginning down at the bottom, a constructive work that might have been begun years ago and been felt to-day. We need, as I have indicated, increased membership, that we may declare with more positiveness—at least with more force—the Gospel of peace.

The statistics show that seventy per cent. of all the people that become Christians, become so before they are eighteen years of age. I have no doubt that seventy per cent. or more of those of us to-day who stand for the subject of peace, stood so before we were eighteen years of age. The principles that we are trying to carry out were implanted in our minds in childhood. It is not difficult, therefore, to see where our field of labor lies. It belongs to that period in the life of the individual when he is most susceptible to impressions.

If, then, we would be strong in the future for peace, so far as numbers are concerned, we must reach and win to our church the children and young people. I know there are some who think that it is not numbers but character that Friends want. "Quality and not quantity," they tell us. Quality is good, but quality and plenty of it is a great deal better. We need a stronger ministry, for the proclamation of the Gospel of peace. The strength of the ministry is planted in childhood and early life, and is further developed in the college and university.

We need men, as has been indicated in this Convention, who are able to stand in the Congress of the United States with a force able to stem the strongest tide in times when the excitement of war is on. It was said the other day that one of the difficulties in getting men of peace principles into Congress was the lack of a constituency. If we had the numbers we should have the constituency that would put men into Congress where their voices could be heard as John Bright's was heard in the Parliament of England.

There are many of us here whose voices can be heard only by petition; but every one of us is in touch with childhood somewhere and can thus make ourselves heard in the future. There has been a tendency where I have known the Society to bring children into touch with our church and its agencies, get them interested and then allow them to go to other denominations to be cared for. In this way many of them have been led away from peace principles, and brought into the spirit and advocacy of war. If we had put them under the training of our own denomination and kept them there, we should have had more men of peace to stand for the principles and the cause of peace. Let every individual of us put forth efforts not only that the children of the church may be rightly taught, but that the children that come in contact with us may be brought in and made lovers of peace, so that in the years to come we may have largely increased numbers to declare our principles and render them more effective in the life of the nation.

ROBERT E. PRETLOW: A number of times during this Convention I have thought of an estimate of Jesus Christ by two prominent Jews whom I have recently seen. Both of them conceived the essential principle of Jesus Christ to be that which we Quakers hold—the principle of love, of brotherhood, of peace. One of them says the Jew rejects Jesus Christ as a dreamer, an idealist, because this idea of His good-will and peace is impracticable in a world such as ours. The other regards this as the chief and most beautiful point in the character of Jesus, and says that the light was too dazzling for His nation; they could not stand the blaze of the sunlight, and so rejected Him. But he closed with the pertinent query, " Has Christianity accepted Him? "

Some of our discussions have seemed to me to echo a little of that first estimate, that Jesus Christ is the bringer of ideals and dreams, which are exceedingly delightful to contemplate, but which in a world of men are impracticable. If Jesus Christ's teaching was true—and I do not need to discuss its truth before an audience of Friends—if the principles which He enunciated are right, they not only ought to be obeyed, they can be obeyed. Whatever ought to be done can be done. God does not demand impossibilities in this world. It is quite within the range of possibility for those who name the name of Jesus Christ not only to have peace in their personal and social relations, but to demand it in the State, and get it.

Our attention has been drawn this morning to some of the failures of Friends. It seems to me that they have been very pertinently put before us. One of our great failures has been extreme individualism. We have seen the vision of Jesus for ourselves; we have felt some transformation in our own natures as we have contemplated Him; and then we have drawn the robe of our sanctity about us, withdrawn ourselves, wrapped ourselves up in ourselves, and let society go its way. We have set ourselves on a pedestal, as the old saint did, for the world to gaze at as a specimen of the best and holiest; but we have not got down with Christ's spirit among men and inculcated that spirit among our brethren as brethren among them.

The Friends' Church, it seems to me, needs a rejuvenation, a refilling with that old spirit that was in Fox and Penn and other early Friends, that made them not content to hold views themselves and enjoy them, but made them sacrifice the comforts of life, social position, means, and go out to bring the truth to all men everywhere. Peace cannot be secured among men unless we bring it to them in a living form. When Jesus Christ came to the world He found religion congealed. There was no flowing of the spirit Godward. Traditionalism reigned. When George Fox came, he found the world again wrapped up in tradition and following what other men had thought and said and done. I want to ask the question here for our candid and serious consideration, whether the time has not almost gone for us as Friends to keep talking about peace as Fox and Penn saw it, and reviving what they did, instead of bringing it into living contact with the affairs of this time and this day.

It has been brought out in these discussions time and time

again that there can be no peace without righteousness. For us to go into the world and simply make a plea, when war breaks out, that that war shall stop, that our ideas shall now be put into practice, and that this particular piece of fighting shall cease, seems to me short-sighted and unwise. If the Friend longs for peace in government, he must begin at the root and seek righteousness in the government as the necessary antecedent of the peace which shall be lasting. The Friend who withdraws himself from political activity, who cuts himself off from his relations with men in the affairs of government, or compromises with iniquitous political machines and condones and takes part in things which are in themselves ungodly, loses all possible influence for peace at a later date.

JOSEPH ELKINTON: We have had the scourge of small cords applied very beneficially and stimulatingly this morning. One phase of the subject has been sufficiently dwelt upon. I thought it might perhaps be my place to hold up the other. We are all under bonds to this Conference to preserve sweetness of spirit; but peace of mind depends upon justice and truth of statement.

When I think of George Fox standing before Cromwell; of Mary Fisher going to the Turk, hazarding her life in that perilous journey; when I think of Isaac Norris on this side handing up his lonely vote against a warlike measure; when I think, also, of John Pemberton and others in the assemblies of the people here, and remember how Dr. John Fothergill and David Barclay on the other side appealed to George III. not to go into that greatest of all mistakes in the line of war; when I remember the history of our Society and what a magnificent record it has made for peace, the force of fact is far greater than the force of words.

There have been thought and action in this generation, just as truly as in any before. There have been in this house to-day men who have stood before successive presidents of the United States pleading that they would not endorse any warlike measure. I have looked upon their gray hairs with the greatest veneration; and I know that the spirit of the fathers is in them. I know that the appeals of the Meeting for Sufferings of this Yearly Meeting have gone out time and again in behalf of peace, with no uncertain sound and with no uncertain effect, ultimately. I know that the Meeting for Sufferings in London has done its duty, and is doing its duty now.

I know there is indifference to this great subject in our membership, and I wish all to be stimulated to do their duty; but I believe this duty is only to be performed as we have the spirit of the prophets in us; as we stand with the convictions that they had— alone, it may be, sometimes, but nevertheless willing to be alone. But I believe that the fervor of their spirits wil come down, has come down, to us, so that we shall send our message ringing through the ages, accumulating force; I doubt not it will accumulate rapidly henceforth; it will not go down with the thunders of Sinai; it will not go down with those misconceptions of our loving Father, who has been so long called the God of Battles; but it will go down with all the sweet reasonableness, with all the irresistible persuasiveness of the spirit of Christ.

I want these newspaper reporters to know that this Society is yet alive, has a testimony to bear, is bearing it, and if any other society in 250 years has borne equally well any such testimony, I want to know it. I do not say this to congratulate ourselves, but to give credit to the efforts of our fathers and our forefathers, and to those in this Conference who have steadily withstood up to this very time all war measures. I believe if the severe test of the past were again put upon us to-day, we should stand it faithfully, some of us at any rate. With all deference to those who have expressed the view that we have seriously failed in important ways, I hope that they will go away from this place knowing that there is a living peace testimony still extant among us.

JOHN B. WOOD: In William Pearson's remarks he says, " Paul's testimony was, ' Ye shall not strive.' " That word was the Greek word " fight." Paul said, " Ye shall not fight." Of course, the Christian translators had to put it " strive," because they believed in fighting; but the word in the Greek is " fight," and not " strive."

The Conference then adjourned till 3.30 p.m.

Eighth Session.

SEVENTH-DAY AFTERNOON, TWELFTH MONTH 14TH.

The Conference re-assembled in Twelfth Street Meeting House at 3.30 p.m. Susan W. Janney, of Philadelphia, presided during the afternoon. The session was opened by a season of devotion.

THE CHAIRMAN: I desire very briefly in the moment allotted to me to endeavor to summarize and to re-sound a few of the signal notes of encouragement that have been struck during the interesting sessions of the conference.

Doubtless many of us already find ourselves thinking of the time, near at hand, when, this notable occasion concluded, we shall undergo individual questionings as to its results. Whither do we seem to be tending? Are we looking forward or backward; towards a higher evolution of industrial civilization, or towards a revival of "reactionary militarism" in our social and political life?

Personally, I rejoice to believe that all who go forth to continue their labors in the cause of peace will have found fresh courage, increased breadth and enlightenment, and a renewed faith in pacific influences and conditions which have here been so intelligently presented.

I think it has been clearly shown that the tendencies of civilization are towards peace; that science, religion, commerce, facility of intercourse, almost a common literature, common friendships and common interests are overcoming the antipathies of nations, whose interdependence grows constantly more marked, and whose solidarity in great emergencies has noticeably increased.

It has been demonstrated, also, that under modern political, social and economic conditions the growing difficulties from the very developments that have taken place in the mechanism of war, and the unmanageability of immense masses of men mobilized at the outbreak of war, are some of the outward and visible signs of its growing impracticability.

The deepening sentiments of human brotherhood and the prevalence of the conviction that upon the welfare of the individual depends the elevation and the happiness of the whole, coupled with the fact that the tribunal of public opinion is more and more exacting and more and more deferred to, have been dwelt upon.

But if it is true, as our most ethical economists show, that the elements contending in the wars of the future will be all the moral and intellectual forces of nations, all the modern civilization, all technical improvements, feelings, characters, minds, and wills—the combined fruit of the culture of the civilized world—is not this the brightest promise of the future, the most practical argument of all against a continuance of wars?

It is not a dream, not an ideal only, but the result of surely developing conditions, a stage in evolution which all the spiritual God-given forces of man should contribute to hasten.

> " . . . . There is a story told
> In eastern tents, when autumn nights grow cold,
> And round the fire the Mongol shepherds sit
> With grave responses listening unto it:
> Once on the errands of his mercy bent,
> Buddha, the holy and benevolent,
> Met a fell monster, huge and fierce of look,
> Whose awful voice the hills and forests shook.
> ' Oh, Son of Peace! ' the giant cried, 'Thy fate
> Is sealed at last, and love shall yield to hate.'
> The unarmed Buddha looking, with no trace
> Of fear or anger, in the monster's face,
> In pity said : ' Poor fiend, even thee l love.'
> Lo, as he spake, the sky-tall terror sank
> To hand-breadth size; the huge abhorrence shrank
> Into the form and fashion of a dove;
> And where the thunder of its rage was heard,
> Circling above him sweetly sang the bird;
> ' Hate hath no harm for love,' so ran the song,
> ' And peace, unweaponed, conquers every wrong.' "

THE CHAIRMAN: The first paper of the afternoon is on "The Relation of Quaker Women to Peace," by Emilie U. Burgess, of Highland, N. Y.

THE RELATION OF QUAKER WOMEN TO PEACE.

BY EMILIE U. BURGESS, HIGHLAND, N. Y.

There is a marked impracticability in my subject. Quaker women are less distinct from the Church than the women of any other religious organization. They are a part of the legislative body of the Church, and of its controlling force. There is none the less a peculiar fitness in the subject, for woman is the shaper of destiny—an appropriateness in the thought of the relation of Quaker women to peace, for woman sets the moral standards, and is always found in the reformers' camp, even if it be in the foulest prisons. Elizabeth Fry was told that the women of Newgate would attack her, and a cannon was loaded and ready at the gate as she entered, but she declined all protection and appeared before those miserable creatures like a vision from a fairer world.

Christian people are grouped into organizations according to their principles and preferences. The carrying out of our principles thus expressed naturally leads to an attainable ideal of brotherhood and mutual helpfulness. Representing the Society of Friends, I am to touch briefly upon the relation which we bear to the whole Christian Church in common. Friends have never professed any separate theological or historical creed. There are certain points of Christian practice upon which we have been accustomed to lay stress. Certain "testimonies," conscientiously adopted, have been handed down among us from generation to generation with jealous care.

One of the most important and best known of our special testimonies is that which has been steadily borne by our organization against all war. Friends have ever maintained and acted upon the belief that war and strife of all kinds are opposed to the spirit and teaching of Christ, and have felt as his disciples precluded from participating in them. They have steadfastly refused to take up arms at the bidding of human authority. That course has brought them at times into collision with the civil authorities. To maintain this ideal has tested our strength. So long as our country is so imperfectly Christianized we recognize that conflict may at any time arise between the demands of our loyalty to the spirit of Christ and our obedience to law.

We are confronted, of course, with this question: Is the view of one's duty as held by a religious body higher than that of the nation at large? To abstain from participation in warfare is quite different from laying down any general theory as to the unlawfulness of war. We do not blame those who are acting in obedience to their own views of duty, however much they may differ from ours. To many people war is justifiable. A fully Christian nation has never yet been seen.

The question upon which we Friends differ from other Christians is not whether peace be desirable, whether it be the goal of political effort, but what are the means by which it is to be attained. Other Christians agree with us that quarreling is contrary to the spirit of Christ; but we regard the opposing of violence by violence as a hopeless method of procedure. Many others do not. Our place is surely to teach, not to govern, the world. The world, through Christianization and enlightenment, must become the kingdom of the Lord and his Christ, before wars and fightings will cease from among men.

In the beginning of Christianity it was felt by most believers to be as clear as daylight that " Christians cannot fight." So now, not only among Friends, but in many another Christian body, the same spirit is working, and consciences are awakening to the utter incompatibility of strife and retaliation and reckless self-aggrandizement with the spirit of brotherhood which lies at the very foundation of Christianity. Frances E. Willard said: " We all believe that one of the choicest fruits of Christianity will be the growth of a bond of brotherhood so close, among all nations, races and peoples, that we shall become truly kindred each to the other, and that the great word humanity, like a rolling wave of the ocean of God's love, shall wash out from the sands of time the words caste, creed, sex, and even that good word patriotism, because we shall feel that the whole world is our country and all men are our kin." Every utterance of appreciation, affection and friendship—every act of co-operation, every stroke of honest, hard work undertaken by the side of another, helps forward this beautiful day that we call the " coming of the kingdom of Christ."

The year 1898 was momentous in events and experiences. Beating drums and booming cannon marked an occasion which was termed " love of liberty," as our country tried to break the shackles of oppression from a neighboring people. The same year a great conference was called by the Czar of all the Russias to discuss and decide upon some practical means of lessening the burdens and miseries of war. It was a wonderful scene in the House-in-the-Wood at The Hague, when this body of representative men, statesmen and diplomats, gathered under the cupola of one of the most artistically decorated halls in the world, to perform a task which, if carried to its logical conclusion, will win for them the blessings of untold generations.

The nursing of this new institution, the Permanent International Court of Arbitration, and the bringing of it into operation, is our present duty. Just now various influences are working against it. Cannot our Quaker women do something in this important issue? Baron de Staal, in his farewell address, said of this conference, which had provided for this court, that " the work done, while not as complete as might be desired, was sincere, wise and practical." He affirmed that "in time to come institutions which had their origin in the need of concord would be the dominating influence, and that thus the work of the conference was truly meritorious." At the same meeting Dr. Beaufort said that " if the conference had not realized Utopian dreams, nevertheless it had disproved pessimistic forebodings, and the moral effect would more and more influence public opinion and governments to solve the question of the limitation of armaments, which still remains a source of grave consideration for statesmen of all countries."

We all lament that in the closing years of the last century there should have been war and famine, massacre and pestilence; still we believe that the nineteenth century was the best the world has ever known. In previous centuries there were continuous wars, duels, private wars. The latter have now been abolished altogether, and scores of cases of differences between nations have been settled by arbitration. We may confidently believe that we are already far on the way toward the general use of the International Court of Arbitration, now set up.

If wars are allowed to continue in the future the heaviest part of the burden will have to be borne by women, as in the past. They suffer most, because they are robbed by war of companionship and support. We Quaker women, as part of the great human sisterhood, are vitally concerned in this matter. Our profession lays upon us a very great duty. We think it is late in the day to begin arming and drilling boys in our public schools. The arbitrament of reason instead of passion ought to be a part of our inextinguishable purpose, in order that the good of life may be realized by all. Mothers prefer that their sons should not bleed their lives out on the battlefield, but should live to enjoy the kindly fruits of the earth and to help to make it the garden of the Lord.

The voice of the people in this age in all great nations is what directs the governments. The people are learning slowly that the " True Grandeur of Nations " consists in dealing fairly and patiently, and maintaining long periods of peaceful years. The closing words of President McKinley's address at Buffalo make doubly dear to many the great subject of peace. He said: " Our interest is in concord, not conflict, and our real eminence rests in the victories of peace, not those of war." The words of President Grant to an Eastern prince on the subject of arbitration are entirely in harmony with the teachings of the Society of Friends: "Arbitration between nations may not satisfy everybody at the time, but it satisfies the conscience of mankind, and must commend itself more and more as a means of adjusting disputes." We women must use our utmost influence in the spheres in which we move to bring all the people to believe this, and to insist that the government shall believe it.

Higher in importance than our Houses of Congress, our public institutions, our armies or navies, are the homes of the nation. The home is a republic within a republic, a church within a church, a world within a world. Study the history of the past, and you will find that no nation has risen any higher than the general level of its home life, and no nation has fallen below that level. Lord Shaftesbury, the greatest philanthropist of his time, declared that " the direction of his character and his life was fixed by his nurse, a devoted Christian woman, before he was seven years old." Abraham Lincoln loved his mother so well that, lonesome little fellow that he was, he walked a long distance to bring a preacher who would pray at the grave, after her body had been buried a year. How revered and cherished is a hallowed motherhood! Around this are clustered the holiest scenes the heart can know. In the reign of England's gracious Queen we see combined the wise ruler of monarchy and the priestess of the home. The mother-heart of this Queen shaped the destiny and controlled the policy of the woman sovereign.

Where is the emphasis of Christian duty placed to-day in Christian homes? Where does your life and mine put its true emphasis? Is it for making the world better? Is it for training the boys of the nation to love, and self-sacrifice, and peace, instead of strife, and selfishness, and unholy ambition, and disregard of others? With the heritage of our Quaker testimonies, with our ardent confidence in divine guidance, shall we not recognize the whole world as our country, every family as our interest, and help thus to establish that golden era of brotherhood, which will be the introduction of His kingdom, for which we pray?

THE CHAIRMAN: The second paper on the program is "War Inconsistent With the Genius of Quakerism," by President Charles E. Tebbetts, of Whittier College, California. The paper, in the absence of President Tebbetts, will be read by President Unthank, of Wilmington College, Ohio.

BENJAMIN F. TRUEBLOOD: Before President Unthank reads I think I ought to say just a word about the absence of President Tebbetts. He has been extremely interested in the Conference and would have liked very much to be here; but he found his work pressing, and he felt that it was too much to have the committee pay his traveling expenses for such a long journey. He thought his paper would do as well without him. I assure you that he is not away from any lack of interest. He is one of our most faithful and capable peace workers on the Pacific Coast.

WAR INCONSISTENT WITH THE GENIUS OF QUAKERISM.

BY PRESIDENT CHARLES E. TEBBETTS, WHITTIER COLLEGE, CAL.

In a leading editorial of one of our most prominent journals * occurs the following:

"Did General Funston do right? Was he justified in deceiving Aguinaldo and capturing him by this deception? The answer is simply the answer of war. It is wrong to lie, and wrong to steal, and wrong to kill. But in war men must lie and steal and kill. Then war is wrong? Certainly—wrong for somebody—for the party that is in the wrong, and whose act involves both parties in all these wrong acts. War is an accursed thing: 'War is hell'; but all is fair in war and hell. There was no violation of the laws of war in General Funston's conduct."

The amazing logic of this quotation, which would make it right for a Christian to violate all the laws of God because some other party is in the wrong, is altogether too prevalent among Christian people, even in this enlightened twentieth century.

The above statement suggests a fact most serious in its consequences, which I will state in a proposition, thus: To become a soldier in a modern army requires the individual to surrender his *conscience* into the control of his superior officer.

---

* "New York Independent," April 4th, 1901.

This fact is specially true under the discipline of modern times. In ancient warfare an Achilles might retire to his tent and refuse to take part in the conflict if it did not suit him; but in these days a soldier is made a part of a vast machine, under the absolute control of his commanding officer. I am aware that there have been noble instances of the exercise of conscience in minor matters, as in the case of some young men who declined to go on duty as bartenders for the army canteen, and were excused by a lenient officer because of conscientious convictions. Yet it is true that in all things essential to the successful carrying on of war, the conscience must be surrendered; for " in war men must lie and steal and kill," and destroy property and burn homes and violate the Sabbath day, and subject women and children to disease and death, and whatever else of cruelty the commanding general may regard as essential to final victory.

Another proposition equally serious with the above is this: To become a soldier requires the abrogation of the human reason in all matters pertaining to the issues of the conflict. A soldier might become convinced that the right in the contention was with the enemy, and that he was fighting with a side wholly in the wrong; and yet there is no honorable way to escape the dilemma. To state his convictions would lead to suspicion; to desert the army means dishonor and death. Rather would he be likely to yield to a sentiment altogether too common, " My country, may she be always right; but my country always, right or wrong."

What can possibly be more disastrous than this dethronement of conscience and reason? The suffering incident to death upon the battlefield or disease in camp is usually soon ended. The heartpangs caused by broken home ties and loss of loved ones will heal. Entire lives subject to the loss of limb and weakened physical energies have their compensation in human thought in the honors and glory consequent thereto. But what compensation is there for the moral degeneration, the debased manhood, the lowering of conscience, the impairing of reason that follows in the train of the conflict of war, and is entailed by the laws of heredity upon future generations?

Nor does the soldier alone suffer in the cessation of reason and conscience. From the beginning of the war until its end every voice of argument or of protest that does not harmonize with the attitude of the government must be hushed, or taint of treason rests upon one who lets that voice be heard. Even the preacher of the word, who ought to stand unflinchingly for righteousness and the inviolability of the law of God, becomes too often an apologist for the barbarism of war, or even an enthusiastic instigator thereto.

Does it need any argument to show that this enslavement of conscience and reason is inconsistent with the genius of Quakerism? Can we by any stretch of the imagination think of Fox and his associates as submitting themselves to the mechanical movements of a modern drill-master, and degrading manhood to the level of an inanimate machine? Their conception of the dignity of the individual man was so high that they would pay homage only to God himself, and carried it to the very extreme in their refusal to remove the hat, or use the plural pronoun when addressing an individual. No man could ever stand between them and God, or dictate to them the lines of duty. God's law was supreme, and no human plan was allowed to interfere with their obedience to the divine voice. The conscience must ever be kept tender to the least intimation of duty. No command of God was trivial; no human authority could for one moment abrogate the divine command. What others regarded lightly was to them a solemn obligation. They spent months and sometimes years in foul dungeons, rather than take an oath. For them to have submitted their conscience or reason to the will of another would have been to sell the very birthright of their manhood.

Three things, at least, were fundamental to early Quakerism: the supremacy of the divine law over every human authority, the freedom of the individual conscience from all dictation of men, and the right of every man to discover for himself the righteousness of every cause involving human conduct, and when discovered, the obligation fearlessly to espouse the side of right. These principles have made the Friend the uncompromising foe of all oppression and the pioneer in every right reform.

It is no idle boasting to claim for our forefathers their full share of credit for the victories of civil and religious liberty. If they were right in the maintenance of these principles, the obligation rests no less heavily upon us, their children, to condemn war as being always utterly antagonistic to the laws of God.

But were they right? Were they correct exponents of the teachings of Christ and his apostles? Only a few days ago I heard the assertion, in a most excellent Thanksgiving address, that a Christian was bound to obey every command of his government. This was based upon Paul's words in Rom. 13, " Let every soul be in subjection to the higher powers. . . . He that resisteth the power resisteth the ordinance of God "; and also upon Peter's injunction, " Be subject to every ordinance of man for the Lord's sake." Did they mean that a man could shift responsibility from his own conscience for any act, however foolish or wrong, because of the command of those in authority? Daniel and his companions certainly did not so understand God's law; and Peter is his own best interpreter, when in answer to the command of the authorities " not to speak at all or teach in the name of Jesus," he replied, " Whether it be right in the sight of God to hearken unto you rather than unto God, judge ye."

We may then not shrink from the assertion that we cannot become soldiers and recognize God's supreme authority over conscience and reason. May it not be ours to so persistently enforce this truth, that all Christians shall come to see that war is inconsistent with Christianity? This time will come; and when it comes war will have become a barbarism of the past.

THE CHAIRMAN: The next paper, "Constancy in our Peace Sentiment and Effort," is by President Edwin McGrew, of Pacific College, Ore.

CONSTANCY IN OUR PEACE SENTIMENT AND EFFORT.

BY PRESIDENT EDWIN M'GREW, PACIFIC COLLEGE, OREGON.

In every movement of reform there are periods of greater or less hopefulness and periods of greater or less discouragement. There are times when the sunlight of possible success seems ready to burst forth to ripen faith into sight and hope into possession, and again the unbroken cloud of despair seems to shut us from the possible realization of the thing hoped for. The crowds depend upon conditions, but the heart of the true reformer is moved by a more constant power. We sit in a peace conference and follow some one in a well-prepared paper that outlines a hopeful view; we watch the development of the national peace idea from its germination, until, cultivated and nourished, it comes to mature fruitage in a powerful peace congress, and we are all men and women of peace.

But we go from these great meetings, and in the mighty onward progress of the nations of the world there comes a clash—a battleship is sunk, the flag is insulted, what then? Oh, the mighty provocation is a sufficient cause for war—we are people of peace, but for all that shall we not defend our flag? Certainly, as we respect and love our flag we must defend it, and demand that other nations respect it; but shall it be by way of the bloody and dead-strewn field of carnage, contrary to the teaching of the Christ whom we profess to love above father and mother, houses and lands, nation and national emblem?

As Christian men and women, rich in inheritance from a devout peace-loving ancestry, rich as subjects of the Prince of Peace, there is but one position for us to take, and that is—war is, first of all, morally wrong, regardless of conditions. A second proposition, which I will consider only briefly, but one worthy of careful consideration, is that from a social and economic standpoint war is not a satisfactory means toward the end desired. The moral question has been discussed until perhaps the discussions have well-nigh lost their power to move the hearts of men. Yet in the opening days of this great new century, under the steady glow of the light of our boasted civilization, touched by the radiance of the cross of Jesus Christ, which must soften hatred into love, and balance justice with mercy, it is not difficult to find men of high

Christian profession and church standing ready to favor the use of armies and navies, and to advocate government legislation for their support.

In a most peculiar way has the " right " of the matter been presented, and a " righteous and Christian " war has been entered into for the " sake of humanity " and those oppressed by tyranny. It has been urged that the position one may take concerning this question measures unerringly his loyalty to his country and his love for the flag. It has been with some effort that some of us who represent the West have urged that it is as much a mark of patriotism to pay taxes as it is to fight, and with great difficulty have we restrained some of our earnest young men from enlisting. May the church of Jesus Christ remember the lesson from her earlier history and never attempt military engagement with the cross at the columns' front. A fatal day was that to the Christian Church. Unwonted results will follow the propagation of the Christ-spirit by Satan's methods. Let the tempting one still be rebuked with scripture message, while we catch the words from the lips of the Nazarene—the Son of God—my kingdom is of another character. " Put up thy sword."

The Society of Friends has ever been recognized as an uncompromising champion of the cause of peace. Much of our literature is upon this subject; with no uncertain sound we have cried out against war. We have advocated the doctrine that peace is a fundamental principle of Christianity. I say, we have done this if we have been true representative Friends, for we meet on common ground these days of blessed and helpful intercourse, because this doctrine of peace is one of the great distinguishing features of Quakerism.

Just here, by her permission, I incorporate in my paper some lines written by our friend, Elizabeth B. Miles, who is the most zealous advocate of peace in Oregon Yearly Meeting:

" The consideration of the great principle of peace is the vital question of Christianity, embracing as it does the mission of Christ upon earth as expressed by the prophet, ' For unto us a child is born, unto us a son is given, and the government shall be upon his shoulders, and his name shall be called Wonderful, Counselor, The mighty God, The everlasting Father, The Prince of Peace,' and as announced by the angels at his birth, ' Glory to God in the highest, on earth peace and goodwill to men.' It permeates every fibre of our being and enters into every action in every relation in life; into every moment in every period of life; in our walk among men, in our homes, in our neighborhoods, in Church, in State, in nation. Every friction that gives pain to another is a violation of this principle. Christ will manifest peace, promote harmony, heal every offence. As it regulates the hearts of men it gives living force to the powers of influence permeating communities and becomes identified with the angels' anthem, ' Peace on earth, goodwill to men.'

"This living, Christ-begotten principle will eradicate evil and is the only remedy to cause conflict and wars to cease. I believe this great emancipation is increasing in the earth. The Captain of the Lord of Hosts is pressing on to victory."

May such holy sentiment control our great Christian nation. All strife that would work ill to our neighbors—neighbors in the narrow Pharisaic sense and neighbors in the broad Christian idea—all words that tend to stir up hatred, all, *all*, are out of harmony with the Christ we serve. How inconsistent with our conception of his true, generous, loving spirit, how revolting to our thought that he whose message was and is peace, and whose touch was the touch of healing—should lead an army of carnal warfare. Then how can his followers?

Some one has said it was an awful thing for Abel to be killed; but that "it was lots worse for Cain to kill him." Two little pictures have found their way to our home on the Pacific slope; one is a scene in South Africa. The landscape is rough, rocky and broken—only here and there are bunches of low underbrush, while away in the background rise the higher and more rugged cliffs. It is evening time, and, as the sun sinks behind the mountain, a sulphurous cloud of battle smoke hangs around the hill-tops. In the foreground lies the body of a Boer soldier, one of many who fell that day before the awful fire of British guns. He had fallen with deadly wounds, and while the hot sun poured burning heat upon him he writhed in death agony upon his bed of rock and sand. As the day grew cooler, he became insensible to suffering and lay quietly dreaming of the little home away across the valley, where wife and children, with generous love, petition God to provide and care for one who has gone to fight and die for them. He dreams, too, of the morrow and of those who will gather at the church to pray for the cause for which he is dying. Well, right or wrong, we find ourselves saying, it is too bad that a soldier must suffer and die on the battle field away from his home. Yes, but I have thought it was worse for England, civilized England, enlightened England, Christian England, praying England, to kill him. Add to this scene multitudes of like scenes, scenes a thousand fold worse than this, scenes of foulest, blackest crime, and we say they are bad—but O! worse, worse, when laid at the door of a Christian nation.

The second picture is not unlike the first. The scenery is richer, for it is an island of tropical verdure. The sun that seemed to rise out of the deep blue waters to the eastward has gone beyond the palm grove and seems ready to drop into the restless waves of the western sea. American soldiers are reviewing the work of the day. Here a company of Red Cross men are tenderly caring for a wounded Filipino, and here another company of soldiers are looking upon a little lad who has been a victim of one of their shots. One soldier remarks, "He couldn't outrun our bullets"; and again we are ready to say, Too bad he was killed. Yes, but it was worse for Christian America to kill him.

I need not recount the oft-repeated, but seldom exaggerated horrors of war. The Lord preserve us from allowing our feelings to become deadened until we fail to recognize that war at its very best is crime.

Since I represent so distant a section of the work of Friends, it may be interesting to some to know that we are doing something in the line of peace education. Last spring the debating team of the Pacific College won, by the unanimous decision of the judges, in a debate with a team from one of our State institutions, our team taking the peace side of the discussion concerning the Transvaal situation; and at our commencement two orations were given on the subject of peace and arbitration, neither speaker being a member of the Society of Friends. I have been asked if our college is Pacific with reference to size. It is not, but it is none the less Pacific.

A little careful consideration, which time does not admit of in this paper, would be convincing that war, from both the social and the economic standpoint, is a curse to any people. No war can make a wrong right, nor can it be a satisfactory arbiter of justice. In our demands for peace we must not overlook the fact that there will often arise questions demanding justice in settlement, constant wrongs that must be righted. The American people will never respond to a cry for peace that demands a softening of patriotic sentiment. We love a liberty that has in it no loose license, a liberty not of mere beautiful sentiments, but a liberty "established in permanent institutions under the sway of law." The peace which we desire is not such as will make us willing to see our flag insulted and our rights infringed upon, nor such as will sap our patriotism, but a peace that demands justice by wise and righteous methods. I love my country, and, as I walk over these old battle grounds which are so familiar to some of you, they seem like hallowed spots to me, not because I approve of the methods whereby our freedom was purchased, but because I recognize with sorrow the great travail that brought forth this new nation. These old historic buildings are sacred, and I thank God for all that has been done for me. As I ride from ocean to ocean, through rich valleys and over mighty mountain ranges full of unmeasured wealth—over the vast plains where range-cattle graze, and across the great farms of the Middle States, where the granaries are overflowing with their store, over the hills and valleys of Eastern States, with prosperous towns and thriving commercial cities, I am convinced that this flag of freedom and justice and purity waves over the grandest nation that God ever gave man to rule, and I pray it may never again be compelled to wave in sulphurous smoke above the confused noise of battle.

But I am not a prophet to say our nation will or will not ever again engage in carnal warfare. We hope for a better future, but there may yet be wars and rumors of wars. Most hopeful sentiments have been read in our hearing. Some have declared we are near the last days of carnal warfare. Let us hope as much. Sometimes, indeed, it seems we are nearing the fulfillment of the prophecies of universal peace. And so we pray that "come it may," and hope that

> " Come it will for a' that,
> When man to man, the warld o'er,
> Shall brothers be for a' that."

Again we shout with confidence that the implements of warfare are soon to be hammered and beaten into instruments of peace, and the " war drums shall throb no longer," and the great world federation shall be realized, when the ivy shall twine about the half-buried cannon to hold it forever in its place, while the children of peace will fill its silent mouth with roses. I hope with you that the time is near at hand, and I believe that this great and most inspiring conference is to be a help in that direction. But such convention is not enough. Every life from this time forth must be a potent and aggressive force for peace. The Master in his announcement that his kingdom is not of such character as to demand his followers to fight, did not indicate that they need not work. On the contrary, his coming to the world was the birth of a new force, and his every step and word was in service. To his disciples he gave the matchless commission for labor, " Go and herald my gospel." In obedience to his commandment are the greatest possibilities of disseminating our peace doctrine. With all the many things and conditions that make for peace, many of which have been so beautifully set forth, nothing has resulted or can result in so much as the wise, prayerful, vigorous sacrificing efforts of true missionaries and evangelists of the cross, under the leadership of the Holy Spirit.

The great apostle indicated a mighty truth in his rich testimony that the law of the spirit of life in Christ Jesus made him free from another law. The broad truth indicated is simply this: the only thing that can overcome LAW is LAW.

After we meet in one more session of this great and good conference, I think we must return to our respective places of service—in the household, in business life, in educational effort—in this lovely and hospitable city, in the north land, in the south land, on the plains of the West or beyond its rugged mountain ranges, truer exponents of the " law of the spirit of life," which will make the individual and the world " free from the law of sin and death."

THE CHAIRMAN: There is important business to come before this afternoon's session, and it has been thought by the Business

Committee that it had better come at this time and the discussion of the papers be left until later. First is the report of the Committee on the subject of an Address to the President, which will be presented by Dr. Trueblood.

BENJAMIN F. TRUEBLOOD: The Business Committee have noticed during the sessions the expression a number of times of the hope that this Conference would send either a deputation or a message to the President of the United States expressing sympathy with him in his great responsibilities, appreciation of his integrity and high sense of honor, and also encouragement to him to do all that is within his power as the Chief Executive of the nation to further the cause of permanent international peace. The committee have had the matter under careful consideration; and it has seemed to them best on the whole to name a committee of five persons to draft and send to the President a message on behalf of the Conference. It has been impossible in the press of business and other engagements connected with the Conference, for us to have time to draft such a message as we thought would be worthy to be sent. We propose, therefore, that a committee of five, consisting of President Sharpless, of Haverford College; President Birdsall, of Swarthmore College; Philip C. Garrett, Howard M. Jenkins and Rufus M. Jones, be appointed to prepare as early as possible and to send to the President on behalf of this Conference such a message as in their judgment it may seem wise to send to him.

After some discussion, the names of Susan W. Janney and President M. Carey Thomas were added to the list of persons proposed for the committee, and the proposition was adopted.

THE CHAIRMAN: The second matter of business is that of the printing the report of the Conference, which will be introduced by Howard M. Jenkins.

HOWARD M. JENKINS: By direction of the Business Committee, I propose that the proceedings of the Conference be printed; not less than 5,000 copies, and as many more as the funds, in the opinion of the committee, may warrant.

JOSHUA L. BAILY: I want to second that proposition, but to make a little addition. It is very proper that the proceedings as a whole be published, and I hope the edition will be large enough to place a copy in every public library throughout the country. Some of the papers which have been read have a special fitness at this time. I should like to have the committee left at liberty to publish these in separate form for a wider circulation than will be obtained by the proceeedings as a whole. I should like to see some of them printed by the tens of thousands. We Friends who feel interested in the circulation of these papers ought to send contributions at once to the Finance Committee. A thousand dollars has been raised to pay the necessary expenses of the Conference. I think at least another thousand dollars can be usefully employed in the publication and distribution of the papers.

PHILIP C. GARRETT: I think, probably, some of the peace societies of the country would be very glad to take advantage of the opportunity to purchase a considerable number of copies of the report or of certain of the papers, such as will be of special value to them. I hope that the other suggestion with regard to the public libraries will take hold of Friends generally. Bound copies of the proceedings might well be placed in the Library of Congress, in the libraries of the Legislatures of all of the States, and in many other public libraries. A fund, it seems to me, could easily be made up for that purpose.

The proposition of Howard M. Jenkins was then adopted.

THE CHAIRMAN: Philip C. Garrett has a further matter of business to introduce.

PHILIP C. GARRETT: It is manifest that between the reading of the papers and their publication there is a large amount of work to be done by some one. It will be necessary to assign the editing of them to somebody. My motion is that a committee of three, with power to add to their numbers, be appointed, who shall take the papers and edit them, and do whatever is necessary in the way of deciding the number to be issued and every other question relating to publication. I would propose that Dr. Benjamin F. Trueblood, Howard M. Jenkins and Rufus M. Jones be the committee of three, with power to add to their number.

The proposition of Philip C. Garrett was approved and the committee appointed.

THE CHAIRMAN: There is a further report from the Business Committee, which Dr. Trueblood will present.

BENJAMIN F. TRUEBLOOD: One of the subjects assigned to the Business Committee at the opening of the Conference was the consideration of resolutions that might be offered and the preparation of such a declaration as we might think it wise that the Conference should issue. The committee have had these matters under careful consideration and have decided that, in addition to sending a message to the President of the United States, it is wise to issue a short declaration, setting forth the convictions of the Friends here gathered on the important subject for the promotion of which the Conference was called.

In preparing this declaration we have had several things in mind. In the first place, we felt that it must be brief, for now-a-days people will not read anything that is very long. In the second place, it seemed to us clear that the document should be fundamentally a restatement of the views the Friends have always held in regard to war. The committee believed, further, that our utterance should contain a positive statement of the power and efficiency of the moral forces which create peace in the world. The committee also thought that it was not wise to let this occasion pass without expressing an appreciation of the remarkable gain which the cause of peace has made in recent times. It also felt that it was the duty of the Conference at least to utter its serious regret at the wars which have recently been going on in the world and in some measure still continue; and, lastly, that an appeal should be made to Christians of all names in our country to be more faithful and zealous in setting forth and maintaining the great principles of peace which lie at the very heart of our Christianity. On behalf of the committee, I submit for your consideration the following, and move its adoption:

DECLARATION OF THE AMERICAN FRIENDS' PEACE CONFERENCE, HELD IN PHILADELPHIA, THE 12TH, 13TH AND 14TH OF TWELFTH MONTH, 1901.

1. This Conference of members of the different bodies of Friends in America is convinced that lapse of time has not made necessary any change in the position which the Friends have always taken on the subject of war. Rather have reasons accumulated, with the passing generations, for believing that war in all its forms is not only irreconcilable with the precepts, example and spirit of the Founder of Christianity, but that it is likewise out of harmony with the common principles of reason and morality, whose foundations are laid in the essential constitution of humanity. War, in its spirit, its deeds, the persistent animosities which it generates, the individual and social degeneration produced by it, is the antithesis of Christianity and the negation, for the time being, of the moral order of the world.

2. We believe that love, goodwill, self-sacrificing service, the faithful and courageous inculcation, by teaching and example, of truth and righteousness, are the divinely-ordained means for the promotion of justice and right, for the eradication of error and iniquity, for the creation and maintenance of social and political order, and that the efficiency of these is not promoted but impaired by the instruments and methods of war.

3. We recognize with profound gratitude the progress toward the peace of the world that has been made in recent generations, in the elimination of certain forms of war, in the establishment of peace over wide areas of territory within the nations themselves, in the supplanting of brute violence by Law, and in the progressive substitution of arbitration for war in the settlement of international controversies.

4. The establishment by the civilized powers of the Permanent International Court of Arbitration we gratefully recognize to be one of the

greatest events in the history of human society. The setting up of this institution is the practical adoption by the nations of the principles and methods of settling controversies which have always been advocated by the Friends. The existence of this Court makes it practicable and therefore morally obligatory hereafter to adjust in a pacific way all international controversies that may arise, and therefore takes away every ground that has been urged for considering war a necessity.

5. We deplore the fact that nations making high profession of Christian civilization are at present engaged in war with less civilized and enlightened peoples, and we believe that the time has fully come when the voice of enlightened humanity should make itself heard, calling for an adjustment of the matters at issue by the Christian methods which have in numerous instances of successful operation proved themselves as practical as they are reasonable and humane.

In the spirit of our Master, the Prince of Peace, we call upon Christians of whatever name prayerfully to consider whether they are faithfully holding and advocating, as fully as their profession demands, the great principles of love, brotherhood and peace, which lie at the very heart of our common Christianity, and the faithful maintenance and propagation of which by all who call themselves Christians would, we firmly believe, speedily make all war impossible and bring in the reign of permanent and universal peace.

THE CHAIRMAN: We shall be glad to hear the expression of the Conference on the subject of this declaration.

PHILIP C. GARRETT: I am glad to second the motion which has been made for the adoption of this paper. One feature of it, which strikes me very pleasantly, is the tactful way in which the committee has touched the question of existing wars. No nation is named, but the condemnation of the wars that are existing is direct and emphatic, and will be understood as well at the seat of government of our own country as at the court of St. James.

CHARLES H. PENNYPACKER: I should like to suggest a thought that occurs to me relative to the fourth section of this Declaration of Principles. It is all right as far as it goes; but does it go far enough? The fourth section commends the establishment of a court of arbitration. Would it not be wise to deplore the fact that the English nation refuses to accept any arbitration of its difficulties with the Boer Republics? While we commend the establishment of the court of arbitration, should we not express our great disappointment at the refusal of the leading Christian nation of modern times to agree that its difficulties with those republics shall be submitted to that court?

GEORGE A. BARTON: I feel very thankful that the deliberations of this Conference have, through the medium of the Business Committee, taken form in a set of resolutions so brief, so pointed, so thoughtful as those to which we have just listened, and I heartily approve, personally, of their adoption by this Conference.

HENRY W. WILBUR: The resolutions seem to be adequate to the case. I think sometimes that teachers and preachers make a mistake in presuming that they must tell all they know in a single sermon. The philanthropist has fulfilled his function when he has cut and made the coat. It is no part of his business to put it on the man that it fits. I believe that we can send out these resolutions safely. Rest assured that the common wit of a common race will make the application where it is needed.

JOHN H. DILLINGHAM: I think we have passed the four resolutions and that virtually in them we have adopted the fifth. I think that there is no need for raising special feeling over special wars. We ought to say all that we have said about the general system of war. I think this will go forth before the country better on its own merits if we do not seem to reflect on the policy of any special war. We all have our private feelings about those two wars; but I fear the expression of opinion upon them will frustrate the reception of about all that we have said about war as a system.

General expressions of approval of the Declaration were given from many parts of the house.

THE CHAIRMAN: After the general expression which has been given in favor of accepting the Declaration as presented by the Committee, we will consider it adopted as it stands.

BENJAMIN F. TRUEBLOOD: We had a friend in the house this morning whom we are not likely to have again. He rose a time or two to speak and was not noticed. If he is here this afternoon, I should like to ask that we give him two or three minutes before we close. I refer to Willis R. Hotchkiss, of the Friends' African Industrial Mission.

WILLIS R. HOTCHKISS: I appreciate the courtesy which has given me this opportunity. Certain considerations would impel me to remain silent during this Conference; yet there is one feature of the subject that perhaps has not been dwelt upon with the force that it might call for. There is no doubt that the language of peace is greatly needed in this land, as well as in those lands where none of the restraints of civilization are thrown about men; for if in this country, where the restraints of civilization and Christianity are thrown about men to keep them from evil, we yet read such shocking details of crime and debauchery, what shall we expect in a land where none of these restraints are felt, where men are left to pursue the evil bent of their natures to the last limit, where the brute in man shows his teeth in the brutalized countenance and vicious life?

I bring to you the question of peace from the savage standpoint and from the missionary standpoint. Some words have been spoken during the Conference with respect to this side of the question. But it has not been dwelt upon as it ought, perhaps, to have been. It seems to me that in these strenuous days the most signal testimony to the effectiveness and the practicability of peace principles has been given in the lives and conduct of those who are out upon the frontier of civilization, amid the conditions that are so strictly against these very principles. Against the dark background of recent events in China there has been painted a story of fidelity and of sacred adherence to these very principles, not on the part of Friends alone, but on the part of those of every denomination, which might well inspire us to renewed effort and renewed diligence. Great numbers of missionaries, rather than strike a blow in their own defence, have peaceably bowed their head to the Boxer's sword. These examples ought to inspire us to a new and fresh heroism in the work that we have been considering here.

Again, the fling has been thrown out against the native Christians, many a time, that they were "Rice Christians"; in other words, that they were in it for what they could get out of it in a material way. But that fling may never be thrown at them again in the face of the magnificent heroism of these last days, when multitudes of them have laid down their lives in defence of the principle of non-resistance which they have received through the Gospel that has been borne to them, not by Friends' missionaries alone, but by other missionaries. I myself in Africa have seen the missionaries of other denominations, of the Church of England, refuse utterly to take up arms when their institutions were attacked by Arabs and by hostile natives; I myself passed through four years in the most savage part of Central Africa, and was ambushed numbers of times by savage natives. I have faced their spears and their arrows, their bows and drawn bowstrings; and yet I never raised a weapon in my own defence. It is still true that the Golden Rule and the Sermon on the Mount are effective in a remarkable way. They are not things of centuries ago, but they are very practical to-day.

Another thing or two: What is the difference between the influence of David Livingstone and that of Stanley? Why is it that the one is spoken of and remembered with affection throughout the length of the Dark Continent wherever he traveled, while the other is forgotten, or, if remembered at all, is remembered with dislike because of his deeds of blood? Because the one played the part of the strenuous, worldly man who goes through at any cost, trampling up the rights of his fellow-man, and the other that of the loving man of God, who recognizes that beneath even a black skin there is a soul that lives throughout eternity; that, though he dwell in the rude hut of a savage, and though he be so bestial that he bow before a stone and call it God,

"A man's a man, for a' that,"

and has inalienable rights, rights which every man must respect—every man, at least, who has a spark of manhood about him.

One incident and I close: A few years ago two young women sisters, were sent by their mother from Australia to Central China. Some time after this one of those numerous outbreaks which have sent a shudder of horror throughout the civilized world occurred, and these two sisters were murdered, with the others at that station at Cochin, in China. Did that mother, away in Australia, bear a spirit of revenge toward the murderers of her lovely daughters? No; but Mrs. Saunders, for that was her name, immediately sold out her possessions, and to-day she is in Cochin in her daughters' place, proclaiming to their murderers the principles of the Prince of Peace. We are finding out that the principles that we Friends stand for are practicable to the very extreme.

After a few moments of waiting up God, during which prayer and thanksgiving were vocally offered by Mary Chawner Woody, the Conference adjourned till 8 p.m.

Ninth Session.

SEVENTH-DAY EVENING, TWELFTH MONTH 14TH.

The ninth and last session of the Conference met in the Twelfth Street Meeting-house, under the presidency of Dr. Isaac Sharpless, at 8 p.m.

A period of silent devotion was observed at the opening of the session.

THE CHAIRMAN: The first paper on the program this evening is by Josiah W. Leeds: "Remedies for the Prevailing Militarism," to be read by his daughter, Lucy Leeds.

REMEDIES FOR THE PREVAILING MILITARISM.
BY JOSIAH W. LEEDS, WEST CHESTER, PA.

It is one of those propositions which "goes without saying," that when seeking to apply the remedy to any disorder, we need to have clear knowledge of the complaint, its symptoms and features, in order to a discovery of the root of the trouble. We know for a certainty what are the *characteristics of war*. All the adjectives of woe might be exhausted in truthfully portraying it, while we need scarcely cast about for better authority upon the generation of the wretched brood than that of the Apostle James. He tells us, in asking, "Whence *come* wars and fightings?" "Come they not hence, even of your lusts that war in your members? Ye lust and have not; ye kill and desire to have, and cannot obtain: ye fight and war, yet ye have not, because ye ask not," or ask, only to "consume it upon your lusts"; and so he goes on to declare, in pointing towards the remedy, how that "the friendship of the world is enmity with God," that it is "a spirit that lusteth to envy," and is only to be effectually met by that grace of God which will potentially "resist the devil," and, inferentially, the devil's work of war.

So here is a disease affecting the whole system, whether we consider it as of the body individually or the body nationally, and the correction, to be effective and lasting, must run all the way through; nay, it will not suffice to "have healed the hurt of the daughter of my people slightly, saying, peace, peace, when there is no peace."

A most singular suggestion for bringing within bounds the war spirit and the spirit of anarchy, a suggestion which was *seriously* broached, perhaps, only the present year, is found in the proposal to bring about a general softening of people's hearts and sweetening of their tempers through a great development of *music*. How ill-supported must be such an expectation! Consider that the Athenians of old, who developed plenty of the war fever, were a music-loving people; and in our own time, none more so than the Italians, yet we hardly look upon them as a nation ardently anxious for peace. Reading, years ago, a series of brief biographies of noted musical composers, I remember to have been struck with the fact that, despite the atmosphere of constructive harmony in which they lived, the inspiration of dulcet symphonies did not suffice (with many of them at least) to subdue the tempest in the human breast. Indeed, the quality of irascibility seemed to be quite pronounced. Clearly we cannot look for the panacea here.

A well-intentioned Chinese writer, in a lately-contributed magazine article, quotes a saying of Confucius that " Peace is a condition that must be born of war." Applying the maxim to this country, he recommends that we provide ourselves with an unsurpassably powerful navy to police and protect our coasts, and to thence dictate peace to all the world. But ruined Phœnicia, that once great maritime power, essayed this role of supremacy many centuries ago, and its splendid sea port of Tyre—well, we only know the sunken site of it as *under* the sea which it sought to rule.

A recent letter received from one who had had long experience of literary and political life, gives expression to a quite popular belief, that the *intensification of war enginery*, together with the *exceeding expensiveness* of its production, must ere long operate to bring to an end the fighting habit of the nations. " The taste for war," he says, " is being gradually cured by its indulgence. The cost of the destructive agencies of war has been so enormously increased that I think the experience of nations during the last three years will have demonstrated that there is nothing to be gained by an offensive war that will not cost more than it can possibly be worth; and that diplomacy will be substituted for guns and powder before the world is many centuries older."

Well, the economic argument ought to help along the remedy, and it certainly has influenced many advocates, as publicists, parliamentarians, Socialists, and even Anarchists; for it must be kept in view, now that the cure of anarchy is being diligently sought after, that there are those among the ultra-agitators, who, driven to frenzy by brooding over the insatiable demands of the war monster ever crying, Give! Give! have brought themselves to believe that the extinction of the rulers will by-and-by abolish conscription, minimize taxes, and bring release of the proletariat from military service,—a good sequence, but an impossible way to attain it.

There are those among the wise ones of the world who may have a persuasion that the stimulation of learning, public improvements and utilities generally will effect much in overcoming the war spirit; but the great and now fallen empires of the past had their libraries, gymnasia, public baths, and—when Rome came to represent almost the then known world—their famous stoned highways that ran to all parts of the vast domain. We may have all these useful public possessions in greatest abundance, but, lacking the underlying principle founded on the love of God and man, they will not avail as any *final* remedy for war and assurance of peace.

Nevertheless, as the Law was a schoolmaster in bringing to Christ, the spread of the humanitarian motive, with its leavening of Christianity, will serve as a handmaid in hastening the advent of the reign of peace. But the one essential remedy which I believe we need above all others to look to is this: " The gospel of Christ [which is] the power of God unto salvation." Not simply the Glad Tidings of the letter, be it said, for well we know it has been charged upon the greatest of the nations claiming this knowledge— " See what fighters these Christians be!" So that, notwithstanding the Glad Tidings was proclaimed nearly two millenniums ago, do we not in this day, this very year, witness the fulfillment of what Paul testified in his epistle to the Romans, that " the name of God is blasphemed among the Gentiles through you, as it is written "? For thus it had been written by Israel's seer, in telling how those who made claim to be " the people of God, and are gone forth out of his land," that his holy name " was profaned among the heathen, whither they went." Oh, what a change is wrought with the *power*, " the power of God unto salvation," which brings only blessing and not blasphemy!

This effectual remedy, as said before, must run *through the life* —whether it be of the individual or the nation. The word which came to Jeremiah when judgment upon the favored nation hung in the balance, was " Thus saith the Lord of hosts, the God of Israel, Amend your ways and your doings, and I will cause you to dwell in this place," repeating to them the promise that this should be so: " If ye *thoroughly* amend your ways and your doings, if ye thoroughly execute judgment between a man and his neighbor"; saying further they must cease from oppression and come away from idolatry,—in other words, out of the lust of those forbidden things which are the roots of war.

Now, this necessary amendment in order for the *remedy*,—must it not begin with the child? With the twig that will bend? In large showcases in the basement of a great department store in this city may be seen *military playthings* for the juveniles, some of them elegant and costly, representing platoons of mimic soldiers of the infantry, and gaily-caparisoned cavalry, lumbering artillery, bristling ramparts, and all the scenic make-up of actual warfare. We shall not be likely to see these things in the playrooms of the children of Friends, yet they are common in the community, and as educators their influence must be pronounced.

It is an easy step from playing soldier in the nursery to *march-*

ing in brigade along the streets, with real undersized guns, and fife and drum, and the contented thought that if we may do this as pupils in the Sabbath School to the chant of " Onward, Christian Soldiers ! " we are in the right road to the overturning of the bulwarks of Satan. The remedy applicable here is a closer teaching of the truth that the Christian warfare is not carnal, but spiritual, to the overturning of the strongholds of evil; so, if the active brigade be wanted for the boys, let it be with other implements, as for the *saving* of life—a substitute which has been adopted in various directions. The amended drill may also properly be with the Indian clubs, affording excellent exercise, whether for boys or for girls, in the line of calisthenics.

In *field* athletics, the intense rivalry, tending to many serious abuses, as jealousies, recriminations, love of publicity, stimulation of the betting habit, and fierce contests marked by maimings, and, at times, loss of life, betoken the cultivation of a lust for acquisitions which are not happily educational. A remedy here, recommended, but far too infrequently put in practice, is the discontinuance of the *publicly-heralded match games* of the colleges and other scholastic institutions. This would easily deduct a *tenth* from the reading matter of the daily papers, but it would be a needed step backward in the direction of peace.

In the schools, lust of fame, glory, empire, and the uplifting of a patriotism wrenched out of place, is very much fostered through the *teaching of war in the text-books of history*. Not so much in the salient facts concerning any particular war, especially its causes and effects, but through the manner in which the mere fighting details are exaggerated, so that the battle-loss of our so-called enemies becomes a thing to exult over. I know this well from my youthful experience. As to the *battle pictures*, while the frightfully realistic canvas of a Verestschagin may partly lift the illusion of glory by a glance at the hideousness of the field of carnage, the popular class-book of history sufficiently drapes the repulsive part, and the young mind is left to its visions of the special prowess, triumph and renown of the heroes of battle. However, I believe there has been an amending in this particular. The Sumner bequest to Harvard, creating a prize for approved theses on the settlement of disputes without resort to war, was a valuable educational precedent. Similarly commendable was the effort of Lafayette College, some years ago, to substitute for one of the courses in pagan classics, with its pro-war and often immoral ideals, one in which the classical exponents came closer to the Christian standard. (A failure of the specially-contributed fund, I believe, was the cause of the dropping of this rarely-tried course.)

As our student reaches manhood, and embarks, mayhap, in commerce or manufactures, and perchance finds his country engaged in war, there may open a choice of courses in which he will need to reckon closely with his conscience. If he has rightly appropriated the lessons or influences conducive to peace which have heretofore been laid in his way, he will not make gain through furnishing goods or material to be used in carrying on war. To instance but a few: The Rotch family, of Nantucket, with their neutral shipping and whale oil commerce during the Revolutionary and later wars; an Allen, of England, who, as manufacturer of chemical products, declined a very lucrative contract for certain goods to be used in the war in which his country was engaged; a Cadbury, who, a little while ago, though willing to supply, at cost, the Queen's special gift of chocolate for her soldiers in South Africa, refused thereafter to furnish supplies upon regular contracts of profit; the Hustons, iron manufacturers, who could not be persuaded to furnish armor-plate to the government during the Civil War, even though such action may have been looked upon as unpatriotic, as well as unnecessarily self-denying.

Further, our fair-minded citizen who would wish practically to apply the Scripture obligation to love our neighbor as ourselves, would welcome such *harmonious commercial relations* with other nations as would be of reciprocal benefit, and not be heavily weighted with the selfish maxim of *take all* and *give nothing*. Of such wisely-adjusted international traffic, which must prove a great conservator of peace, it was happily remarked by Elihu Burritt: " Commerce has no country but the world, no patriotism but an earnest interest in the well-being of *all* the nations. Its genius in this respect runs parallel with the genius of Christianity, though in a lower course—just as subterranean rivers run parallel with those that show their silver currents to the sun. Commerce repudiates *war* as an outrage upon its domain. It will not obey the laws of war, nor recognize any nation as an enemy with which it has or may have intercourse." The benevolent thought of Burritt in this direction is suggestively indicated by the caption of some of his cogent essays, as that on " The Waste of War and the Winnings of Industry "; another, on " Cotton, Commerce and Civilization "; a third, " Wardrobe, Webs and Table-Ties of Brotherhood." What a bulwark, what a remedy would be found here, could we apply the touchstone of Christ's commandment to this which is destined to be an uppermost topic of general discussion, and most urgent subject for diplomacy and legislation! And so likewise in the matter of oppressive trade combinations, the fertile source of endless angry contentions.

In conscientiously manifesting his Christian citizenship, the citizen and voter will *thereby* directly provide, and speedily so, a foremost remedy against the outburst of war. The rule of political action recommended may be concisely expressed by that vigorous Anglo-Saxon word, *straightforwardness;* for, as Secretary of State Hay tersely stated it the other day, in speaking of the better diplomacy, " There is nothing like *straightforwardness* to beget its like." " We believe," was the conviction hereupon adopted by the National Woman's Christian Temperance Union last month, at Fort

Worth, " we believe that in a right apprehension of the ideals and demands of Christian citizenship lies the hope of the nation; that no citizenship is worthy the name of Christ which is not founded upon divine ideals of righteousness."

Thus, I conclude, *applied Christianity is the only assured remedy for war*, because it alone has its foundation on the immovable Rock. There have been formed for the *arrest* of war—beneficially operative after their measure—arbitral councils, and treaties, and truces in the old time, in the middle ages, in our own day especially —even up to the hopeful Pacific Tribunal at The Hague. But there have never been, as there are now, and as many observers are remarking, such legions of men in camps or in reserve in readiness for the fray, or such vast treasure applied on account of wars present or that threaten to come, or as interest and pensions due to those that are past. Nevertheless, solemn pacts will be made to be broken or evaded, while men remain largely unsubjected to the limitations of the cross. John, the disciple, was still unescaped from the law, when he plead that the Lord Jesus should smite with his wonderful power the offending village of a people who had no dealings with the Jews. In the same mood was Peter, when, with his sword, he cut off the ear of the servant of the high priest. Later along in life, better instructed of the Spirit, we behold John breathing only love, and the naturally-impetuous Peter discoursing how to " be pitiful, be courteous." Ezra, the scribe, and his company, in carrying unguarded over the desert the temple treasures, and Penn and his people in founding a State without one weapon of defence while surrounded by those accounted as hostiles, found equally the remedy against fighting to be in him of whom it was declared, " The government shall be upon *his* shoulder, and his name shall be called Wonderful, Counselor, The mighty God, The everlasting Father, The Prince of Peace." While faithfully laying hold of every proper aid, let us especially exalt the effective, divinely-appointed remedy, " The Gospel of Christ: for it is the power of God unto salvation."

THE CHAIRMAN: " The Influence of Quaker Peace Ideals in Our National Life," is the title of the next paper, by Dr. O. Edward Janney, Baltimore, Md.

THE INFLUENCE OF QUAKER PEACE IDEALS ON OUR NATIONAL LIFE.

BY O. EDWARD JANNEY, M.D., BALTIMORE, MD.

The Quaker ideal of peace is well expressed in the prophetic words, " They shall beat their swords into plowshares, and their spears into pruning hooks; nation shall not lift up sword against nation, neither shall they learn war any more." " They shall not hurt nor destroy in all my holy mountain; for the earth shall be full of the knowledge of the Lord, as the waters cover the sea."

Acknowledging, with other men, the necessity for government in order that there may be an enjoyment of life, liberty and the pursuit of happiness, and acknowledging further that orderly government requires an organized civil force to control the unruly, Friends have always maintained a consistent opposition to warfare and warlike preparations.

To what extent has this ideal of peace influenced our national life and affected our every-day affairs?

MILITARY SERVICE.

The Friends who founded Pennsylvania and those who controlled its affairs for seventy-four years bore a strong testimony against conscription and the organization of a militia, although frequently urged thereto by the English government, by their successive governors and by the clamor of the militant majority of their own community.

Although wars raged about them and invasions threatened, and although the colonies to the north and to the south suffered from the horrors of warfare, Pennsylvania refused to authorize movements of aggression and found little necessity for measures of defence. At last, when unjust encroachments on the rights and property of the Indians had roused them to reluctant revenge, and popular clamor among the colonists demanded war, Friends voluntarily relinquished the government to their opponents rather than prove false to their peace principles. "When the crucial nature of the question became clear, and either place or principle had to be sacrificed, their decision was in favor of the sanctity of principle. . . . The Yearly Meeting never gave any uncertain sound." (Sharpless.)

Thenceforward, although Friends did not take part in the administration of the Colonial or State government, yet the principles in which they trusted continued in force to a considerable extent, and do so yet. This influence is shown to be greater when it is made clear that the Frame of Government wrought out by William Penn and his counsellors, "though changed in form many times, shaped all future constitutions of Pennsylvania, of other States, and of the Federal Union." (Sharpless.) To the Friends of Penn's colony, therefore, the people of the United States are indebted, in great degree, for their present form of government, and some of the principles which underlie good government.

It would not seem to be taking too much for granted, therefore, to ascribe to this Friendly element, thus introduced, some of the beneficent traits of the American people. Among these are opposition to a large standing army, to compulsory military service in time of peace, and exemption from such service in time of war. To this influence, also, may perhaps be traced in part the generally peaceable character of the American people, who have never entered into war except when reluctantly forced into it by the pressure of circumstances, and then always in opposition to a strenuous protest from a large number of our citizens. The attitude of our nation towards others, with rare exceptions, has been one of peace, justice and good feeling.

When we compare the happy condition of our citizens, as to compulsory military service, with those of France and Germany, where the military spirit is rife, it must be admitted that an influence has been at work among us that has not been felt on the continent, and some of this has been exerted by Friends.

THE INDIANS.

The just and peaceable relations with the Indians established by the Quaker colonists produced and ensured harmony so long at it was continued, and trouble with the red man arose only when unjust and warlike encroachments were permitted.

Although an unrighteous Indian policy has been continued for 150 years, with its inevitable evil consequences, yet the Quaker ideal has been kept ever before the American people, and slowly, slowly our government has advanced toward it, until in President Grant and some of our recent administrators the friendly method of dealing with the Indians has been approached, with much success and with great hope for the future.

COURTS OF ARBITRATION.

For the prevention of disputes and as a substitute for armed conflicts Friends have offered arbitration between individuals and between nations as the ideal as well as practical Christian method.

Here again mankind is slowly emerging from darkness into light, leaving behind the trial by duel and, we believe, the trial by warfare, and advancing towards the frame of mind that is willing to accept arbitration as a just and proper method of deciding contests.

In the history of our nation many international disagreements have been so decided, some of them involving millions of money and preceded by heated arguments and antagonistic opinions that would ordinarily have led to bloodshed.

Numberless disputes between individuals are now settled by arbitration and lawsuits are thus often avoided. The court of arbitration is gaining popularity, and, being of equal standing with the law courts, is being appealed to more and more. In Baltimore, for instance, the Board of Trade, proceeding under an act of Legislature, has established such a court, whose decisions are as binding as though made by the courts of law. Indeed, it is not unusual for disputants to agree to abide by the legal opinion of a judge or eminent counsel, thus adopting the principle of arbitration. There is also constant demand for the settlement of all disagreements between employers and their employees by this method, of the application of which there have been some recent instances.

In all of this advance towards the peaceful settlement of disputes Friends can certainly claim that their unswerving testimony in favor of arbitration has had influence.

THE CHURCH.

It has often been asserted that the principles and testimonies of the Society of Friends have been so generally adopted by religious people everywhere that the need of our continued independent existence has vanished. An answer to this may be found in the attitude of the religious world toward war. The ideal of peaceableness expressed by the Master in the Sermon on the Mount, and made their own by the Society of Friends, is realized but inadequately by most Christian denominations, whose leaders are apt to weaken in the face of a strong popular demand for war, and too often give their support to measures of conquest or bloody retaliation. Very few churches would discipline a member for engaging in military service; the thought of doing so would hardly occur to them. Strange as it may seem, in the Church, the representative of the Prince of Peace, his message of non-resistance finds but tardy acceptance.

EDUCATION.

The well-known testimony of Friends in favor of the guarded education of the young was as far removed as possible from military training in schools, and in this a consistent course has always been followed. It is not claiming too much to say that their ideas have influenced those who have had charge of education in this country, especially as there have always been Friends who, as teachers and superintendents of instruction, have extended our Friendly thought.

However this may be, it is evident that the advisability or necessity of military education has never taken hold of the American people. The army has its West Point, to be sure, and the navy its Annapolis, and so it must be as long as the people allow an army or a navy to exist; but aside from these, it is only here and there, especially in reform schools, that military discipline is enforced, and in these it is the habits of attention, order and obedience and physical development that are sought, rather than the inculcation of a warlike spirit.

Owing to the accession of military feeling caused by the late war with Spain, a number of attempts have been made recently to introduce military training into the public schools; but the sentiment, as well as the judgment, of the people is opposed to this endeavor, which is doomed to failure.

CURRENT LITERATURE.

It is much to be regretted that the war spirit is so prominent in weekly and monthly journals. Most of this is to be accounted for by our experience of the past four years, as before that period there was little of it. Especially unfortunate is it that the juvenile press is so full of war stories and the glorification of warlike deeds. In fact, the most popular monthly of this class is one of the greatest sinners in this respect.

When the present attack of temporary insanity has passed and reason has once more regained its throne, our ideal of peace will seem all the more beautiful, and the young will be taught that the victories of civil life often far eclipse those of war, and do not leave behind remorse, nor the scars of conflict, nor the moan of the widow and orphan.

On the whole, it may be concluded that the Quaker ideal of peace has spread among the American people and deeply influenced our national life. May this high ideal continue to be held aloft until all people shall come within its ennobling influence, and the spirit of peace shall hover over the nations with healing on his wings!

The Chairman: "Peace as Involved in the Christian Method," by Rufus M. Jones, of Haverford College, is the last paper on the program of the evening and of the Conference.

PEACE AS INVOLVED IN THE CHRISTIAN METHOD.

By Dr. Rufus M. Jones, Haverford, Pa.

The scientists of the century have been forcing us to realize that Nature's method is ruthless competition. She gives success to the strong and extermination to the weak. Her realm is an endless battlefield—a fierce struggle for existence where the weak fatten the strong, and the unfit are mercilessly sacrificed to the fit. Every step of the slow advance from the lower forms of life has been marked by the weeding out of the helpless and the survival of the strong and physically fit. "Red in tooth and claw," Nature proclaims that strength, power, force, might, fitness to survive, are the only qualities for which she cares. Few have any conception of the awful slaughter which goes on day by day beneath the peaceful waters of the sea. Here everything lives on something else, and in the act of seizing its prey it is dodging its own foe. There is no corner of the ocean which is not a veritable Indian jungle where each lives on the life of another. This law of the jungle, this merciless method of nature, everywhere marks primitive man. Anthropology, archæology, ancient history, all tell the same tale— everywhere tribe at war with tribe, man arming himself against his enemy. The very divisions of the earth among the peoples of it have been made with an eye to protection and defense. But the little new-born child comes with an even surer record of this age-long warfare than any which the monuments of Assyria or the ruins of Karnak give us. His hereditary instincts are the deepest scars of these centuries of strife and survival of the strong. The primitive instincts are fear and anger; followed by the hardly less primitive instinct—love of power. They are egoistic, self-preservative instincts. They are in the very structure of the race, and they have their roots deep in an immemorial past, when human life meant struggle for existence and survival by the law of might. Nature's whole concern has been to produce a physical being with a fitness to survive in a competitive struggle for existence.

Now Christianity reverses this whole idea. Christ introduces a type of life which advances on precisely the opposite principle. He declares that in the kingdom where he rules a selfish struggle for existence carries with it extinction—" He that seeks to save his life shall lose it,"—and its very method of advance is by the propagation of love which forgets self in the effort to bless others.

The true way to study the peace idea at the heart of Christianity is not to make a collection of peace-texts, but to develop the Christian view of man and society and to see whether any place is left here for war and strife. Our question therefore must be, What does Christ's conception of man and society involve? What lies prophetic in his revelation of man?

Nothing is surer than that he thinks of man—any man—as a potential son of God. He puts man on a new level. He sets forth his new conception and calls men to it, in order, he says, " that ye may be the children of your Father in Heaven." His new commandment is, " that you love even as I have loved." His " follow me " is no mere call to walk over the same Syrian roads behind Him, but a call to the same attitude of life and an invitation into a brotherhood which has its origin in a Divine Fatherhood. The characteristic feature of the Son of Man is his devotion to the business of saving and perfecting others—his struggle for the life of others. To give, to share, and to transmit what he has received is his unfailing purpose. To win by defeating others is as inconceivable a course for him as it would be for the tiger to win his prey by methods of persuasion. He reverses the whole process of advance. Victories are to be won by the inherent power of light and truth and love, and if they cannot be won that way, then they are not to be won at all. Men are to be drawn to God on the simple ground alone that He loves them; and then, in their efforts to overcome a world organized on the principle of the power of the strongest, they are to make their appeal to the silent but invincible power of love and truth.

There can be no mistaking the fact that this was his method. There can be as little doubt that he bequeathed this method to his followers. I shall not now ask whether such a method is practicable in a world like ours or not, though one can say that so far it has had no adequate trial, and we must expect such transformations to be slow. But I shall consider the question, which is of some interest, namely, Why is the law of competition reversed by

Christianity? Why do we here go over from the law of struggle for existence to the method of love and sacrifice for others?

The first reason is that humanity found a new goal in Christ which could be attained only by some new method. So long as the goal is the attainment of material goods there must be a sharp competition and an occasion for warfare. The supply of good things is limited, and whatever one gets diminishes what the rest can have. The demand for such things exceeds the supply. The struggle, from the nature of the case, becomes a keen one. The whole breed of selfish passions are pushed to the front. It is for the vital interests of the stronger to put down the weak, and, by a certain natural selection, those who can fight best survive and produce a race like themselves. But the moment the goal becomes the attainment of some spiritual possession, the supply of it exceeds the demand! The more of it one gets, the more of it there is for others. It increases in proportion as it is possessed. When one man rises to the height of a new idea, the whole world is richer for it forever, and all souls feel the power of it. When one soul sees some new beauty and learns how to share it, he has made it at once the common possession of the race. When one individual by stricter obedience has caught a new truth and voiced it, all men everywhere feed upon it and add cubits to their stature. When some one person puts his life into an heroic deed, that becomes a universal legacy. If it can be revealed that God is love and that men can partake of his nature, then no amount of sharing can ever exhaust such a possession, and there will be no competitive struggle to win one's own share.

But the truth is deeper than this and involves more than we have yet touched. For as soon as the human goal is shown to be the possession of a spiritual attainment, it becomes clear that this can be attained only through the method of sharing. The surest way to shrivel and dry up is to live for self-perfection alone. In the spiritual life it is an eternal fact that no high quality can be won if it is directly sought for self. If it is impossible to catch a spinning top to see what the motion is like; if it is impossible to turn on the light to see what the darkness is like, it is equally impossible to produce the saintly spirit along any line of self-interest. To gain any pleasure from any action one must forget all thought of pleasure and become absorbed in the act. To become spiritual one must throw his life into the work of helping others win their victories, and lo! he finds that nothing he gives is ever given away. By losing his life in the glowing purpose to help men come to the possession of their true selves, he finds his own life enriching and deepening, and he enters upon an ever-heightening life. The loss is gain, the giving makes rich, the sharing increases the possession. This principle lies at the very heart of the Christian religion, and, because it is true, no one who fully enters upon the higher levels of Christian experience can consent to live by the law of might which breeds war and sets men everywhere against each other.

The struggle now will be not to see how much one can get, but rather how much one can give, not to see how many men's share one can seize and appropriate, but rather to see how many one can help to enter and share the common blessings of the Father's gift.

But there is still another reason why Christianity supplants war with a method of peace and love. Christ introduces the organic idea of society. We pass at once and forever from the individual as an atom to the individual as a member of the whole. There can be no isolated personal perfection, for our lives are so tightly linked that when one member suffers all suffer, and when one rises all rise. Human destiny is a social affair and no man can live unto himself or die unto himself. There is a gravitation finer and subtler than that which holds the worlds in a universe, and this binds the lives of human beings into a society in which each must share the rise and fall of all the members. It is, then, our end not to realize some little goal of personal attainment for which we live, but to raise, be it ever so little, the whole level of human life and to bring into actual existence a kingdom of God—a society of brothers by the divine right of sonship to God. The sublimest outlook of Christianity is its prophecy of a society founded in brotherhood, and deeper still, in the universal Fatherhood of God, and its most sacred message to man is the call, "by the mercies of God," to join in the work of making that prophecy come true. Now the only way such an ideal can be wrought out, the only way such a new Jerusalem can be brought down from God to become a fact before our eyes, is for a man in this present world to go to living as a son of God and treating all other men as possible sons. This is precisely Christ's method. The strong are to bear the infirmities of the weak, those who have received are to give, those who have seen are to help others see, and those who have found are to become the seekers after others. That such an idea involves peace and makes war impossible is as plain as the sun at high noon, and this is incontestably the Christian position.

But some one says, "This is a remote ideal which will be all right when the heavenly conditions arrive for realizing it, but now we are in a world where men have selfish passions, where the law of competition rules, and where one gets only what he struggles and fights for. No such millennium is in sight. Must we not adjust to the conditions of this present world?" The answer is simple. There never will be any heavenly conditions, there never will be an actual state of brotherhood and love unless those who see the significance of the new method go to living by it at whatever hazard and cost, and so make this ideal less remote, and bring the millennium a jot nearer. The single question to ask is, Which is the true way of life, the law of the jungle, somewhat modified and refined perhaps, or the law of love and brotherhood, the organic society where each lives for all? If man becomes himself and shows his real nature only when he makes his life contribute to the whole total of life and happiness, then there can be no question which course a man should take nor which course is the heroic one, for that course is most heroic which makes a man most a man.

Too long we have allowed the world to think of us merely as non-combatants, as sponsor to the idea of non-resistance, and we have been looked on with pity as a weak and passive folk. This Christian method here outlined is no more passive than is that of the most strenuous fighter on the world's bead-roll. On the contrary, it is gloriously positive. It is no withdrawal from danger or suffering, but rather it involves a genuine sharing of the world's burdens and struggles in a patient labor to make righteousness and peace the very conditions of human life. "Put on the whole armor," says the great advocate of the Christian method, writing from Cæsar's prison. "I have fought the good fight," is his farewell word to his young disciple. "Quit you like men" is his call to those who must take up the banner he is laying down. It is a noble word, but its full power comes out only when we see what it means to be a man. "Quit you like men; be strong." These words must be seen in the light of the new revelation of what it means to be a man—a being who realizes his place in the universe of spirit and who sees that he has a contribution to make to this growing kingdom of God. As fast as such men come the possibility of war diminishes; as man on the new level enters, man on the old level goes out.

"I told them," says Fox, when they were trying to enlist him in the army of the Commonwealth, "that I lived in virtue of that life and power which does away with the occasion for all war." The man who says that has discovered the fundamental idea of manhood. As fast as society becomes composed of such men war vanishes by as certain a law as that which has locked up the pterodactyl and megatherium in the iron hills, and swept the earth of the dodo.

It was on just this sense of the worth of man that our poet Whittier based his opposition to war and his mesage of peace:

> "Give human nature reverence for the sake
> Of one who bore it ; making it divine
> With the ineffable tenderness of God.
> Let common need, the brotherhood of prayer,
> The heirship of an unknown destiny,
> The unsolved mystery round about us, make
> A man more precious than the gold of Ophir.
> Sacred, inviolate, unto whom all things
> Should minister, as outward types and signs
> Of the eternal beauty which fulfills
> The one great purpose of creation, Love,
> The sole necessity of earth and heaven."

THE CHAIRMAN: The discussion of the papers will be opened by John B. Garrett.

JOHN B. GARRETT: It seems to me that discussion implies that there are some thoughts which are to be corrected, or some arguments that are faulty, or some opinions expressed with which one must take issue. No one of these conditions exists to-night; and I feel, for one, that the time for discussion has passed. You will not be surprised if I say that, holding the position I have in reference to this Conference, I have felt a burden resting upon me throughout the past three days. I will not admit that I have had anxiety, for I think that I have had a faith that has enabled me to live above that condition; but I have had a profound and prayerful desire that the best spirit which has pervaded the Conference at any time might live with us to its close. I have certainly desired that this Conference might close with a spirit of peace in the heart God-given, and that we might find rest in one another's company, and that the spirit of devotion might hover about us. I therefore feel that it would be a mistake if I or any other were at this stage of our proceedings to begin to discuss principles or conclusions, or do aught by utterance that would mar the "weight," as we Friends call it, with which we approach the conclusion of our meeting.

So, dismissing from my own mind not a few thoughts that I have felt merit some expression, and which I would have been willing to utter, were the time opportune, I want to say only this: From the fact that we have been together during these three days and have feasted from a richly-laden table, which, by the providence of God, has been spread before us, we have, every one of us, a new responsibility laid upon us, and new privileges likewise given us. We represent many communities, scattered over this continent far and wide. There are within the hearing of my voice many gifted men and women who are accustomed to being the mouthpieces in those communities, and whose influence is potential over the life of communities, the life of States, the life of churches. My appeal to you, dear friends, to-night is that you carry home with you to your several places of abode and of service all that it is possible for your minds and hearts to carry; and that, when you return to your work, you remember the responsibility which arises from the opportunities which are presented to you. Do not go back to your work in the spirit in which you left it when you came here, but go with the sense of responsibility to share in the richest way possible with those among whom you dwell the spirit of that to which we have been listening.

I have already accepted an invitation from one community of Friends not far away to speak to them with regard to this Peace Conference. I hope that similar invitations will come to scores of you. Does anyone doubt that the opportunity which we have enjoyed was not of man's creating? I do not. I believe that it was in the providence of God that we were called together, and I believe that He who brought us together has condescended to our weakness and to our need, and has manifested himself as a very present God and Saviour in our midst, from hour to hour, and from day to day; and that when we come to part He will dismiss us with His blessing.

Nearly three-quarters of a century have passed since divisions began in the Society of Friends, attended in the second quarter of the nineteenth century with many an animosity and many a heartburning. Friends of every connection to whom I speak: I rejoice with thanksgiving that we are not living to-day in that period. I rejoice that out of this Conference shall come blessings that shall tend to peace among ourselves. God has had His holy purposes in bringing us here. If our hearts are open hearts He has begun to fulfil those purposes. As we live in the spirit of self-sacrifice, of devotion, of love one to another that has been so beautifully portrayed to us to-night as the spirit of the everlasting Gospel of our Lord and Saviour, Jesus Christ, that work shall go on to perfection, and this occasion, little though it may have seemed to us as we gathered on the morning of day before yesterday, shall bear its rich fruitage in the progress of civilization, and the winning of the world to the kingdom of the Prince of Peace. God grant it: and may everyone of us who is here to-night be the rich and abundant sharer in the blessing which is already dropping from His hand.

ANNA BRAITHWAITE THOMAS: There is one thing that has pressed upon my heart all day, and I want to speak of it; I mean the loud call that, in the providence of God, comes to this country. I do not think that we have a clear idea of what America was—the ideal of America—to the peoples of the world. It has already been brought before us in the words of that Norwegian who said, " Does that great republic still live ? " That ideal has lived in the hearts of the peoples of the world, especially of those under less favorable conditions. It is the ideal of love and of home, of right and of liberty, of refuge for the oppressed and for the downtrodden. That ideal has been rudely broken to a great extent by recent events.

I have been confronted with the thought recently that the Society of Friends has no special call just now to work for peace. We have not heard that in this Conference; but I know it is the thought of some Friends. But this idea is all wrong. We have a great work before us, and I want to call upon all those who have been members of this Conference to go home and take hold anew of this work. It will require tremendous effort to bring back this country to where it was before it—I was going to say, before it fell—but before the events of the last few years. If we can bring it back it will be a noble work, to say nothing of what we ought to be doing along all the general lines of peace work.

ALFRED H. LOVE: I feel that I must express at the close of this most remarkable Conference my gratitude to the Creator for the privilege of living at a time when there are so many fervent souls dedicated to peace as I have found in these three days. Every word that has been uttered has my commendation. It has been made clear in the Conference that peace is a result, the outcome and recompense of righteousness and well-doing. In order to have peace we must have peace conditions. If we have to-day all the peace that we deserve, let us deserve more by being more fervent, more devoted to the principles of the Master, and in that way we shall realize, perhaps, as I feel that I have realized in measure on this occasion, the hope of the twentieth century. It is possible, dear friends, for us to achieve our conceptions and our ideals. Our Heavenly Father would never have given us the conception of a higher and better condition than that which we see about us, and yet have left us without the means of attaining it. "If the people will to have it so, who shall tell the end thereof?"

FRANKLIN S. BLAIR: I have been a silent actor through all these nine sessions. The prayer of my heart has been that every member of this Conference might have his life hid with Christ in God. The last paper brought that beautifully and wonderfully to our minds. I endorse every word which John B. Garrett has said to us with reference to the whole work of these three days. There has been a wonderful providence of God in the conception and carrying out of the Conference. Like the reader of one of the papers, I go to begin anew, with more earnestness, this life hid with Christ in God, and I ask the prayers of this Conference for us in the Southland, where you know we have had more opposition in many ways than almost any other part of our country, those of us, especially, who began our lives before the war and passed through the great struggle a generation ago. It is our wish to co-operate with you in every way possible in the further extension of the work of peace.

CLEMENT M. BIDDLE: It is not the custom of the Society of Friends to pass resolutions of thanks, or to be as expressive, probably, as we should be to those who work for us. It was my pleasure to be one of the original twenty-six who met at Lake Mohonk, when Benjamin F. Trueblood presented to us the idea of this Conference. We were divided—one earnest, faithful man, and twenty-five in doubt—as to whether it was possible to do what has been done. I wish to say that Dr. Trueblood was the originator of it. He has carried the burden of the work; and with no disrespect to those who have nobly assisted him in making it a success, to him belongs the credit of the plan and of inducing the rest of us to carry it to the successful termination. I desire to give him my personal thanks; and I know I speak for all those assembled.

The Chairman: Dr. Trueblood, say something!

Benjamin F. Trueblood: This Conference is one of the best examples I have seen of the good results that come from the practical application of the principle of Divine guidance, one of the fundamental principles of our Quakerism. The Conference grew out of the simple performance of a very simple duty, that of suggesting the idea of the holding of such a meeting. So strongly had the thought impressed itself upon me for some months, that when I went to Mohonk last spring I could no longer refrain from "opening" the subject to others. There were, of course, doubts about the matter in the minds of some at the beginning, and have been since; but I wish to say that the clearness of the duty of proposing the Conference was made much clearer by the fact that it was approved at once by twenty-five other people who entered into it just as if the call had come to them. Clement M. Biddle, in his appreciation of the little service which I have rendered, has been kind enough to magnify, greatly I think, the doubt and hesitancy of others, including himself. I have no more credit in the matter than the other twenty-five have; for they at once entered into the concern, and everyone of them has stood by it with absolute and unwavering faithfulness to the end.

The outcome so far has been remarkable, and the full outcome is not yet seen. We have had a most interesting and inspiring Conference. A spirit of unity and co-operation has been with us from the first moment to this last. This spirit of unity is one of the growing characteristics of our time; it is spreading everywhere among people who call themselves Christian, and even among others. The era of strife and dogmatic quarreling and division in the Christian church has about gone by. What may come of this Conference other than the moral and spiritual fruit of it, we must leave to the future.

I deeply appreciate what has been said by my friend, John B. Garrett, who has, with the hearty and intelligent co-operation of many others, taken cheerfully so much of the burden of the preparation of the Conference upon himself. What he has said just now is the thing which we need most to remember. This is a great and solemn work in which we are engaged. My friends, we have in the task which is before us in this new century—the task of redeeming the world from hate and war and establishing it permanently in the ways of love and peace—the most glorious calling that one can possibly conceive. The cause of peace has gained much in the past; the principles for which we have stood have already permeated society more deeply than many suppose. That ought to encourage us to throw ourselves with a supreme devotion into the task that is before us. The work of redeeming the world from strife and bloodshed, from the waste of its intellectual and physical powers in the ways of ruin and destruction, and of turning all these energies of thought and feeling and material force to constructive and beneficent ends, is enough, it seems to me, to inspire any soul with devotion and effort of the highest order.

There are great destinies before us. This world is not always to be "red in tooth and claw"; the time is approaching more rapidly than many suppose when the man shall supplant the brute. Great movements advance slowly, so it is said. But every great movement, as it progresses, accumulates power, until, at the last, according to the divine method, it reaches its end as in the twinkling of an eye. The times are moving rapidly, and I want us to move with them. The cause which has brought us together is very near the heart of our Master. It is His purpose that it shall triumph, not in this land only, but in all lands; that America may be saved, and England, and Germany, and Russia, and China, and South Africa, and all the ends of the earth, from the desolations of hate and war, and that the whole world may be brought into harmony and co-operation. What share shall we have in this great accomplishment?

ISAAC SHARPLESS: I think that any one who has attended the meetings of this Conference will come to the conclusion that the Society of Friends of the present day has no disposition to repudiate the doctrines of their first predecessors on the subject of peace. The statements unanimously adopted this afternoon are a strong endorsement of the positions taken by George Fox. We are not sorry we have received these doctrines as a heritage from the past. We have no disposition to apologize for them, nor are we at all ashamed to avow that we are peace men. We are thankful, on the contrary, that this precious legacy has come down to us, and that we are able to meet together here, and in such unity continue to bear up the blessed cause. We propose to continue to hold up the same standard and pass it on endorsed and strengthened.

We regret that we appear to be so nearly alone among Christian professors. So clear does the position seem to us that we are at a loss to perceive how other earnest, honest Christians can differ. We are encouraged when we read the abstract eulogiums on peace; but when war issues come we are surprised and disappointed at the apparent change of ground. We want to keep ourselves open to conviction, and we acknowledge that our lonely position puts upon us a great burden of proof. Can it be that the small minority is right? We have this week asked ourselves this question, and for ourselves we have again soberly answered it in the affirmative, and so we shall continue to answer it always in theory, and in practice just as long as God shall give us strength to be faithful to what we know to be right.

Another feature which must have been noticed during the meetings has been a prevailing optimism,—not a blind optimism which has faith just because we know the strength of our cause, but an optimism based on a knowledge of the advances actually made. The paper of Dr. Trueblood, written on the strength of abundant knowledge, shows conclusively the rapid advance—an advance which prepares the way for a still more rapid advance soon to come. Our optimism is based, too, on a knowledge of the number of forces working for us—the growing acquaintance of one nation with another, the development of world-wide sympathies, the spirit of commerce and industry, the spread of Christianity, the education of the masses, and the development of private morals. Yes, Friends, we are associated with a winning cause, and we know it, and we have the enthusiasm which comes from knowledge. A few more campaigns, a few more martyrs, perhaps, a great deal more energy and wise enterprise, and the cause is won, and other Christian bodies will come crowding each other to fall into the ranks of the peace men.

Friends have not been very active propagandists. The very feeling of their own complete rightness has made many of them slow to take the stump and proclaim the arguments for the good cause. But this is changing. I have been interested in the proposition that a lot of us should go to Congress; that we should get together and say to each other, " Go to, let us enter the Senate." The plan is, unfortunately, not likely to be successful, but I am inclined to believe that for our present purposes it is right in theory, and the way to bring it about is to begin with the humbler politics of the country, the lowly but useful offices and the primary meetings of the political parties. But in this greater activity to which we are called, I should be sorry to lose the typical Friend of the past, the man of tender conscience and guarded life, of simple tastes and quiet manners, absolutely truthful and cautious and faithful and sweet in his life, " Who reverenced his king as if it were his conscience, and his conscience as his king "—the man and woman we have all known and loved. Shall we lose this historic character as we part with the aloofness from the world which perhaps produced it, " if he rides abroad redressing human wrong "?

Not so, I think, if he comes under the spirit of George Fox; if he is a peace man not because he believes war to be wasteful, and productive of suffering, or contrary to some pet theory of morals, but because down in his heart he feels the warm spirit of divine love and power that takes away the occasion and the desire and the possibility of war and revenge and hatred. Pile up your other arguments as you will, such a man can go out doing a strong, active man's full duty to the cause, and not lose one iota of the sweetness and light of our revered Friends of the past. He will be efficient and practical, and at the same time graceful and moderate, generous in his sympathies, and kindly in his criticisms,—an undaunted advocate, a charitable opponent.

THE CHAIRMAN: I think we shall leave this room to-night profoundly thankful, all of us, that we have been here; and with a prayer in our hearts for the blessing of Him without whose help we shall have labored in vain, we will conclude the Conference.

After a time of waiting before the Lord, during which thanksgiving and prayer were voiced by Joseph Elkinton, Jr., and Benjamin F. Trueblood, the Chairman declared the Conference adjourned without day.

Immediately upon the close of the Conference the committee appointed for that purpose (with the exception of President M. Carey Thomas, who found it impossible to serve) prepared and forwarded to the President of the United States the following letter:

LETTER TO THE PRESIDENT OF THE UNITED STATES.

To Theodore Roosevelt, President of the United States:

Honored and Respected Friend:

The Friends' Peace Conference, in session at Philadelphia on the 12th, 13th, 14th of the present month, composed of members of the several bodies of Friends in America, directed that an address on its behalf be sent to thee, and appointed the undersigned a committee to prepare and forward it.

The desire of the Conference was, that there should be expressed its deep sympathy with thee in the arduous duties and great responsibilities which, in so extraordinary a manner, and by so lamentable an event, have devolved upon thee, and its earnest hope that these may be so met and performed as to promote not only the internal concord of the people of this nation, but also good will and consequent peace throughout the world.

We have observed with encouragement and satisfaction, the passage in thy message to Congress in which the declarations are made that "the true end of every great and free people should be self-respecting peace," that "this nation most earnestly desires sincere and cordial friendship with all others," and that "more and more the civilized peoples are realizing the wicked folly of war, and are attaining that condition of just and intelligent regard for the rights of others which will in the end make world-wide peace possible." We earnestly desire that these sentiments, so true and timely, may grow and prevail, and that during thy administration the public opinion in behalf of rational methods for settling international differences may be fostered, and all possible steps be taken to make such methods practical and effective. We are convinced that the stability and true grandeur of the nation can be promoted only by those means and methods which are inherently right, and are in accord with the teachings of Jesus Christ; in this conviction, we would earnestly encourage thee in all thy purposes and undertakings which will make for higher ideals of citizenship and will increase the moral power of the republic.

As it has been the mission of the nation, during its first century, to exhibit and illustrate to the world the principles of true democracy and individual liberty, so may its next contribution to civilization be a demonstration of the fact that there are tried and approved methods of securing justice which makes war unnecessary and that righteousness of intercourse between nations, as between men, will always command peace. May it be thy honorable distinction in coming time, to have helped to build these principles securely in the foundation of our national structure.

Commending thee to the care and guidance of Almighty God, as the source of unfailing Wisdom and Light, we subscribe ourselves, with respect, thy friends.

Signed,

   ISAAC SHARPLESS,   HOWARD M. JENKINS,
   WILLIAM W. BIRDSALL, RUFUS M. JONES,
   PHILIP C. GARRETT,   SUSAN W. JANNEY.

INDEX.

Address of Friends to Washington in 1789, 51.
American Ideal, The, 37, 228.
Arbitration, 45, 155, 158, 160, 208, 220.
Ash, Samuel S., 54.
Attitude of Christians toward Peace and War, 65.

Baily, Hannah J., 119.
Baily, Joshua L., 136, 144, 206.
Barton, George A., 19, 209.
Benham, Ida Whipple, 112.
Bible Schools, Importance of Teaching Peace Principles in, 83.
Biddle, Clement M., 229.
Birdsall, William W., 34, 78, 110, 132.
Blair, Franklin S., 229.
Bond, Elizabeth Powell, 180.
Borton, Joel, 162.
Bright, John, 126, 127, 189.
Burgess, Emilie U., 194.

Chapman, Mariana W., 45, 101.
Chawner, John, 33, 106.
Christian Idea of Force, 70, 105.
Christianity and Peace, 16, 24, 29, 31, 32, 33, 41, 49, 54, 55, 59, 65, 67, 80, 83, 92, 101, 103, 163, 172, 183, 190, 192, 201, 210, 215, 218, 223.
Constancy in Peace Effort, 201.
Cruelty of War, 44, 47, 114, 203.

Declaration of the Conference, 208.
Dennis, William C., 159.
Dillingham, John H., 210.
Disarmament, 145.
Doukhobors, 76, 80.

Early Christianity and War, 59.
Early Friends and Peace, 39.
Elkinton, Joseph, 80, 106, 191.
Encouragements for Peace, 56, 81, 87, 110, 113, 162, 193.

Failure of the Church to Promote Peace, 24, 31, 32, 66, 102.
Ferris, David, 133.
Flitcraft, Allen, 31.
Force, Moral, 71, 81, 105.
Fox, George, 30, 39, 40, 50, 147.

Friends and Peace, 30, 39, 48, 54, 58, 82, 98, 104, 106, 107, 108, 132, 133, 146, 163, 164, 166, 188, 191, 198, 202, 218, 228, 231.
Friends in Political Life, 32, 104, 108, 189.
Friends not Anarchists, 58.

Garrett, John B., 11, 13, 34, 107, 227.
Garrett, Philip C., 146, 207, 209.
Hague Court, 118, 121, 125, 156, 162, 196, 208.
Hatred of Foreigners, 17, 21, 27.
Holmes, Jesse H., 65.
Hotchkiss, Willis R., 210.
Howard Association, 25.
Hubbard, William G., 31, 39.

Individual Responsibility, 66, 78, 172.
Influences for Peace, 81, 87, 110, 113, 193, 218.
Inherent Immorality of War, 45, 49, 53, 55.
Internationalism, 17, 23, 110, 117, 119, 124, 131, 134, 152, 160, 193.

Janney, O. Edward, 218.
Janney, Susan W., 193.
Jenkins, Howard M., 34, 37, 56, 162, 206.
Jewish Ideas of Peace, 17, 20.
Jones, Augustine, 124.
Jones, Rufus M., 29, 104, 222.

Kimber, Anthony M., 54.

Leeds, Josiah W., 213.
Letter to President Roosevelt, 206, 233.
Lloyd, Elizabeth, 105.
Looting, 177.
Love, Alfred H., 229.

Magill, Edward H., 53, 130.
Makers of Peace, The, 180.
McGrew, Edwin, 106, 201.
Militarism, Remedies for, 213.
Morrow, Dr. James, 103.

Neutrality on the Great Lakes, 145.
Newport, David, 101.
New Testament Grounds of Peace, 16, 41, 71.

235

Nicholson, S. Edgar, 98.
Nobel Peace Prizes, 56.
Old Testament and Peace, 19, 29, 31, 32, 33, 78.
Origin and Organization of the Conference, 3, 12, 229, 230.

Patriotism, False, 85, 176.
Peace and Heroism, 68, 175, 211.
Peace as Involved in the Christian Method, 222.
Peace in the New Testament, 16, 41, 71.
Peace in the Old Testament, 19, 29, 31, 32, 33, 78.
Peace Principles in Political Life and Institutions, 124.
Peace, True Spirit of, 183.
Pearson, William L., 102, 183.
Penn's Work for Peace, 132, 146, 161, 162, 219.
Pennypacker, Charles H., 209.
Perry, Arthur, 164.
Philippine War, 43, 89, 95, 99, 198, 203.
Poem "Gentle and Mighty," 112.
Powell, Joseph, 54.
Pretlow, Robert E., 189.
Practicability of Peace, 28, 93, 102, 104, 106, 107, 108, 137, 140, 144, 158, 164, 167, 213, 219, 232.
Price, William L., 163.
Private and Public War, 159.
Program of the Conference, 7.
Progress of Peace, 56, 87, 110, 113, 119, 136, 152, 159, 162, 193.

Raidabaugh, P. W., 83.
Remedies for Militarism, 213.
Reply of Washington to Friends' Address, 52.
Russell, Elbert, 16.

Sanders, Amos, 188.
Sharpless, Isaac, 48, 137, 231.
Shipley, Catharine M., 106.
Smith, Stephen R., 11, 132.
Soldier, A, on War, 54.
South African War, 42, 89, 107.
Spanish War, 27, 37, 47, 50, 83, 99, 107, 203.
Stanley, Edmund, 87.

Tebbetts, Charles E., 198.
Thomas, Anna Braithwaite, 32, 134, 228.
Thomas, M. Carey, 81, 109.
Thomas, Richard H., 55, 70.
Trueblood, Benjamin F., 12, 36, 56, 152, 198, 206, 207, 230.

Unthank, James B., 34, 58, 166.

War Always Evil, 53, 54.
War Inconsistent with the Genius of Quakerism, 198.
Washington, Address of Friends to, 51; Reply of, 52.
Wilbur, Henry W., 172, 210.
Women and Peace, 82, 93, 101, 102, 116, 194.
Wood, James, 59.
Wood, John B., 192.
Woody, Mary Chawner, 24, 102.
Wright, Ellen C., 113.